FOLK ART TOYS
AND FURNITURE
FOR CHILDREN

FOLK ART TOYS AND FURNITURE FOR CHILDREN

Joyce Davies Hundley
and
Jeanne Davies Muller

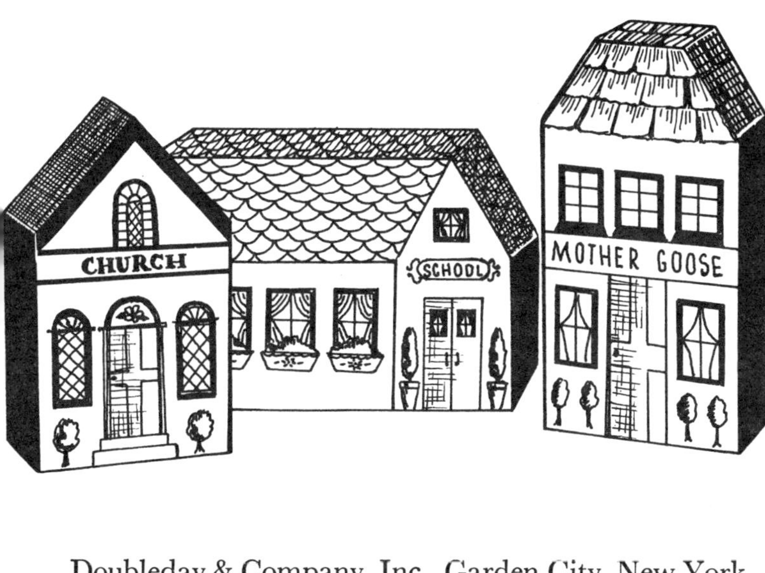

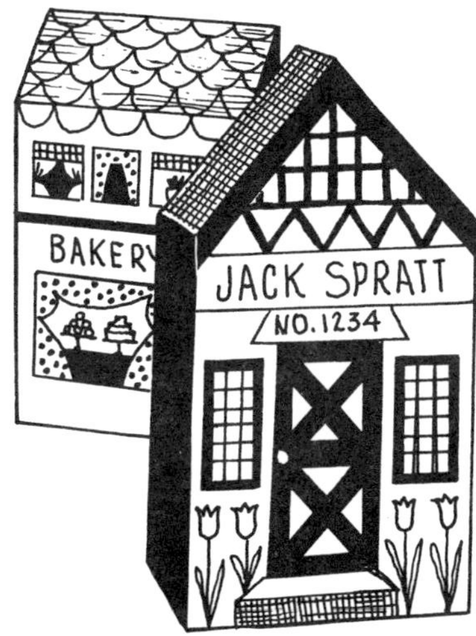

Doubleday & Company, Inc., Garden City, New York

1975

Library of Congress Cataloging in Publication Data

Hundley, Joyce Davies.
    Folk art toys and furniture for children.

    1. Wooden toy making.   2. Furniture making—Amateurs' manuals.
3. Folk art.   I. Muller, Jeanne Davies, joint author.   II. Title.
TT174.5.W6H86   745.59'2
ISBN 0-385-05680-X
Library of Congress Catalog Card Number 74–18809

To Mother and Dad, Bill and Richard
for their patience and understanding

Authors' Note

When the idea to write a book on how to build toys came to us it all seemed very simple. We already had many of the toys we had designed over the years as well as ideas for several others, which we felt should be added to the collection for a good complete selection. Having never really grown up ourselves, we designed the toys for fun and with enthusiasm, the prime requirement, someone once said, of toy designers.

While toy designing does take a certain knowledge of how things fit together, it turned out to be something else again to try to tell our readers how to do it. We consulted with Mr. Al Bartlett, who along with Mr. Fred Tyler, translates many of our designs into working models. Besides, being a business executive, Al is also an artist with a sense of adventure. So he gallantly agreed to write some building instructions for our toy projects.

Add to this fearless trio, Mr. Mal Davies, a retired engineer who is also our father. Actually, he has been trying to retire for the past nine years but is being held prisoner in our studio where he keeps busy with painting and repairing or rebuilding.

The cutting and assembly instructions were first written by Al Bartlett and Mal Davies, compiled by Joyce and Jeanne, and questioned by our editor, who wants to try to build the toys herself. So we threw in answers to her questions too! After all that, the instructions should be quite complete.

ANY QUESTIONS?

Contents

FOLK ART TOYS
AND FURNITURE
FOR CHILDREN

Chapter One

Folk Art Toys

Welcome to the magic world of toys, the beginning of dreams! The painted toys in this book are offered in the hope of inspiring parents to share with their children a rich and too often forgotten heritage, for these toy patterns and designs are our interpretations of time-proven folk toys of the past. We have selected toys that are traditional . . . the kind that have had a continuing appeal through the ages; toys conditioned by local folk art, outstanding in their simplicity, colorfulness, and lack of sophistication. Young children generally prefer the simple toy for it gives scope to their imagination, much more than a perfect reproduction of the real thing. And since colorful objects have a greater attraction to children than plain wood, offer your child the gaily painted toy.

Over the centuries many toys have been made by loving parents or purchased from local carpenters or even a peddler who carried his pack full of bright toys from village to village. Toymaking first developed as an industry in Germany; wood carvers in the rural districts of south Germany had special talent for wood carving, an ample supply of wood from the forests, and the leisure of peasant life in the winters. Eventually the craftsmen around Nuremberg, the international trading center in south Germany, began to organize toymakers' guilds and soon began exporting toys around the world. Over five hundred years ago German toys became world famous and Nuremberg became the toymaking center of the world. Even today the simplicity and colorfulness of many German toys give them the aesthetic quality of folk art toys. Many of the toys we offer in this book were inspired by antique German toys.

AMERICAN TOYS

The toys of America's past are a rich blending of the many traditions of the different groups that colonized the New World. These traditions were combined with the Early American's common sense, determination to survive, and his Puritan work ethic. All this created American toys that were generally stripped of the frivolous, were simpler, more basic than many in Europe at the time, and in essence, a folk toy.

Toys were brought to the New World by some of the earliest settlers. Early American paintings show Indian children holding lovely little English dolls which had been offered as gifts or were traded for grain. In early America, children found little time for play and toys for a family's very survival often depended on the help of the children. Even in wealthier families, children were given household tasks, and if not doing their chores, the girls were kept busy with needlework while the boys went hunting for game.

Eventually, however, Colonial hardships gave way to more security and prosperity, allowing children time for "real" toys. Until then, toys had consisted of those brought over from the Old World or new toys fashioned out of whatever scrap material was at hand; corncob dolls, rawhide balls, whittled tops and whistles. Museums and private collections display a goodly number of toys from the American past. There are painted doll cradles from Pennsylvania, with canopied tops, "to keep out draughts." There are "dining and low chairs" made by eighteenth-century cabinetmakers, and child-size "fancy chairs" that were painted and stenciled by the famous Hitchcock Chair Company in Connecticut.

The hobbyhorse or broomstick horse is a universal toy made of a stick with a wooden horse's head, a rein, and, occasionally, attached wheels. Sixteenth-century silk paintings from China show children on hobbyhorses, and they were also known in Greek times and during the Middle Ages. The rocking horse was a product of the eighteenth century, one being advertised in Pennsylvania by a cabinetmaker, "to teach children to ride and give them a wholesome and pleasing exercise!" Rocking horses, made from a plank of wood with rockers and a carved horse's head, were either homemade or ordered from a local carpenter in the village. The cabinetmaker's horse was undoubtedly more elaborate.

Sledding and skating were favorite outdoor games, and wooden skates and sleds were made by individual craftsmen for many years. Sleds were often painted lavishly with galloping horses, colorful landscapes, or flowers.

Noah's ark was sometimes a simple miniature house set on a block of wood with a group of hand-carved animals. The arks were usually painted with a leaf-and-flower border, and almost always there was a dove painted on the roof. This was considered a satisfactory toy even for Puritan households.

Local cabinetmakers and carpenters made children's alphabet blocks until 1858 when blocks began to be manufactured in quantity.

Doll houses were called "babies' houses" until the middle of the nineteenth century. American doll houses had straight and simple lines as opposed to the European ones which were amazingly intricate and elaborate. The earliest American doll house of which we are aware, dates back to 1744; it was two stories high with a drawer below in which to store more toys.

The past has been infinitely rich in toys of every variety, from the most basic to the very elaborate. But it is the simple painted toy toward which we direct your interest since we feel that for the young child the simple play things are of greater value than the highly technical toys found in toy shops today. The toys we have chosen are likely to bring back nostalgic memories of your own childhood. . . . These are the toys that can be cherished for generations and handed down through the family with pride.

This book was written for those who would like to revive the old tradition of handcrafted toys. These toys are tried and true, inspired by the past and handmade and hand-painted in our studio for a number of years. Many times an eager little visitor has been pried from a rocking horse by his mother so that the horse could be spirited away to appear under the Christmas tree. Doll houses in an endless combination of colors have left the shop with the names of happy children painted above the doors.

So we know that children love these toys . . . and you will love building and painting them for your child. Each toy design includes exact measurements, cutting patterns to be enlarged, and directions for assembly. For decorating the toy you will find painting patterns complete with color guides. The bright colors and happy designs will help make your toy a work of art. You can be sure that your child will think it is the very best toy in the world . . . and it might just be!

Chapter Two

Beginners Only:
Helpful Hints for the Novice Builder

If working with wood is a new experience for you, the following suggestions should help to make your first projects go more smoothly.

WOOD

Generally we like to use white pine shelving for most pieces and plywood when necessary. White pine has a uniform texture and is easy to work with. It finishes well and resists shrinkage, swelling, or warping. Plywood is used when extra-wide areas are needed, thus eliminating the need for gluing lumber widths together. Plywood will also help to avoid warping problems.

TOOLS

To work with wood you will need a basic tool kit which you will also find handy for small maintenance jobs around the house. This kit should include the following items, all of which can be purchased at a building supply store:

Claw hammer
Hand saw with medium teeth
Screw driver
Hand drill with set of bits
Jig saw or saber saw
Carpenter's square
Metal measuring tape
Nail set
Compass
Finishing nails
Sandpaper, medium and fine
White glue
Spackling paste

CUTTING THE PATTERN

Following the instructions on how to enlarge a design (see page 17), make a paper or cardboard pattern of each piece, actual size. Figure the most economical way that these pieces can be cut as you place them on the wood. When figuring, be sure to allow sawing space between your patterns. When you lay your patterns on the wood for cutting, secure them with Scotch tape and recheck all measurements. Use your carpenter's square to be sure that all pieces are 90°-square corners and accurate. Cuts should be square unless the directions specify otherwise.

DRIVING THE NAILS

Start a nail into the wood with light hammer blows. If the nail should bend, pull it out and start another. If the nail begins to split the wood, drill a pilot hole with your hand drill (smaller than the diameter of the nail) before driving the nail into the wood. Do not drive a row of nails in a straight line since this tends to split the wood. Instead, stagger the nails for extra strength. For holding power, use common nails. Where appearance rather than strength is needed, use finishing nails which can be countersunk and hidden.

A nail should penetrate about three fourths of the thickness of the wood in which you are nailing. With finishing nails, hammer the nail until it is almost flush with the wood surface. Then to countersink, use a nail set to drive the nail about one sixteenth of an inch below the surface of the wood. The indent can then be filled with spackling paste.

SCREWS

Screws have great holding power and also the advantage of being able to pull two pieces of wood together for added strength and durability. If the wood is quite soft, such as the pine we recommend, you will have no trouble driving screws into the wood. If you are not using a soft wood, it would be wise to drill a pilot hole before trying to insert a screw. Pilot holes should be large enough to allow the screw to screw in easily, but not so large that the screw cannot bite into the wood.

NAILING AND GLUING JOINTS

For extra strength it is a good idea to both nail and glue all joints. Since surfaces to be glued should not be rough, sand them smooth and clean off all dust. Then apply the glue carefully, removing all excess that might ooze out from the joint after the two surfaces are joined. Wipe the excess glue off with a damp cloth and allow the glue to dry for thirty minutes or more.

FINISHING

We have found that you can save a lot of effort at this stage if you have sanded the various pieces of the toy before assembly. Therefore, we recommend that practice, using medium sandpaper and finishing with fine sandpaper. After the piece is assembled, set all nails with a nail set. Fill the shallow hole above the nail with spackling paste. It is also a good idea to fill any imperfections in the wood. After twenty to thirty minutes, the filler should be dry and can be sanded till smooth. Since plywood edges reveal many layers of wood, any exposed edges should also be filled and sanded smooth. With a brush or vacuum cleaner, remove all traces of dust left by the sanding, and your toy is ready to paint.

Remember that the main cause of poor craftsmanship in woodworking is haste, so avoid carelessness in measuring and in cutting the wood and be sure to fit and glue each piece with extra care. Always keep your tools clean and in good condition. If you follow these simple suggestions, you should find most of these toys surprisingly easy to build and decorate.

Chapter Three

Transferring and Enlarging a Pattern

Whenever possible, the building directions show actual size patterns that can be traced directly from the book with tracing paper. The traced pattern can then be transferred to the wood. Some of the patterns show only half of the cutting design. With a half pattern, measure and draw a center line on the correct size board. Match the center line of the traced half pattern to the center line of the board and draw off half of the pattern. Still matching center lines, flip the paper pattern over to reverse the pattern and draw off the other side.

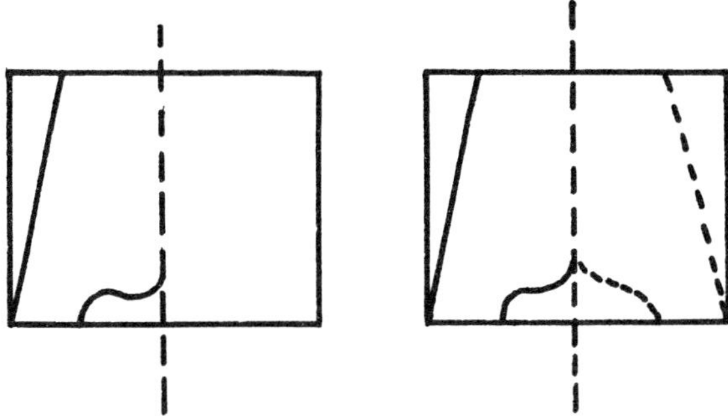

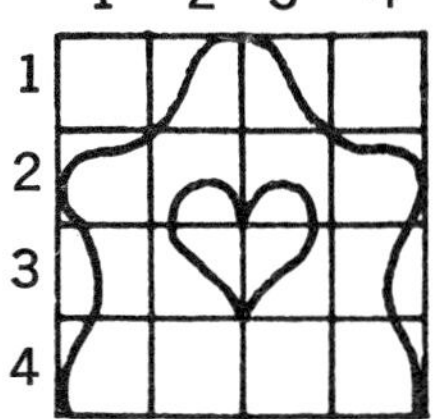

ENLARGING THE PATTERN

Since it is impossible to include actual size patterns for the larger toys, it will be necessary to enlarge some patterns to actual size. To do this, use the following method:

1. The pattern will state the scale size of the book pattern. (For example, 1 square=1 inch.)
2. On a piece of tracing paper measure and draw a rectangle the exact size that the pattern is to be enlarged.
3. Measure and mark off this rectangle with exactly the same number of squares as the graph in the book. (1 square= 1 inch, your squares would measure 1 inch for each square in the book graph.)
4. Number each square both up and down to correspond with the small graph.
5. Copy each line of the design from the original graph onto the enlarged graph, working one square at a time.

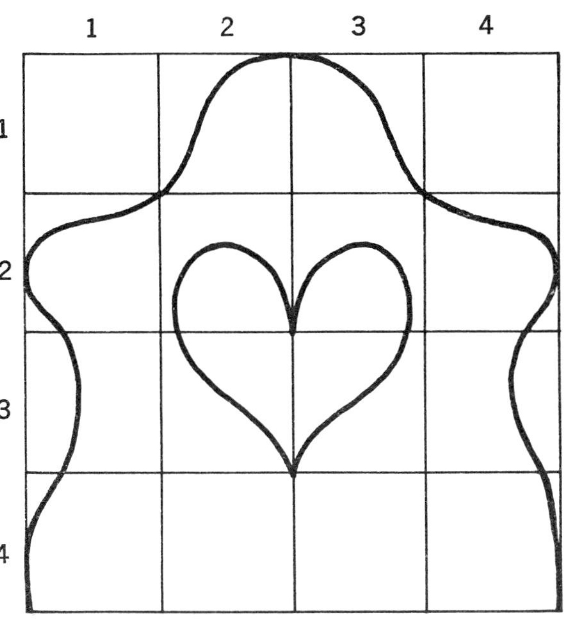

Chapter Four

Painting and Decorative Design

FOLK ART PAINTING

Folk art painting and handicrafts have found a place of honor in the history of decorative arts. The "people's art," or provincial art, is a simple and straightforward expressive form which is highly ornamental. The untrained and perhaps less-talented folk artist copied from the highly trained artist of neighboring cities and in doing so, achieved a naïve rendition which today is most appealing. Urban people had no need to create their own decorative arts for they could buy ready-made goods in the cities, whereas the country people added beauty to their surroundings by painting the everyday things around them, whether furniture, everyday utensils, or children's toys.

The folk art toy was likely to be made of soft pine or fir which were woods available to the peasant. These sturdy toys were given coats of paint and then decorated with characteristic motifs such as tulips, doves, hearts, and floral forms in bright colors. The artist did not always try to be original, often preferring to paint motifs that his ancestors had used for centuries. This is the key to understanding the timeless quality of folk art toys, or for that matter, folk art in general.

The simple and unsophisticated folk toys were painted to brighten and beautify them. The painting was done for the fun of it and to please the children. The designs were painted on a base color rather than the natural wood to make the colors appear richer and brighter. Red is most often chosen by children today as a favorite color, along with other warm bright colors, and if you look at old toys you will find that folk artists showed a preference for red, yellow, green, and blue when painting toys.

So when painting the toys in this book, keep in mind that this is to be fun and that you do not need to be an experienced artist to paint and decorate a folk art toy. Your children will not notice your mistakes but will appreciate the time and effort you have put into decorating a bright and happy toy especially for them.

APPLYING THE BASE COAT

When you have finished building the toy, double check to make sure that all nail holes and imperfections in the wood have been filled. Be sure that all rough edges have been sanded smooth and that all traces of dust have been removed. You are then ready to apply the first coat of paint.

Use satin enamel paint, a good-quality two-inch brush, and either turpentine or mineral spirits to clean the brush after you have finished painting. Before you begin, stir the paint to be sure it is well mixed. As you are painting the surface, be sure to take up any sags or drips with the brush. Apply the paint in any direction, finishing the brushing with the wood grain for a smooth finish. Do not apply the paint too thickly, and allow the piece to dry for twenty-four hours before applying the second coat.

After the first coat of paint is thoroughly dry, sand the piece with fine sandpaper. The first coat of paint has a tendency to raise the grain of the wood, making it rough to the touch. Remove any loose dust left by the sanding and give your toy a final coat of paint. Some shades of yellow paint tend to have poor covering power and you might find that a third coat is necessary.

When the final coat of paint is thoroughly dry, the toy is ready for designs.

TRANSFERRING THE DESIGN

Enlarge the painting pattern in the same manner in which the cutting patterns are enlarged (see page 17). Draw the actual size pattern on tracing paper. If you have had experience with design work or just feel venturesome, we urge you to jump right into the project with gusto and paint the design directly onto the surface of the toy. However, if you prefer an exact tracing, rub a lead pencil over the back side of the enlarged pattern. Then place the pattern over the surface to be painted and secure with Scotch tape. Trace the outlines of the design with a sharp pencil or ball-point pen, being sure to go over all the lines so that the graphite will be transferred from the back of the tracing to the painted surface.

PAINTING MATERIALS LIST

The following list of materials for design painting can be found at an art supply store:

Tubes of artist's acrylic paints
Round red sable water-color brushes; size 2, 5, and 8
Disposable palette (for acrylic paints)

You will also need:

Paper towels
Jar of water

The following tubes of color will be adequate for the beginning painter:

Cadmium Red, Medium
Phthalocyanine Blue
Cadmium Yellow, Medium
Chromium Oxide Green
Yellow Oxide
Mars Black
Titanium White

This is a good basic palette and by mixing colors, you will have an adequate range of colors for the toy designs. If you already have a supply of paints or are unable to obtain the above colors, the following list will be of help as alternates or substitutes:

Red: *Cadmium Red,* Alizarin Crimson, Naphthol Crimson, Acra Red
Blue: *Phthalocyanine,* Ultramarine, Prussian, Cerulean
Yellow: *Cadmium Yellow, Medium,* Cadmium Yellow, Light; Hansa Yellow
Green: *Chromium Oxide Green,* Hooker's Green, Permanent Green
Gold: *Yellow Oxide,* Ochre, Raw Sienna
Brown: Raw Umber, Burnt Sienna, Burnt Umber
Orange: Cadmium Red Light, Cadmium Orange

USING THE COLOR GUIDE

To follow the color guide, use the basic palette to mix the following colors:

Pink: Add white to Cadmium Red
Dark red: Add black to Cadmium Red
Orange: Mix Cadmium Yellow and Cadmium Red
Light or pale yellow: Add white to Cadmium Yellow
Gold: Yellow Oxide
Yellow-green: Add Cadmium Yellow to Chrome Oxide Green
Light green: Add white to Chrome Oxide Green
Dark green: Add black to Chrome Oxide Green
Light blue: Add white to Phthalocyanine Blue
Dark blue: Phthalocyanine Blue
Medium blue: Add a touch of white to Phthalocyanine Blue
Brown: Add black to Cadmium Red
Gray: Add white to black

NOTE: Add colors gradually to obtain desired color.

The color guides accompanying the painting patterns are suggested colors for the separate design elements. The colors are those which were used on the toys shown in the color section. However, other color combinations will work just as nicely, and we hope that you will venture out on your own.

PAINTING THE DESIGNS

When painting the designs always keep in mind that this should be an enjoyable experience and don't worry about making mistakes. If you are not happy with the results, simply wipe off the paint with a damp paper towel and start over.

Acrylic paints are made with a plastic base and are thinned to a painting consistency with water. The consistency of thick cream obtains the best results. The paint dries rapidly so care must be taken to keep the brushes wet while you are working. Do not allow the paint to dry in the brush. Rinse the brush with water to clean it when changing colors. Be sure to clean the brush thoroughly with soap and water when you have finished painting.

Assemble your paints, palette, a jar of water for cleaning your brush, and a paper towel for removing excess water from your brush. Squeeze an adequate amount of paint in the colors you will be using onto your palette. A blob about the size of a dime should do to get you started. Your work will usually begin with the largest brush, ending with a smaller brush for finishing details.

Begin painting the design by establishing the large basic areas, leaving finishing details until last. Lay the colors in flat and smooth. If the first coat is streaked, let it dry and then paint a second coat over it to ensure a rich smooth color. When you have finished painting the design, allow it to dry thoroughly and then erase any pencil lines or smudges that may remain.

Children love to see their names painted on their toys so try painting the name in your own handwriting, and perhaps the date. It will become a part of the design!

Give the finished design a final protective coat of satin finish varnish, which can be done as soon as the painted design is dry to the touch.

Chapter Five

Toy Patterns

Hobbyhorse

Playing cowboys and Indians will be a lot more fun for little kids with this hobbyhorse to ride. The horse and rider has been an important motif in art from earliest times and also has found its expression in toys. Choose between the very quick and simple version with the cutout head and "broomstick" or frill him up with a handhold and removable wheels for a smoother ride.

1″×12″ white pine shelving—18″ long (plywood may be substituted)
3/4″-diameter dowel—36″ long
One leather boot lace for rein—24″ long
One dozen 1½″ finishing nails

STEP ONE: CUTTING

Making sure that the wood grain is running in the direction that the pattern indicates, trace the enlarged pattern for the horse head, and cut with a jig saw or saber saw. Cut the two brace pieces in the same manner.

CUTTING PATTERN

HEAD (cut 1)
1 Square = 1 Inch

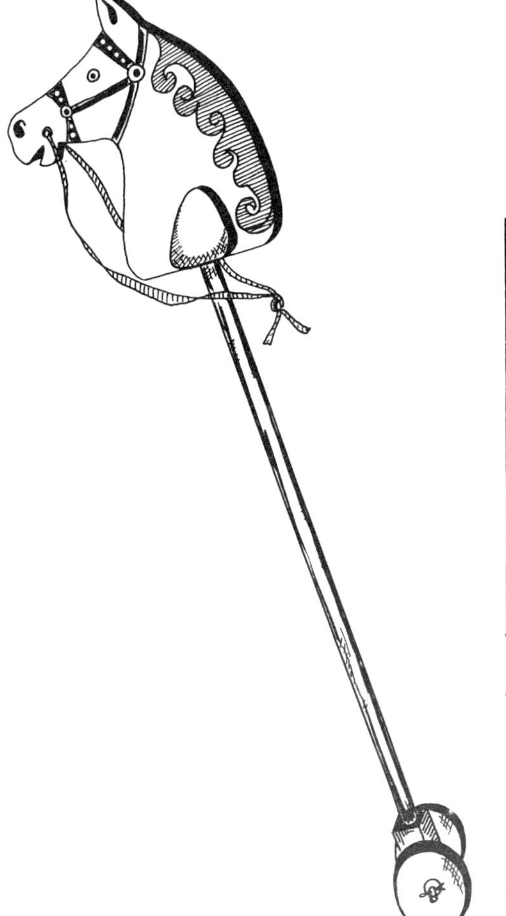

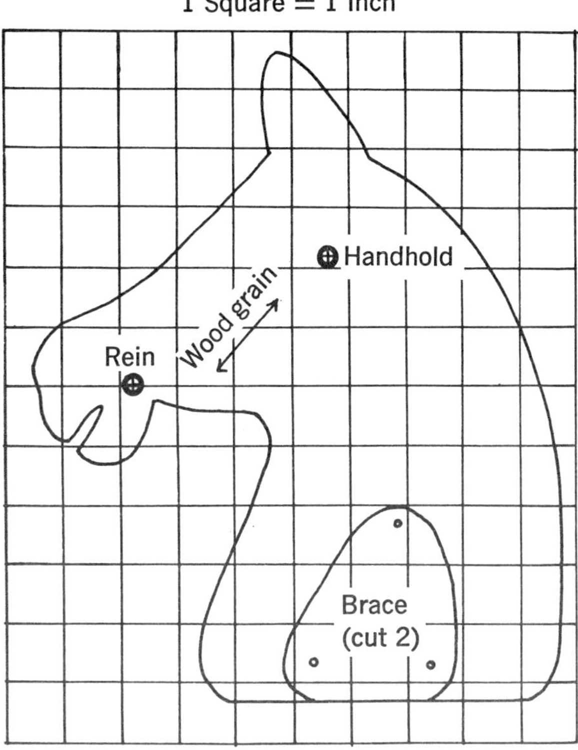

Nail the two braces into place on each side of the head with three nails each. At the center point (in both directions), drill a ¾″ hole up into the lower straight edge of the head piece. Drill to a depth of about 1″ to 1½″ (Diagram A).

Glue the three foot length of dowel into the hole. With sandpaper smooth the other end of the dowel. Drill a ¼″ hole on the horse's mouth for the rein. See the cutting pattern for location. After the hobbyhorse has been painted and decorated, insert the leather boot lace through this hole and tie the loose ends together.

DIAGRAM A

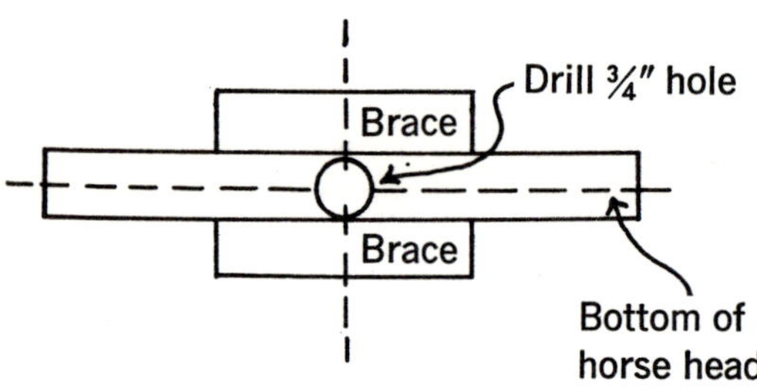

DIAGRAM B

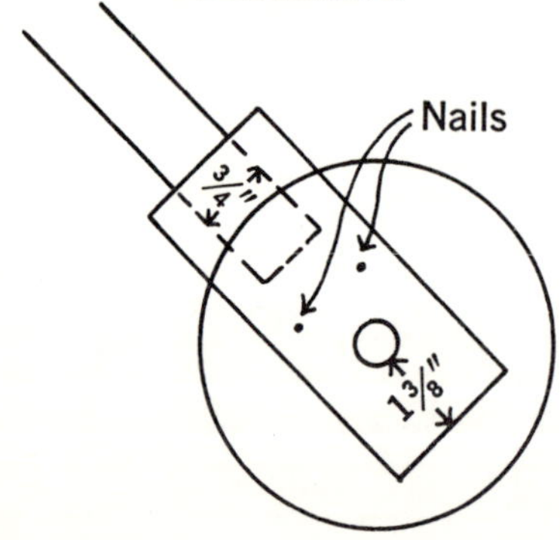

WHEELS AND HANDHOLD

MATERIALS:

One piece ⅜″-diameter dowel—11″ long
Four ⅜″ washers
Two ¾″ cotter keys

STEP ONE: CUTTING

Cut two pieces shelving—1½″×4″
Cut from shelving—two 3″-diameter circles
From ⅜″ dowel:
    Cut one piece—4⅜″ long (axle)
    Cut one piece—6¾″ long (handhold)

STEP TWO: ASSEMBLY

To make the axle block, glue and nail together the two pieces of 1½″×4″ wood, creating a square block measuring 4″ long. Do this by driving one nail through the middle of the block on each side. In this location, the nails will not interfere with future drilling. Allow four hours for the glue to dry. Then, in the exact center of one end of the block, drill a ¾″ hole about 1½″ deep. Then turn the block on its side and mark a center point 1⅜″ up on the end opposite the hole (Diagram B). At this point, drill a ⅜″ hole through the block. Center the 4¼″ dowel through this hole to serve as the axle.

For the wheels, drill a ⅜″ hole through the exact center of both 3″ wood circles. Wrap a small piece of sandpaper around a pencil and carefully sand the inside of the holes to allow the wheel to fit loosely on the axle.

Insert the 4½″ length of dowel (axle) into the axle block. Center the rod so that it is equal on each side of the axle block. Near the ends of each dowel, drill a 1/16″ hole to insert the cotter keys (Diagram C).

Finally, on each side of the axle block place a washer, then a wheel and then another washer before inserting the cotter keys. The assembly is now complete and can be put on the horse. Do not attach with glue so that the child can use the horse both with wheels or without (Diagram D).

For the handhold, drill a ⅜″ hole in the location shown on the horse head pattern and insert with glue, the 6¾″ long dowel so that it is an equal distance on each side of the head. Sand the ends of the rod until they are smooth.

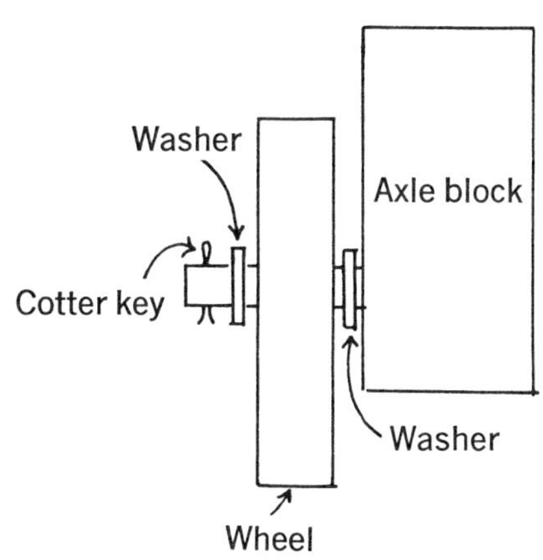

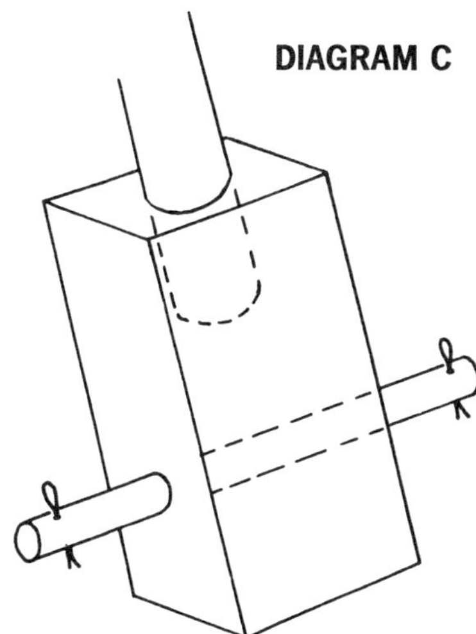

PAINTING PATTERN

1 Square = 1 Inch

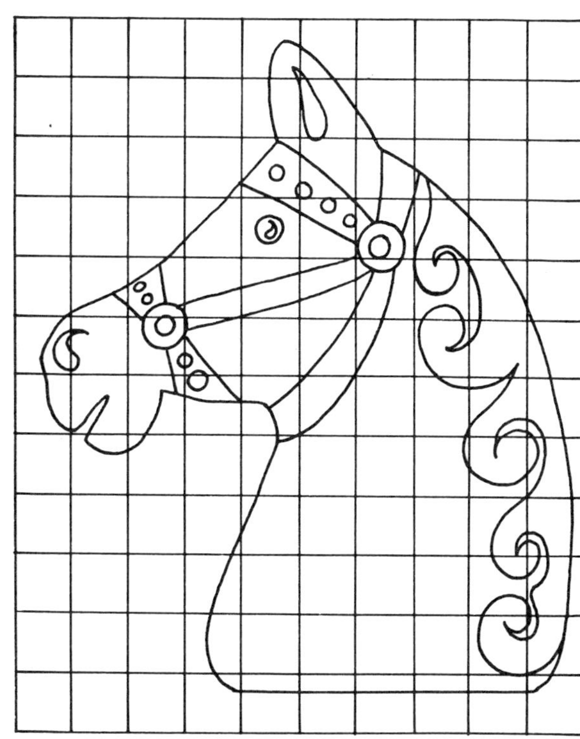

COLOR GUIDE (See color print 1)
Harness: black with red dots
Nose and ear strokes: black
Mane: gold
Eye: blue with white highlight
Harness rings: gold

Rocking Horse

Our gentle little horse is fun for children to begin riding when they are about two years old. Although we have painted these rocking horses in a rainbow of colors, they seem to be at their best when painted white and gaily decorated with hearts and tulips in bright cheerful colors. The horse may be built entirely of plywood or if you prefer, use white pine shelving for the body and cut only the head piece from plywood.

MATERIALS:

¾″ plywood (good on both sides)—24″ ×48″; or,
1″ white pine shelving—12″×60″, and
¾″ plywood (good on both sides)—12″ ×12″

½″-diameter dowel—7″ long
Four No. 8 flat-head screws—1½″ long
Two dozen finishing nails—2″ long
One dozen finishing nails—1½″ long

STEP ONE: CUTTING

Using the Suggested Layout for Cutting as your guide, measure and lay out the following pieces on your wood:

Head: Cut one piece from plywood—12″ ×12″
Seat: Cut one piece—7″×16½″
Tail: Cut one piece—5″×2½″
Stringer: Cut one piece—3″×12⅜″
Rockers: Cut two pieces—4½″×30″
Rocker Separators: Cut two pieces—1½″ ×10″
Legs: Cut two pieces—9¾″×5½″

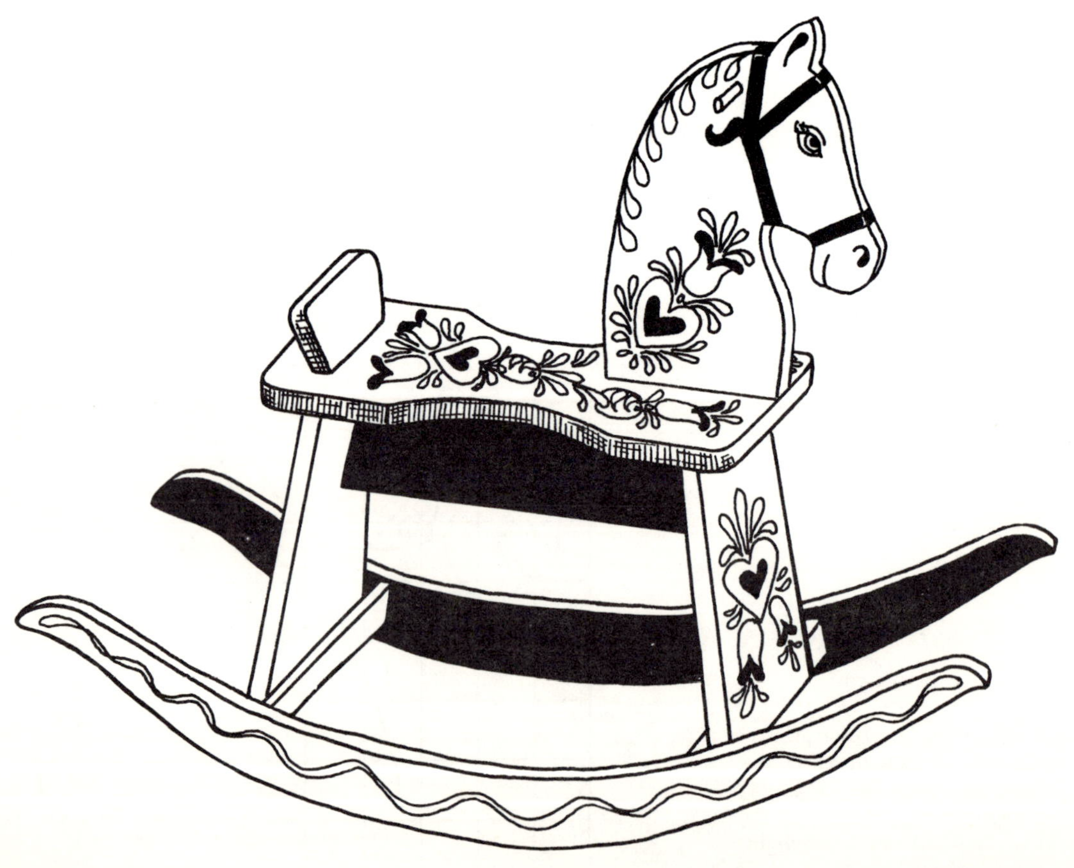

SUGGESTED LAYOUT FOR CUTTING

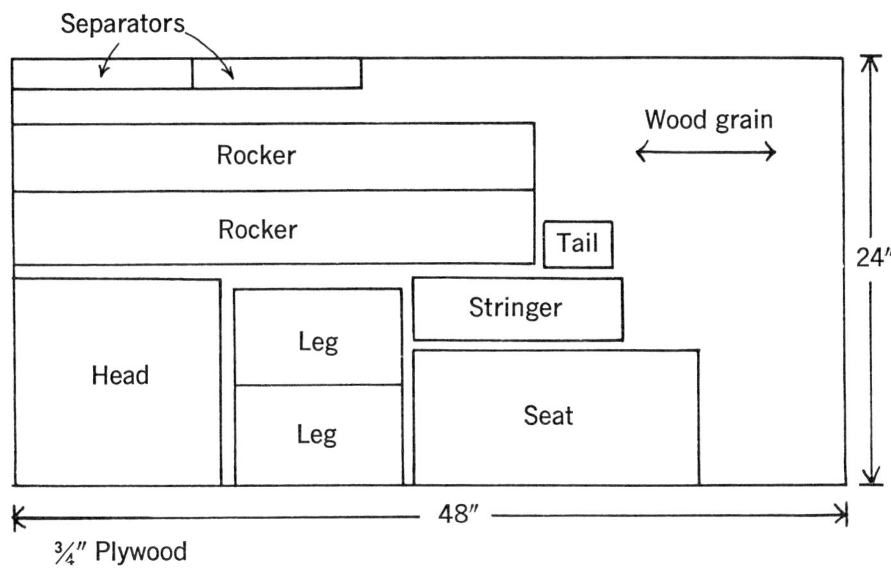

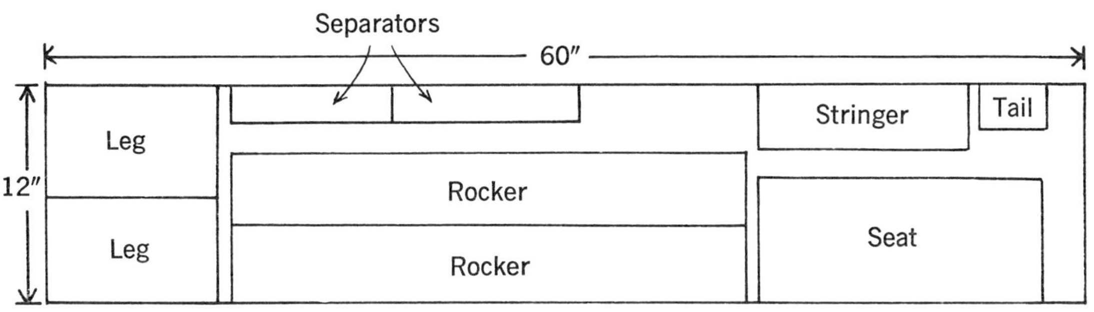

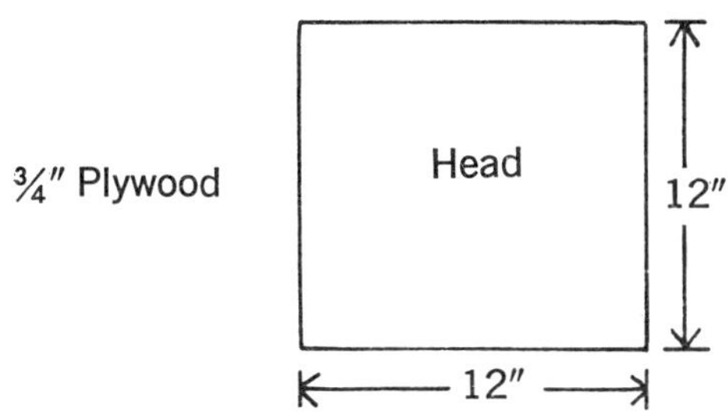

ROCKER (cut 2)
1 Square = 1 Inch

½ Pattern   Center line

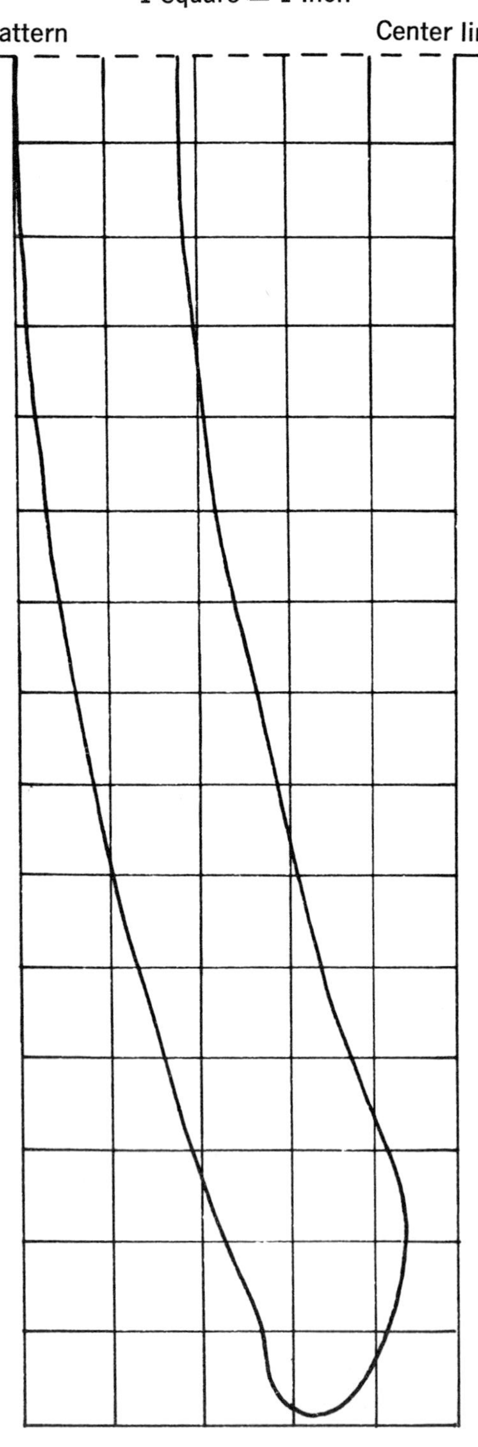

Enlarge the cutting patterns for the rocker, head, and seat and transfer to the corresponding pieces of wood. Also transfer the actual size pattern for the tail (Cutting Pattern D). Cut these pieces with a jig saw or saber saw. Notice that the tail piece is angled on the bottom edge (see side view with cutting pattern). To do this, measure 2¼″ down on one side to establish the angle and cut the bottom edge as shown. After all pieces have been cut, locate and draw center lines on both sides of all pieces except the head piece.

CUTTING PATTERN B

HEAD (cut 1)
1 Square = 1 Inch

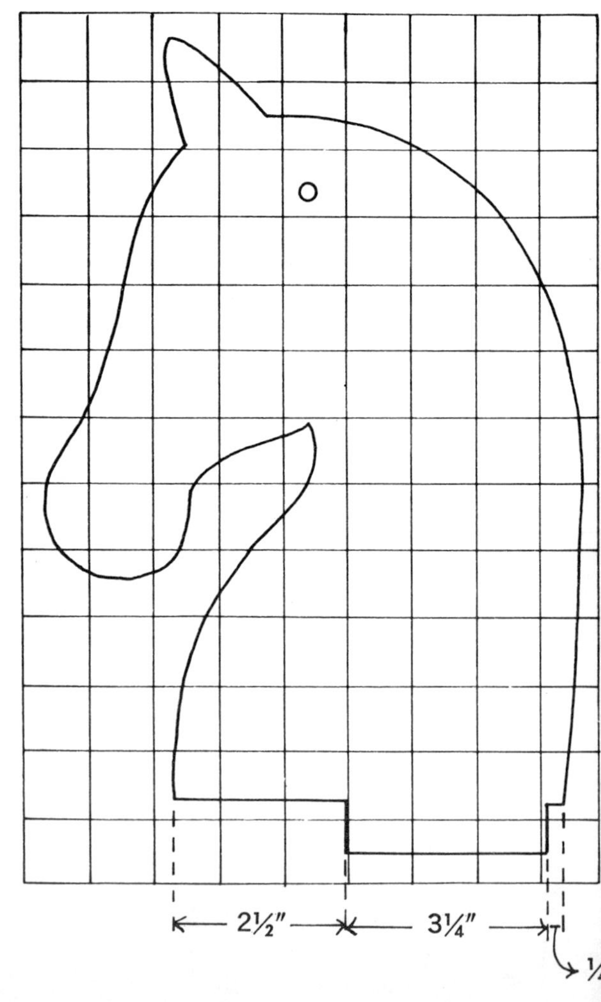

CUTTING PATTERN C

SEAT (cut 1)
1 Square = 1 Inch

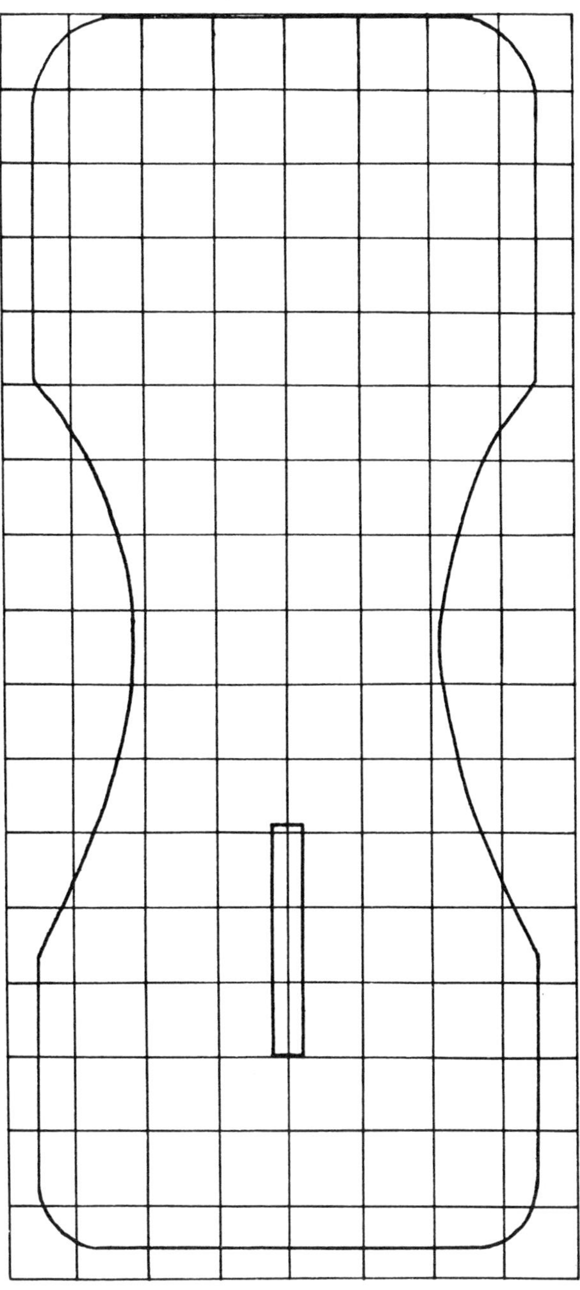

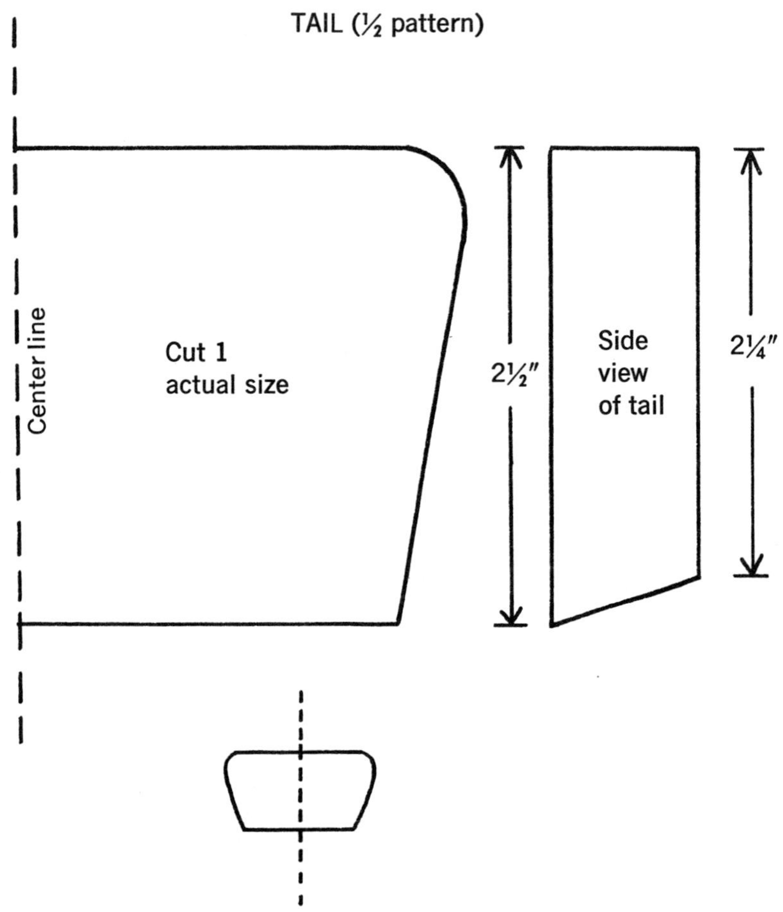

Now cut a ¾"×3¼" slot for the head in the seat. To do this, drill two ¾"-diameter holes, locating the first hole on the center line, 2⅞" back from the front edge of the seat. Locate the second hole on the center line, 2½" past the center point of the first hole (Diagram A). After the holes have been drilled, finish cutting the slot with a saber saw or jig saw. Follow the cutting pattern to round the seat corners, or use a compass to scribe a 1¼" radius on each of the four corners and cut the rounded edges. The seat is now ready for assembly.

To taper the leg pieces, measure 1⅝" from the center line toward the sides and mark on the top edge. At the other end, measure 2¾" on each side of the center line and mark. Connect these top and bottom points on each side of the board and cut along these lines (Diagram B).

To cut the angle on each end of the stringer, measure 5¾" out from each side of the center line on the top edge, and measure 6³⁄₁₆" out from each side of the center line on the bottom edge. Connect these points and saw on the lines (Diagram C).

Either clamp or nail the two rocker pieces together, side by side, and sand the

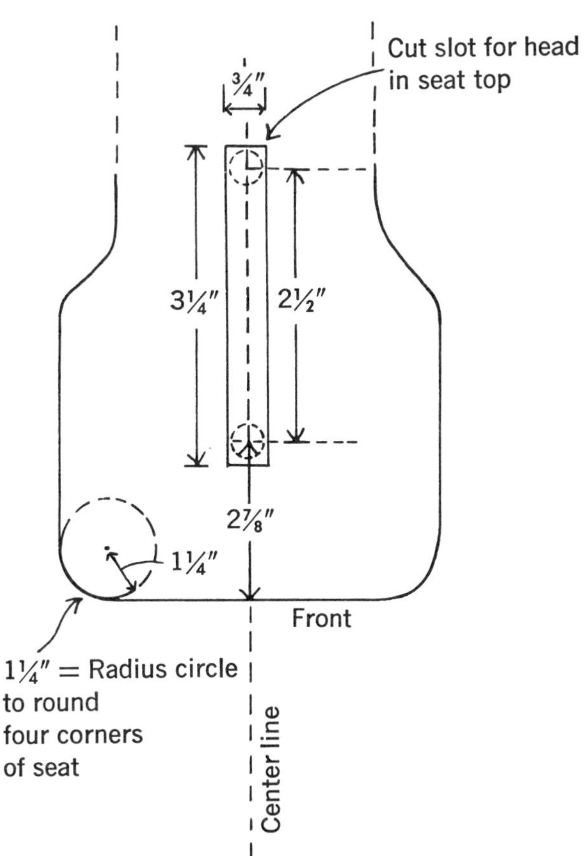

DIAGRAM A
Cut slot for head
in seat top
3/4"
3¼"
2½"
2⅞"
Front
1¼"
1¼" = Radius circle
to round
four corners
of seat
Center line

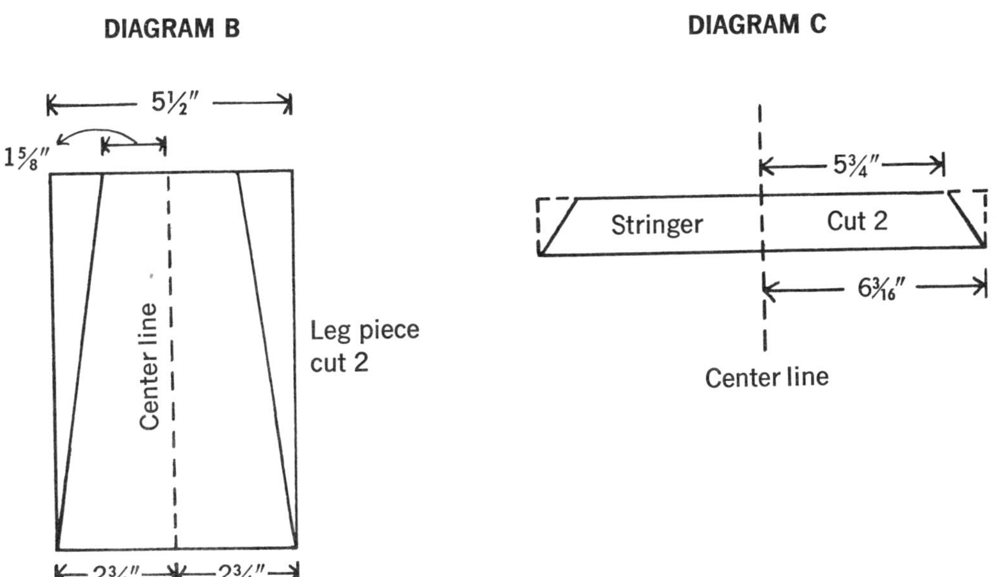

DIAGRAM B
5½"
1⅝"
Center line
Leg piece
cut 2
2¾"
2¾"
DIAGRAM C
5¾"
Stringer
Cut 2
6³⁄₁₆"
Center line

bottom edges so that they match as closely as possible. This will ensure a smooth rocking motion.

Double check to be sure that you have drawn center lines on both sides and edges of all nine pieces, and you are ready for assembly.

STEP TWO: ASSEMBLY

Apply glue to the bottom edge of the head piece and fit it into the slot in the seat by lightly tapping with a hammer or soft mallet until the head sits flush on the seat. Turn the seat upside down and drive a 2″ finishing nail through the seat into the forward part of the head piece. Drive a second nail into the back part of the head at a 45-degree angle (Diagram D).

Next, using glue and two 2″ finishing nails on each leg, nail through the legs into the stringer with the center line of the legs matching the center line of the stringer. The top lower edge of each leg piece should be flush with the top edge of the stringer. With a hand saw, cut down the protruding top edge of the leg so that it will be flush with the stringer. This will create a flat surface from front to back on which the seat will rest (Diagram E).

Place the rocker separators on the insides of the leg pieces, bottom edges flush and center lines matching. Glue and nail into place using six nails, 1½″ long, on each of the two legs. Nail three nails through the leg piece and three nails from the other side through the separator (Diagram F).

Now, apply glue to the top edges of the leg assembly and place the seat on top, matching center lines in both directions. Drive two 2″ nails through the seat on the center line into the stringer. Drive two nails into the front leg piece on each side of the head, and two nails through the seat into the back leg piece as shown in Diagram G.

Place the rockers, still held together, flat on your work bench. Place the horse on its side, supporting the head to make it

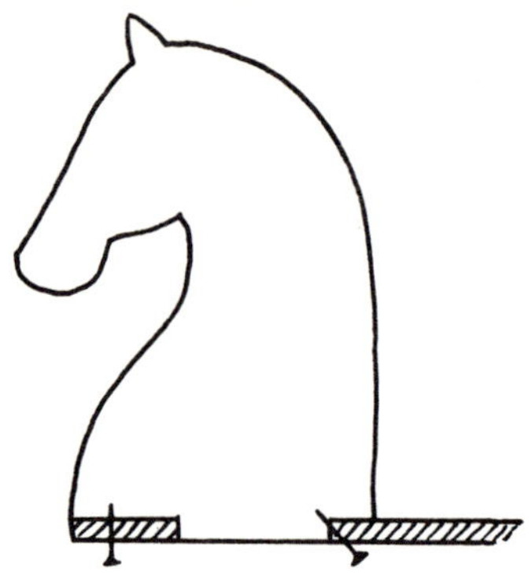

DIAGRAM D

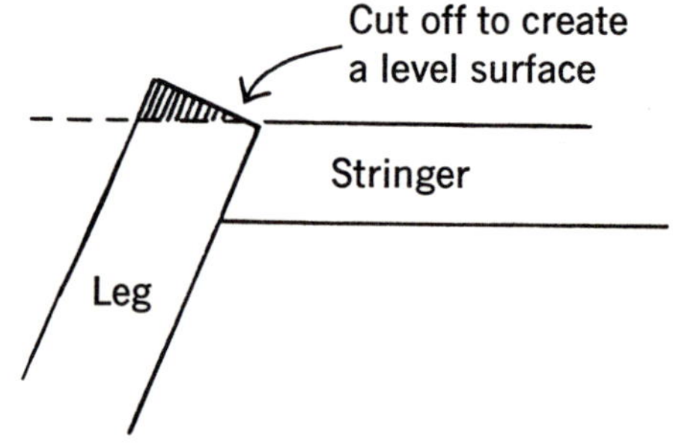

DIAGRAM E

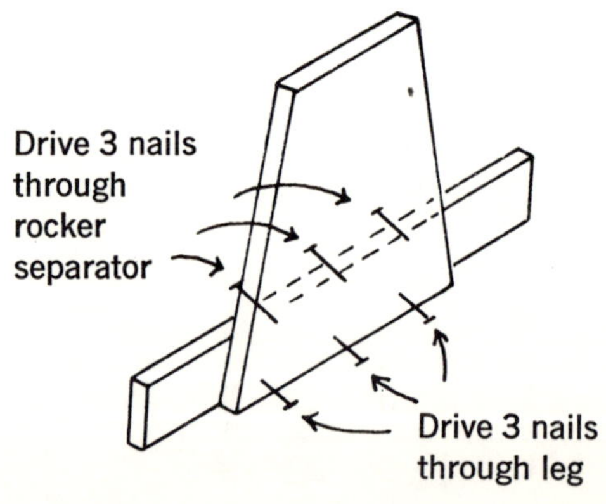

DIAGRAM F

level, and place the ends of the rocker separators an equal distance on each side of the rocker center line. The top edge of the separators should be flush with the top edge of the rocker. Draw the shape of the separator ends onto the rocker. Drill pilot holes through both rockers in the exact center of the separator shapes. The pilot holes should be somewhat smaller than the No. 8 flat-head screw.

Separate the two rockers and fill the nail holes with spackling paste. Countersink the pilot holes on the outside of the rockers so that the screws can be covered with spackling paste after they have been screwed into place. With the horse lying on its side, continue the pilot holes through each rocker into the separators and screw the rockers into place.

To locate the horse's tail, measure 1¼″ from the back edge of the seat on the center line. Match the center line of the tail to the center line of the seat at this measured point. Using three 1½″ nails and glue, nail through the tail at an angle into the seat. Drive the nail from the front side of the tail as shown in Diagram H.

To install the dowel as a handhold, drill a ½″ hole through the head piece as indicated on the cutting pattern. Round the ends of the 7″ dowel with sandpaper and glue into place, centering it through the hole so that it is an equal distance on both sides.

Set all nails and fill with spackling paste, sand thoroughly, and the rocking horse is ready for painting.

DIAGRAM G

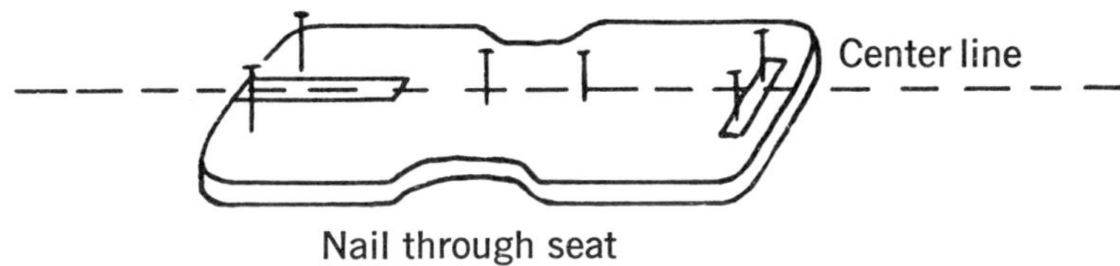

DIAGRAM H

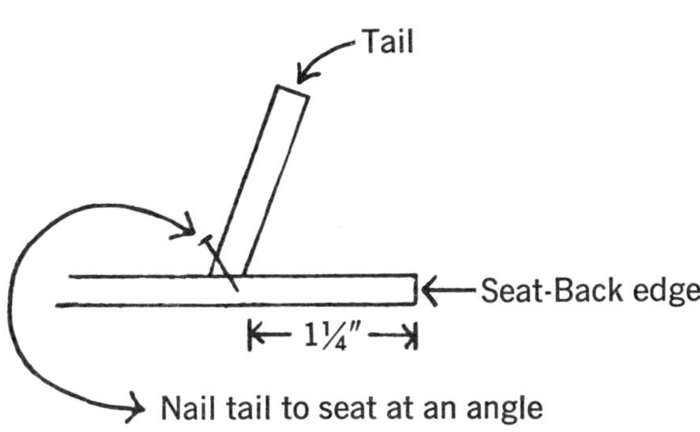

1 Square = 1 Inch

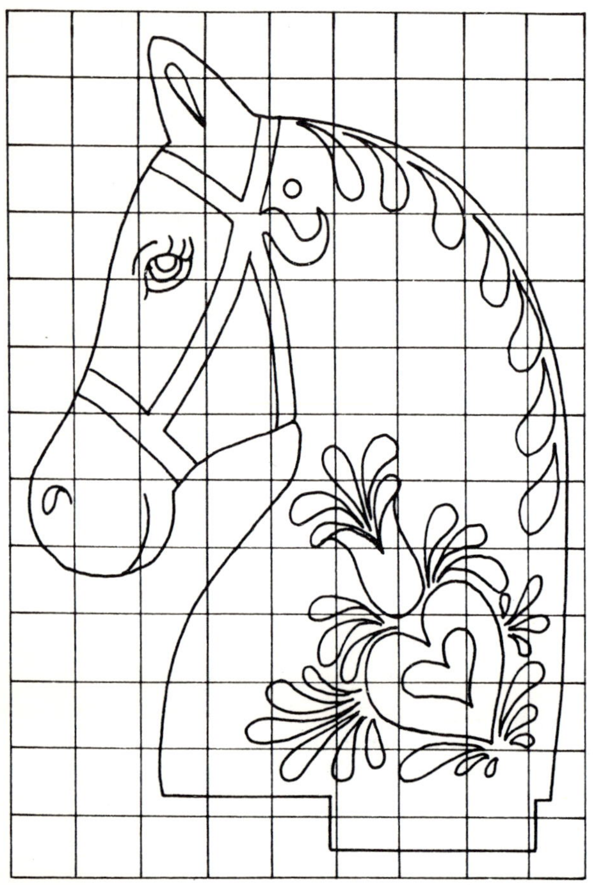

COLOR GUIDE (See color print 1)
Hearts: pink with red hearts inside
Tulips: light blue with dark blue tips
Roses: pink with red accents
Strokes at end of tulips: gold
Leaf strokes: green
Mane: gold
Harness: pink, red, or blue
Handhold: to match harness
Rockers: ribbon line to match harness
Ear, nose, mouth: black brush strokes
Eye: outline in black, light blue iris, black pupil

PAINTING PATTERNS

1 Square = 1 Inch

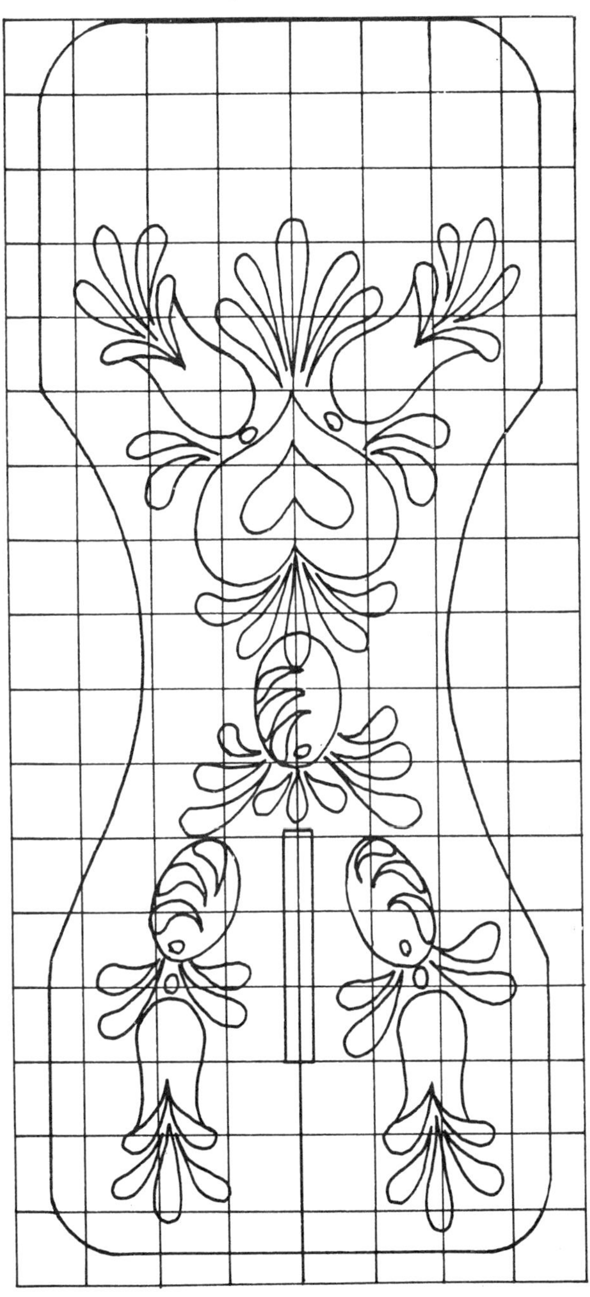

LEG
1 Square = 1 Inch

Doll House

This simple design is an excellent selection for a little girl's very first doll house, reminiscent of Mother Goose, fairy tales, and all these good things that little girls love. The door opens but the windows are painted on which makes it imaginatively cozy. We paint these houses pink with red roof, pale blue with Dutch-blue roof, yellow with green roof, or white with the roof any color of the rainbow.

The shutters look best when painted the same color as the roof. The horizontal dividing line should be in a contrasting color, such as a blue line on a pink doll house that has a red roof and shutters. Be sure to paint the little girl's name just under the upstairs window.

MATERIALS:

One piece $\frac{3}{8}''$ plywood (good on both sides), $4' \times 4'$

Two butt hinges—$1''$ size

One wooden knob for door—$\frac{1}{2}''$ or $\frac{3}{4}''$ diameter

Three dozen finishing nails—$1\frac{1}{4}''$ or $1\frac{1}{2}''$ long

One dozen $\frac{3}{4}''$ finishing nails for door trim

One flat-head screw—$\frac{3}{4}''$ long

STEP ONE: CUTTING

Lay out and cut the following pieces from the four-foot-square piece of plywood;

Front: Cut one piece—$24'' \times 21''$
Floor: Cut two pieces—$20\frac{1}{4}'' \times 8\frac{7}{8}''$
Roof: Cut one piece—$10\frac{1}{8}'' \times 17''$
    Cut one piece—$10\frac{1}{8}'' \times 16\frac{5}{8}''$
Door: Use piece cut from front
Sides: Cut two pieces—$13\frac{3}{4}'' \times 8\frac{7}{8}''$ (Cut top edges at 45-degree angle for sloping roof.)

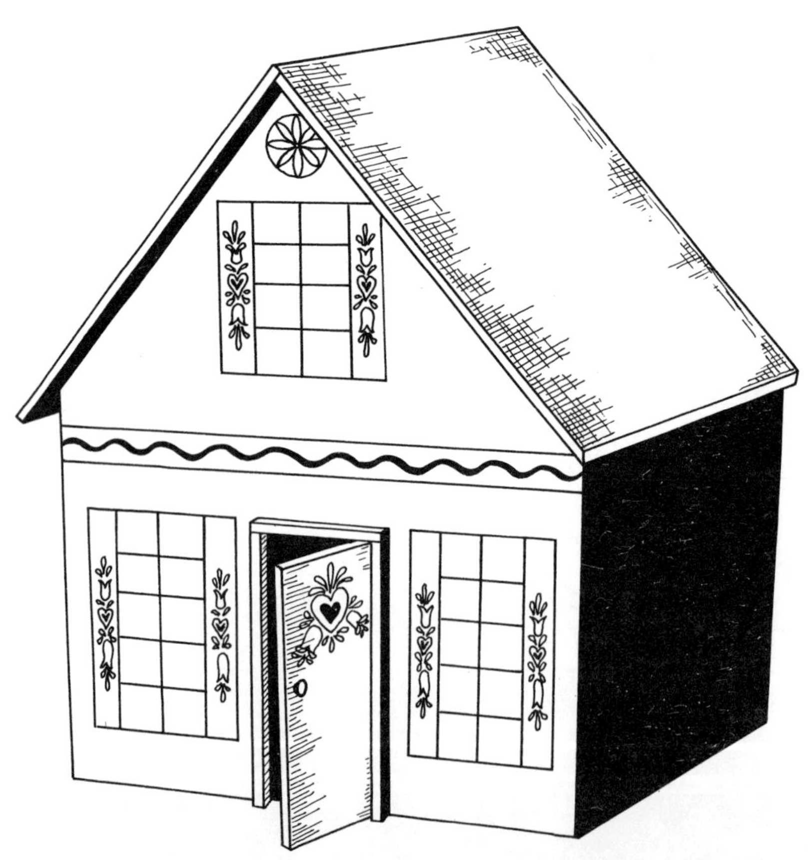

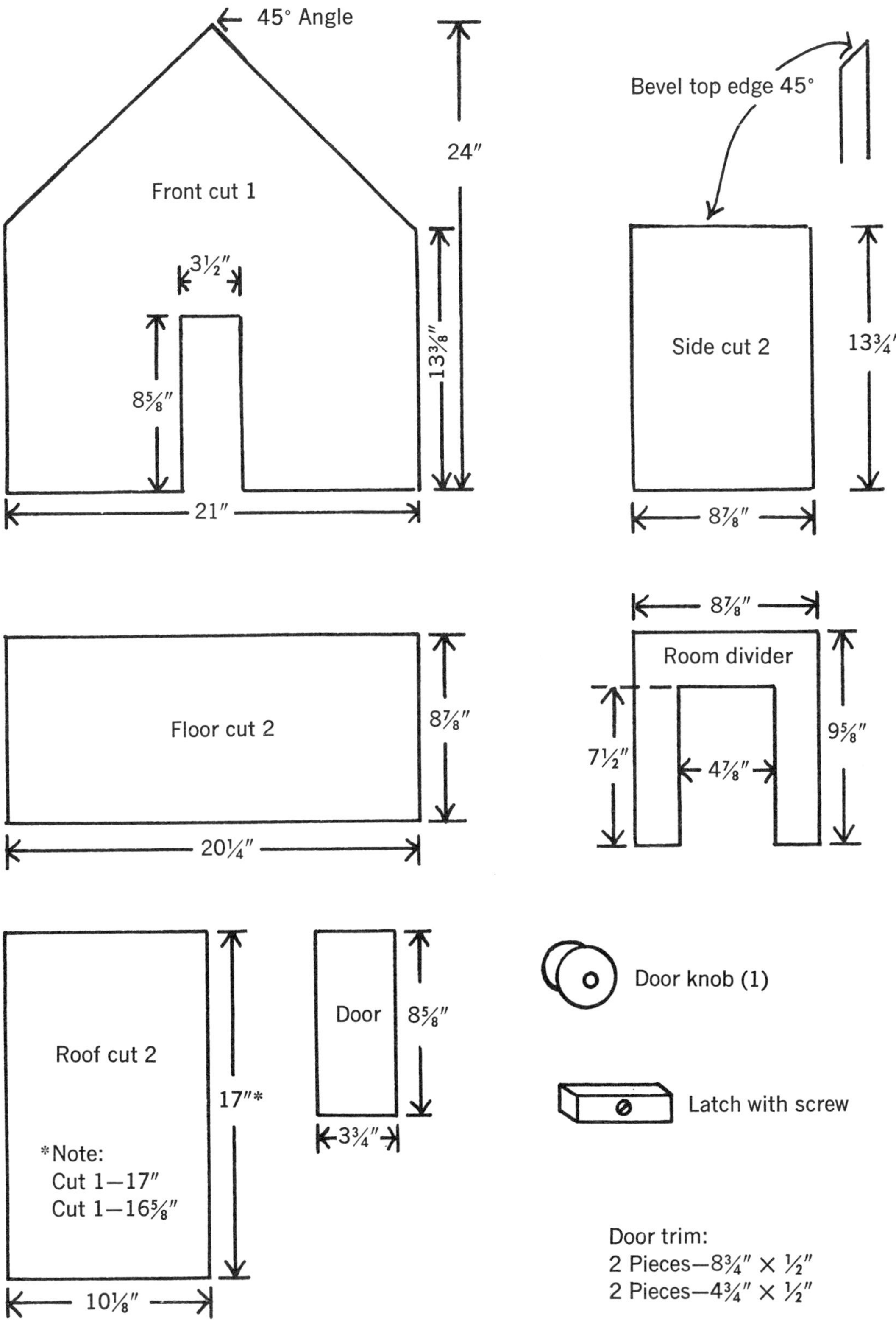

45° Angle
Front cut 1
24"
3½"
13⅜"
8⅝"
21"
Bevel top edge 45°
Side cut 2
13¾"
8⅞"
Floor cut 2
8⅞"
20¼"
8⅞"
Room divider
7½"
4⅞"
9⅝"
Roof cut 2
17"*
*Note:
Cut 1—17"
Cut 1—16⅝"
10⅛"
Door
8⅝"
3¾"
Door knob (1)
Latch with screw
Door trim:
2 Pieces—8¾" × ½"
2 Pieces—4¾" × ½"

Divider: Cut one piece—8⅞″×9⅝″
Door trim: Cut two pieces—8¾″×½″
    Cut two pieces—4¾″×½″
Door latch: Cut one piece—1″×½″
Roof strips: Cut two pieces—Cut one
    piece—8⅞″×1¾″
    Cut one piece—8⅞″×1⅜″

STEP TWO: ASSEMBLY

Begin the assembly as you would any house, from the ground up. Nail the bottom edge of the room divider to the floor, locating it 7¾″ from the right-hand end of the floor. Drive four nails through the floor into the divider. The top floor is now placed on the divider in the same manner and nailed into place (Diagram A). Next, nail each side piece in place making sure that the 45-degree angle is at the top and sloping down to the outside to match the roof slope as shown in Diagram B. Use three or four nails through each side into both the bottom and top floor.

Now, lay this portion of the assembly on its back (this will put the small room on your left) and nail the front piece to the sides and upper and lower floors. Use four or five nails in each side and across the front into each floor piece (Diagram C).

Now place in front of you the two roof pieces with the longer piece on the right. Nail the widest roof strip ⅜″ down from the top and flush with the right-hand edge of the longest roof piece, as shown in Diagram D. Nail the narrower roof strip ⅜″ down and flush with the left-hand edge of the shortest roof piece. Now stand the house upright, with the back facing you (small room on the right). Take the longest roof piece and nail it to the front and right-hand side piece with three or four nails on each edge, making sure that the roof is flush with the back face of the house and projects ⅜″ above the high point of the house front. Follow this by nailing the remaining half of the roof in the same manner (Diagram E).

The house is now complete except for the door and door frame. Lay the house flat on its back and place one of the short

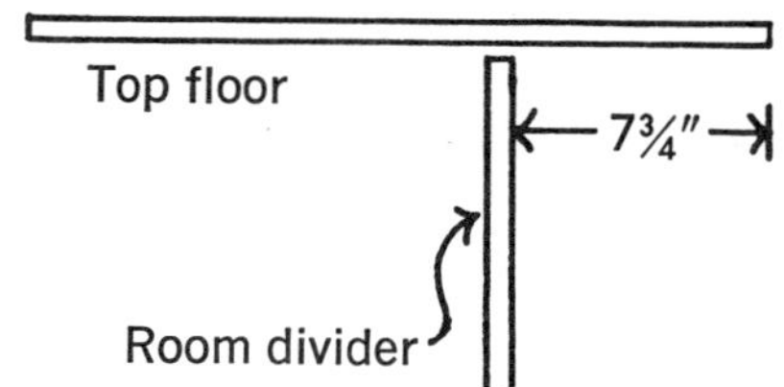

DIAGRAM A

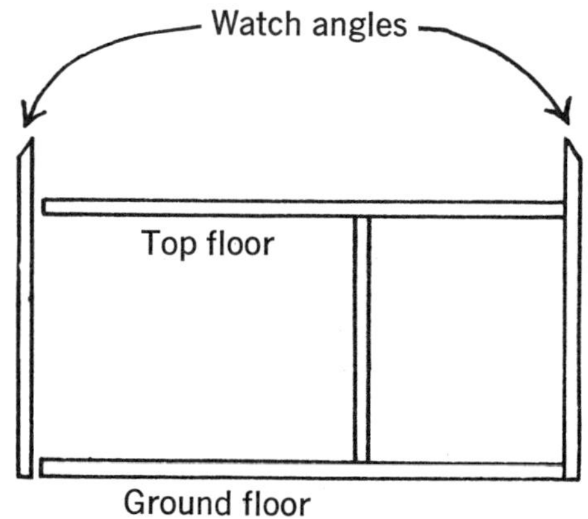

DIAGRAM B

When ground floor is in position, nail in top floor already assembled

DIAGRAM C

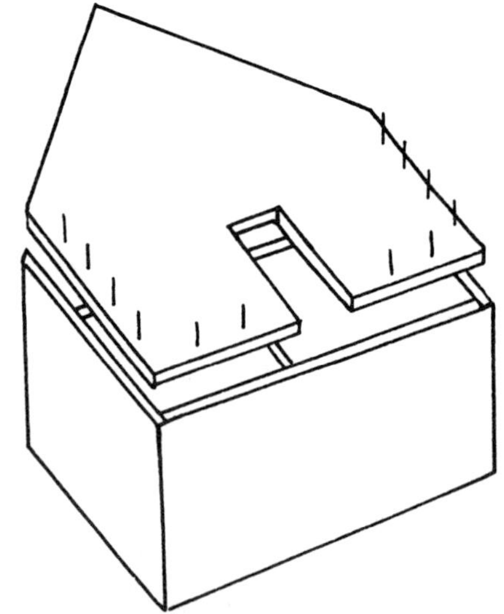

Place back side of house flat in order to nail front piece on frame

pieces of door trim flush with the bottom floor and across the doorstep. This should leave 8⅛″ from the ends of the piece to the sides of the house. Nail this strip in place with two short finishing nails. Next, locate the two long door trim pieces, one on each side and flush with the ends of the bottom strip already in place. Nail each of the two pieces with three nails each. Now nail the top door strip in place. Note that the door opening in the front piece of the house is about ¼″ narrower than the distance between the trim pieces; this provides the door stop (Diagram F).

Place the door in the opening and attach the two small butt hinges locating them 1″ from the top and bottom of the door. The doorknob is located ⅝″ from the edge and 4″ down from the top of the door. The latch is located on the left-hand door-trim piece, 5½″ down from the top of the door framing and is held in place with a ¾″ flat-head screw. The screw should not be screwed in so tightly that the latch cannot move freely.

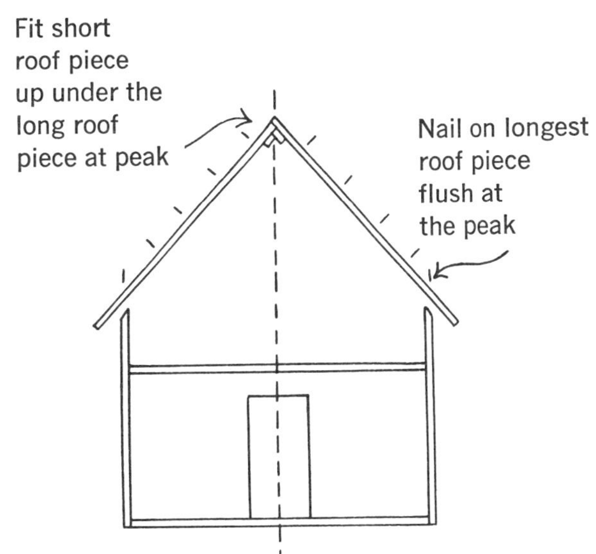

Nail straight down into side pieces flush with back edge of side, allowing front of roof to overhang

DIAGRAM D

Lay roof pieces side by side—nail on roofing strips flush to the outside edges

DIAGRAM F

Fit door into opening and install hinges

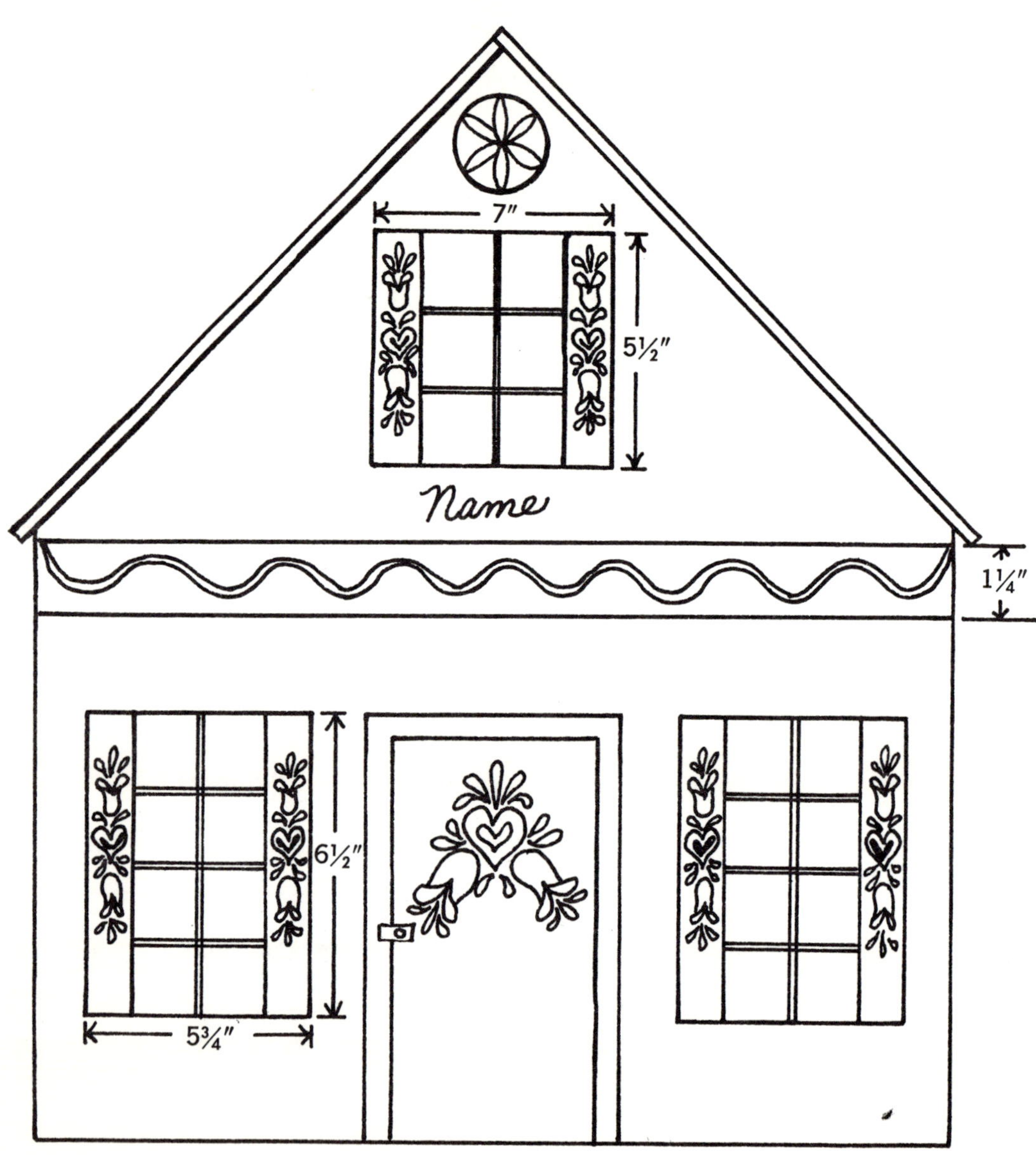

COLOR GUIDE (See color print 6)
Hearts: pink with red heart inside
Tulips: light blue with dark blue edge strokes
Leaf strokes: green
Strokes at end of tulips: gold

Actual size

Shutter design

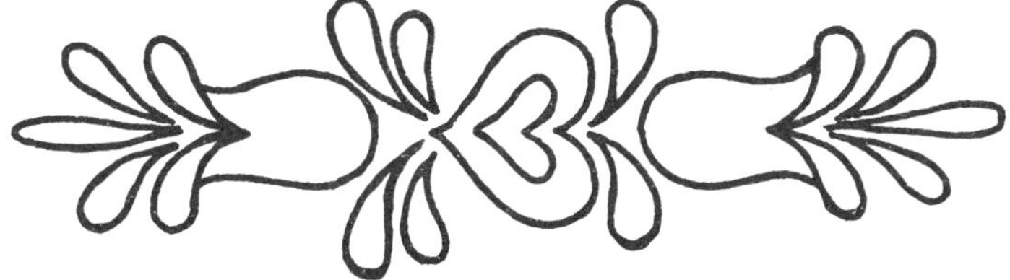

Use a yardstick to draw shutters, windows, and dividing line in place. Center windows in correct areas

Hex sign —PEAK OF ROOF

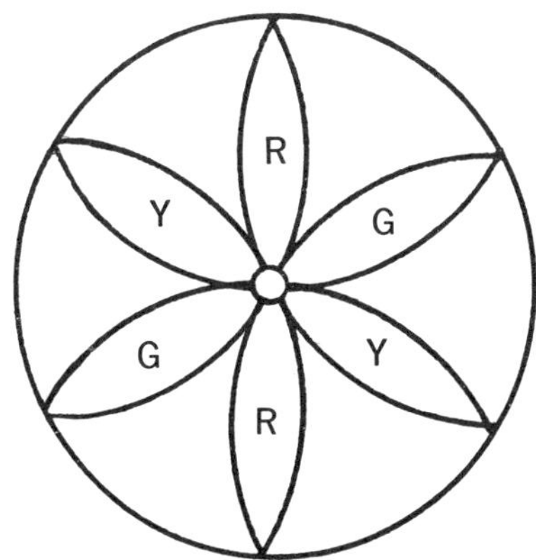

COLOR GUIDE
R: red
G: green
Y: yellow

Door design

Town House

This little town house with its six rooms is a de luxe item for doll house fans. It can double as a cabinet or bookcase, so consider using it as a piece of furniture also. Our town house is painted a rich ivory color with a chocolate-brown roof and a soft pumpkin interior.

MATERIALS:

3 lengths of 1″×12″ white pine shelving —10′ long
⅛″ Masonite board—24″×48″
Two wood knobs with screws—1″ diameter
Two pairs of flat cabinet hinges with screws—2″ size

Two spring-type cabinet door latches
Four dozen finishing nails—2″ long
One dozen finishing nails—1¾″ long
Three dozen common nails—1″ long

STEP ONE: CUTTING

Measure and cut the following lengths of board-width pine:

Sides: Cut two pieces—30″ long (Cut top edge at an angle as shown in Diagram A.)
Doors: Cut two pieces—38⅝″ long on one side and 27⅝″ long on the other side as shown in Diagram B
Floors: Cut four pieces—21″ long
Partitions: Cut two pieces—8″ long
Roof: Cut one piece—16″ long
   Cut one piece—16¾″ long

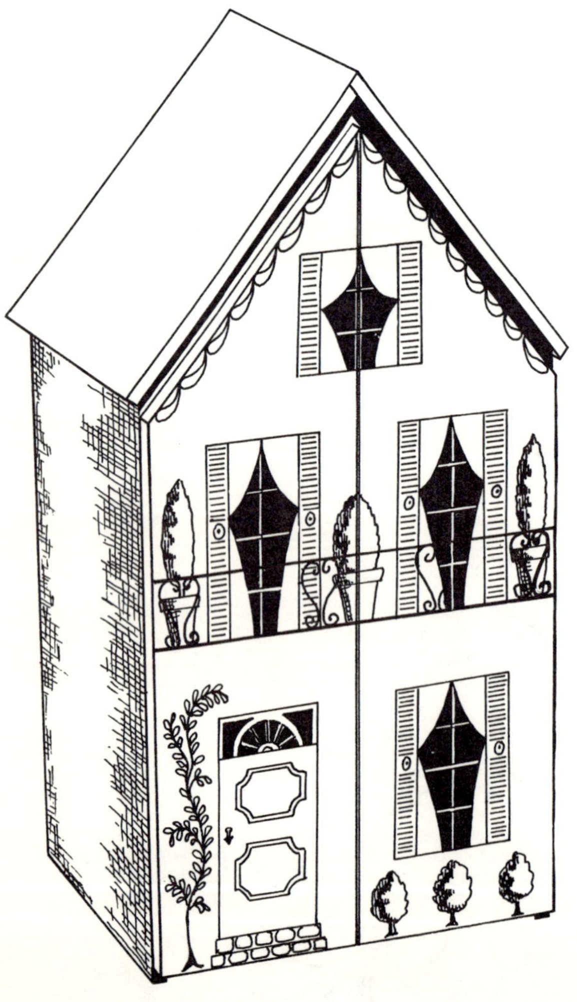

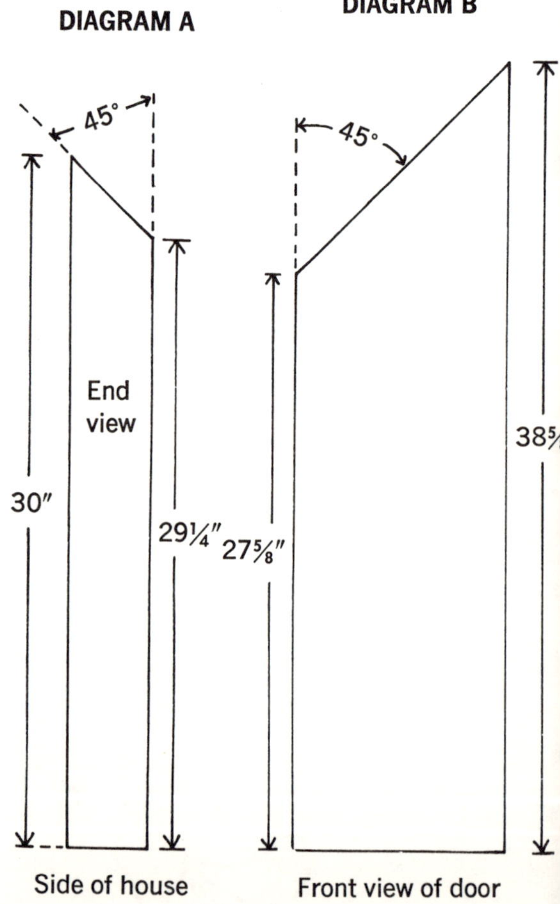

Now cut the remaining pieces to the following measurements:

Door stops: Cut one piece—1¼″×16″
Cut one piece—1¼″×14¾″
Roof extension strips: Cut one piece—¾″×¾″×16″
Cut one piece—¾″×¾″×16¾″
Roof brace: Cut one piece—4″×8″
Back: Cut one piece from Masonite—22½″×40½″

First, following Diagram C, cut a doorway in each partition. Cut one end of each door stop at the angle shown in Diagram D. Now, following Diagram E, cut the two sides of the roof brace at a 45-degree angle to match the roof pitch. Finally, finish cutting the back piece of Masonite according to the measurements in Diagram F.

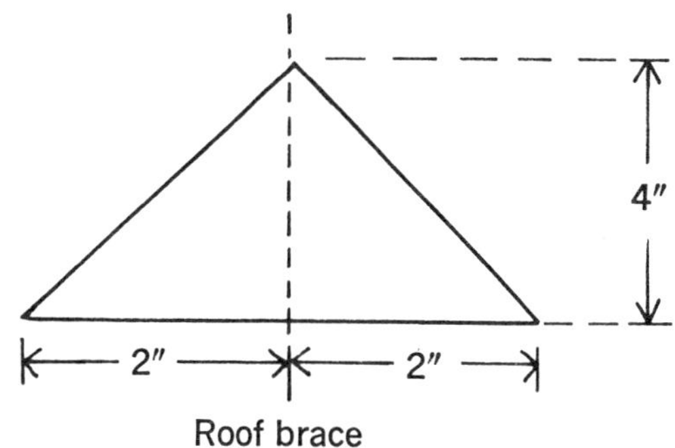

DIAGRAM E

Roof brace

DIAGRAM F

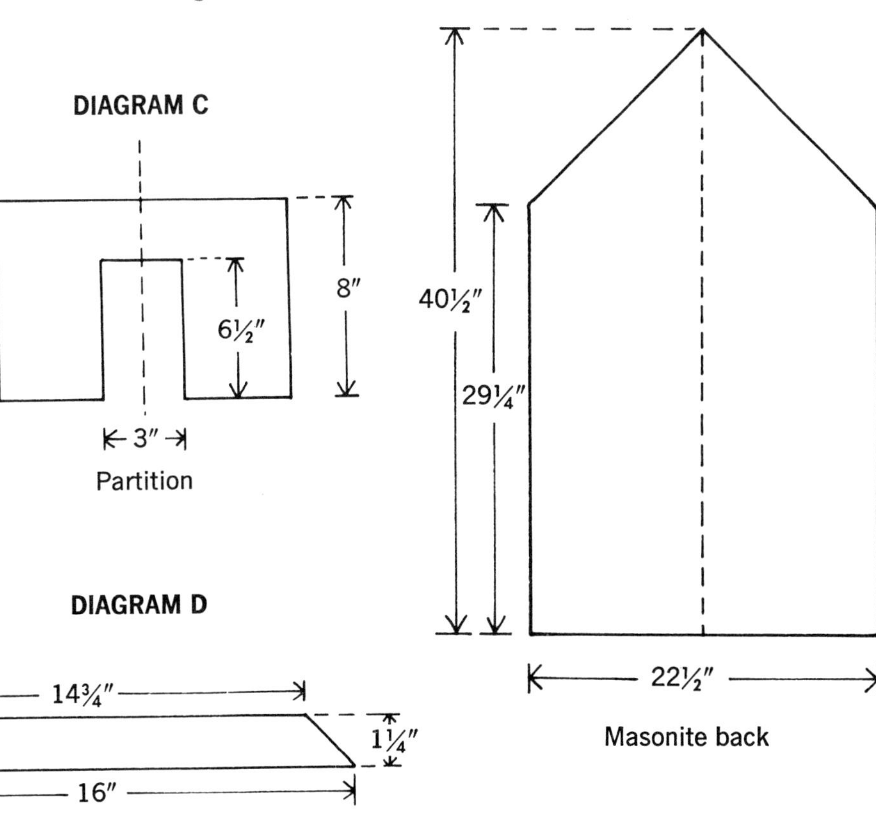

DIAGRAM C

Partition

DIAGRAM D

Door stops

Masonite back

The width of the roof boards must be increased to 12″. Do this by gluing and nailing one roof extension strip to each roof piece using three 2″ finishing nails through each strip.

Lay the two side pieces flat on your workbench with the edges together, side by side, and the bottom edges accurately lined up with each other. The tapered top edge should be on the underside. Begin at the bottom edges and following Diagram G, measure and draw lines across both side pieces to locate the floors.

Apply glue to one end of a floor piece, locate it accurately along the first bottom line, and with three 2″ finishing nails, nail the floor into place through the side piece. Nail the other three floors into their proper locations in the same manner. Now, turn the assembly over and with the floor facing up, glue and nail the other side piece to the floor ends. When all the floors are in place, draw a center line from the front to back and on the edges of the first and third floor to locate the partitions. Glue and nail the partitions on the center line by driving two 2″ nails through the floors both from above and below the floors into the partitions.

With the house on its back, use a carpenter's square to adjust the assembly so that it is square, and temporarily nail a 4′ piece of wood diagonally across the house (from corner to corner) with a nail in each of the four floors. This will keep the house square while you attach the back piece.

Now turn the house over on its face and position the back piece evenly at the top and sides and drive six 1″ common

DIAGRAM G

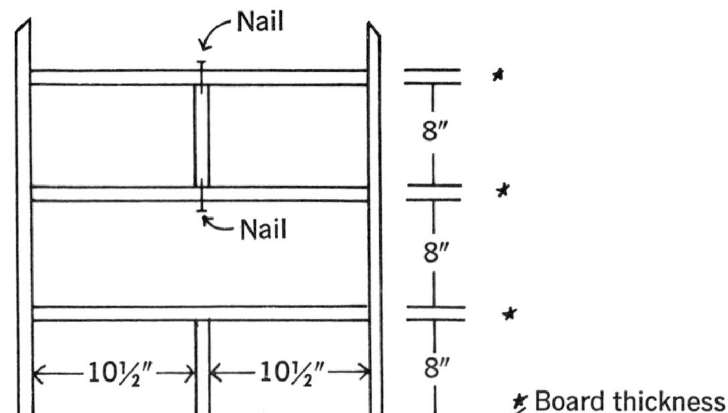

Floor and partition placement

nails into each side and three nails into each floor.

Apply glue to the edge of the short roof piece and place the long roof piece on the glued edge, flush with the top of the short roof piece. Nail into place with three 2″ finishing nails as shown in Diagram H. Nail the roof brace at the back of the roof in the peak (against the back piece), driving two 2″ finishing nails through the brace into the roof.

Lay the house on its back, place the roof into position against the back piece and nail into place, driving three 2″ nails through the roof and straight down into the side pieces. Turn the house over and nail the back piece to the roof edge.

Turn the house upside down so that it is resting on a roof surface. Place the longest door stop 3/4″ back from the front edge of the roof with the tapered end flush with the side of the house. Glue and nail in place using three 2″ finishing nails through the edge of the door stop into the roof. Tip the house onto its other side of the roof and nail the short door stop into place in the same manner (Diagram H).

Temporarily nail the two doors together with all edges aligned, and with a hand plane, shave off approximately 1/16″ from the short side of the door pieces being careful to not shave any more than that. Separate the doors and place them on the house with the short sides flush with the sides of the house and 3/4″ above the bottom of the house. Temporarily nail into place with two nails in each door. There should be a 1/8″ space between the doors in the center, and about 3/4″ between the roof and top of the doors.

DIAGRAM H

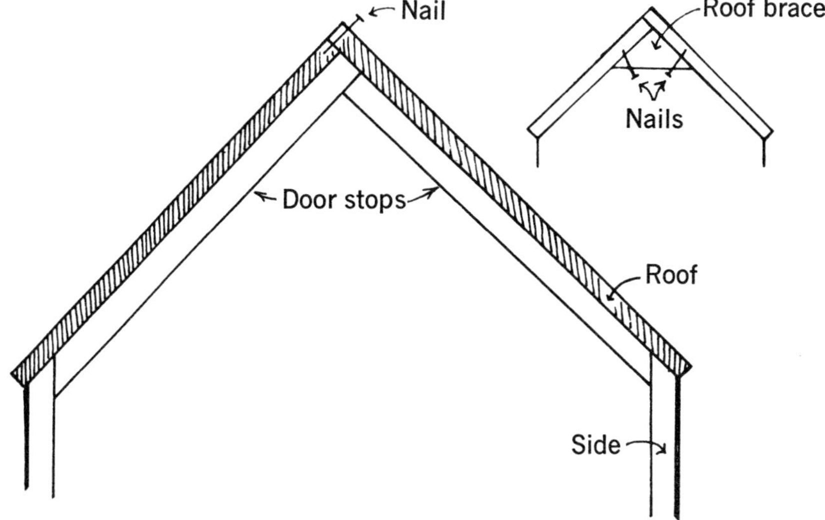

Following Diagram I for location, attach the door hinges and doorknobs. Attach the door catches on the underside of the third floor, 1½″ each side of the center line of the floor.

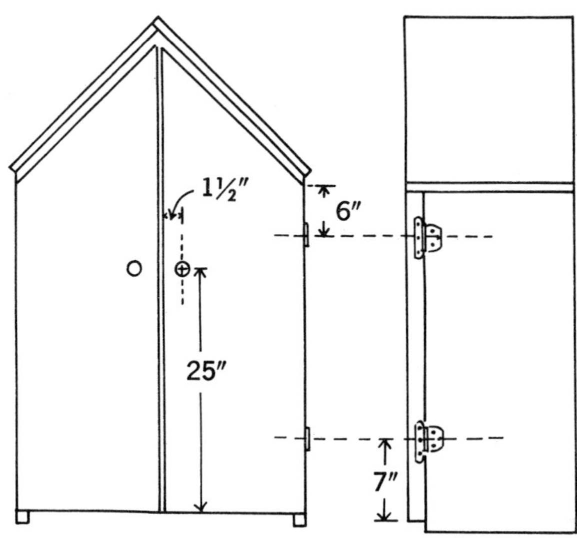

Knob and hinge placement

COLOR GUIDE (See color print 6)
Shutters and door: medium blue, dark gray detail on door
Doorknob: gold
Windows: black with white lines
Curtains: white
Overdoor: blue border and half-circle, black inside with white detail
Plants: green with dark green shading, brown stems
Flower pots and brick steps: rosy brown and pink (Cement: outline bricks with gray)
Scallop trim at top: gold
Balcony: black

PAINTING PATTERN

1 Square = 1 Inch

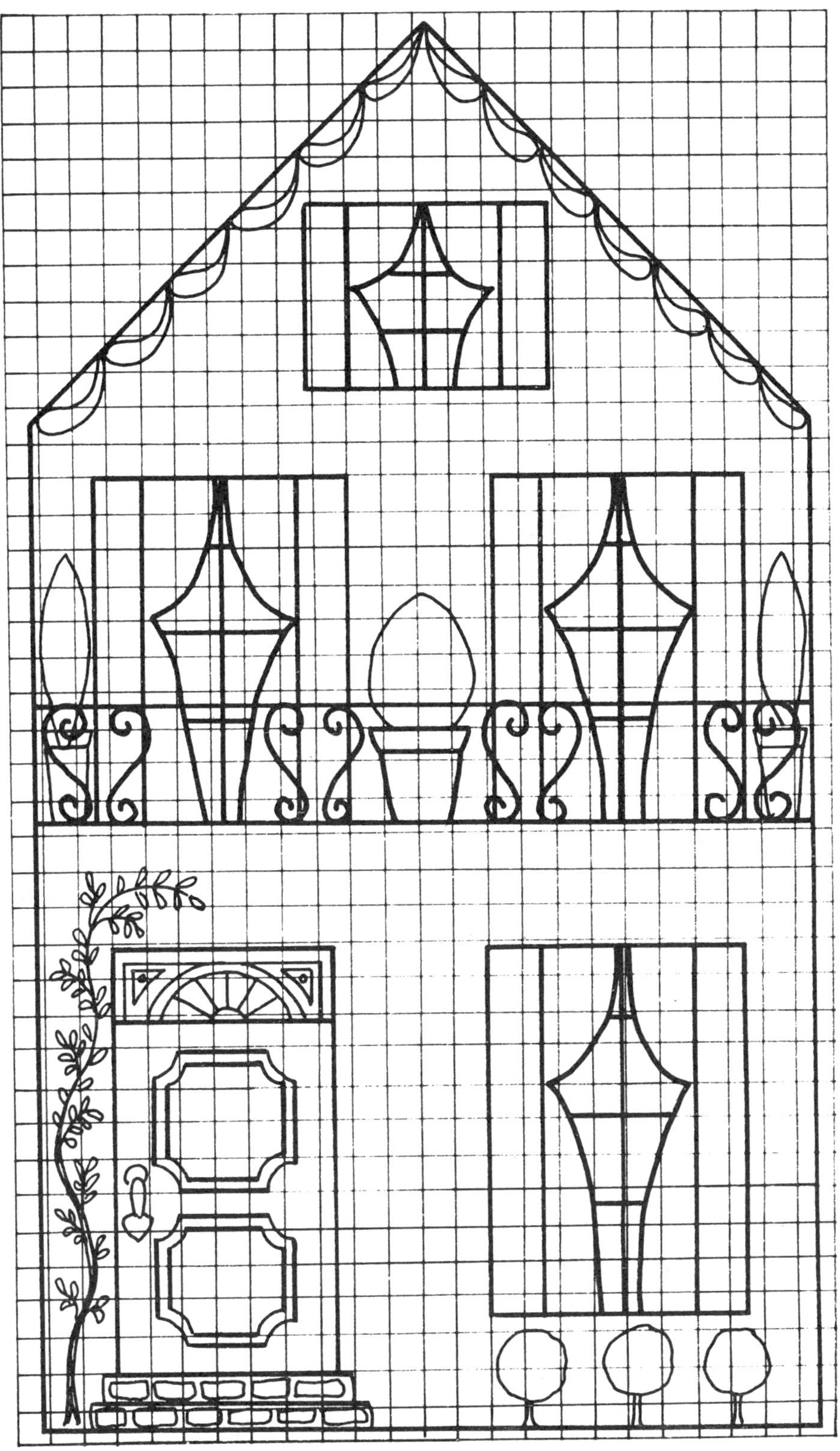

Doll Cradle

Our doll cradle is large enough to hold a good-size doll baby and is ideal for painted designs. The cradle also makes a very fine magazine holder for informal rooms. The heart-shape handholds were a favorite with the Pennsylvania Dutch and serve nicely when moving the cradle about.

MATERIALS:

One piece ¾″ plywood (good on both sides)—42″×42″
About three dozen finishing nails—2½″ long

STEP ONE: CUTTING

Lay out the following pieces on plywood:

Foot of cradle: Cut one rectangle—15½″ ×16¾″
Head of cradle: Cut one rectangle—15½″ ×18¾″

Sides: Cut two rectangles—9″×19¼″
Bottom: Cut later to fit, one rectangle— about 16¼″×9¼″

In order to draw the fancy cutout design for the head and foot of the cradle on the cut rectangles, make tracings of Patterns A and B on the following pages. Draw a center line on the head and foot by dividing the 15½″ width into equal sections of 7¾″. Match the center line of the patterns to the center line on the wood and trace off the pattern, which will give you half of the design. Flip the pattern over and trace off the other side.

Trace rocker Pattern C in the same manner at the other end of the rectangle. After the cradle top and rocker design have been traced onto the wood, use a ruler or yardstick to connect the two starred points on the patterns with a straight line. The hearts can be cut out first by drilling two overlapping circles, each 1¼″ in diameter. See Patterns A and B for placement. After the holes have been drilled, finish cutting the heart with a jig saw or saber

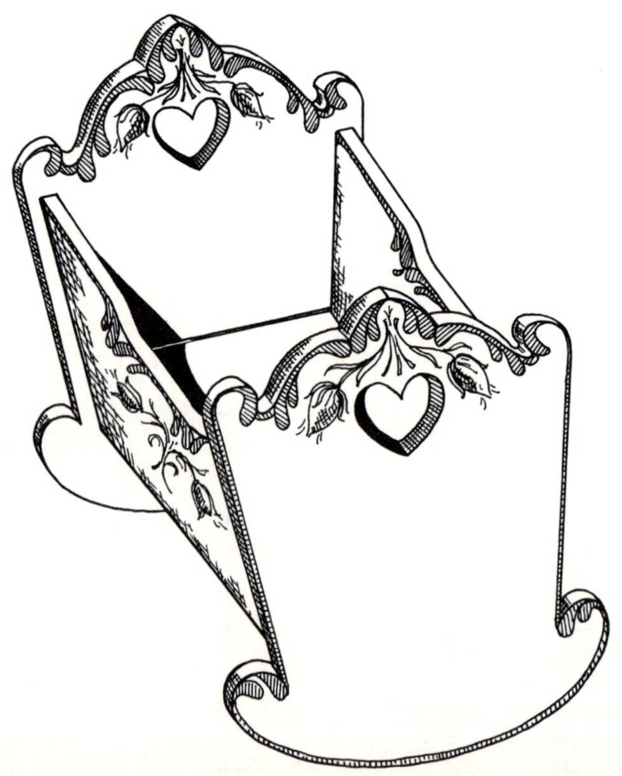

saw. Complete the cutting of the head and foot of the cradle.

Now, to make the design for the side piece, locate the center line of the 19¼" width by measuring 9⅝" from the edge to the center. Draw the center line on the board. To get the proper angle on each end of the side piece, measure 8⅛" on each side of the center line which will give the bottom edge of the cradle a total measurement of 16¼" when cut. Draw the angles with a ruler from the upper corners to the 8⅛" mark.

Establish the dip in the top edge of the side piece using Pattern D. After drawing in the pattern in the two top corners, join patterns with a straight line to complete side piece design. Mark the other side piece to match and use a jig saw to cut the top edges.

PATTERN PIECES

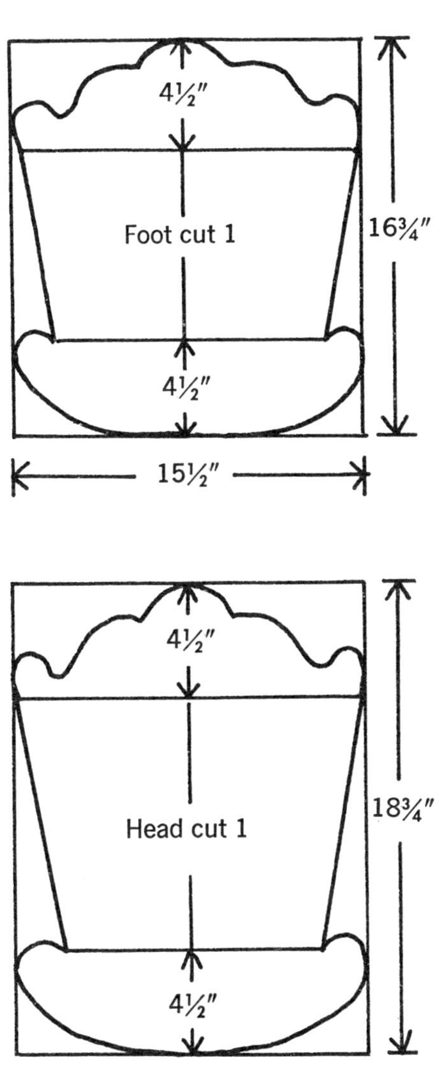

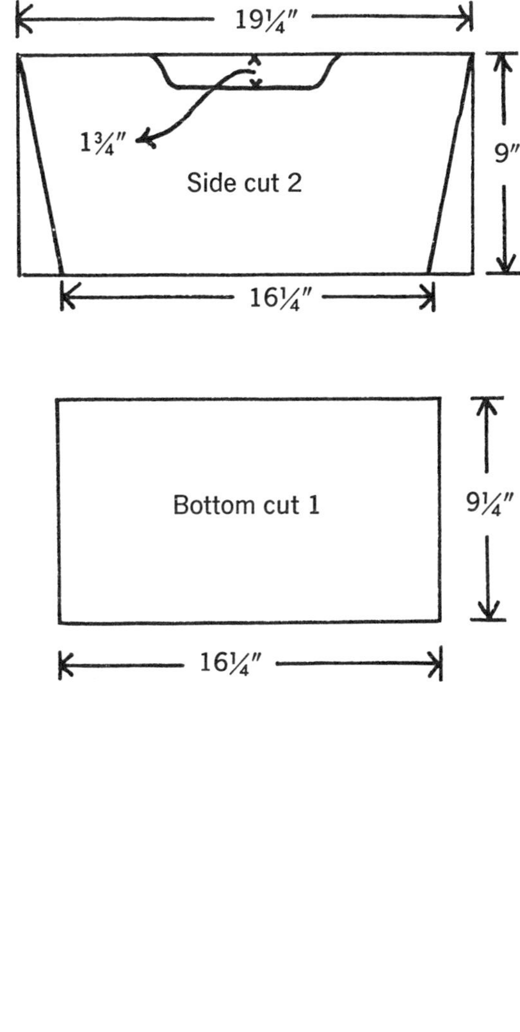

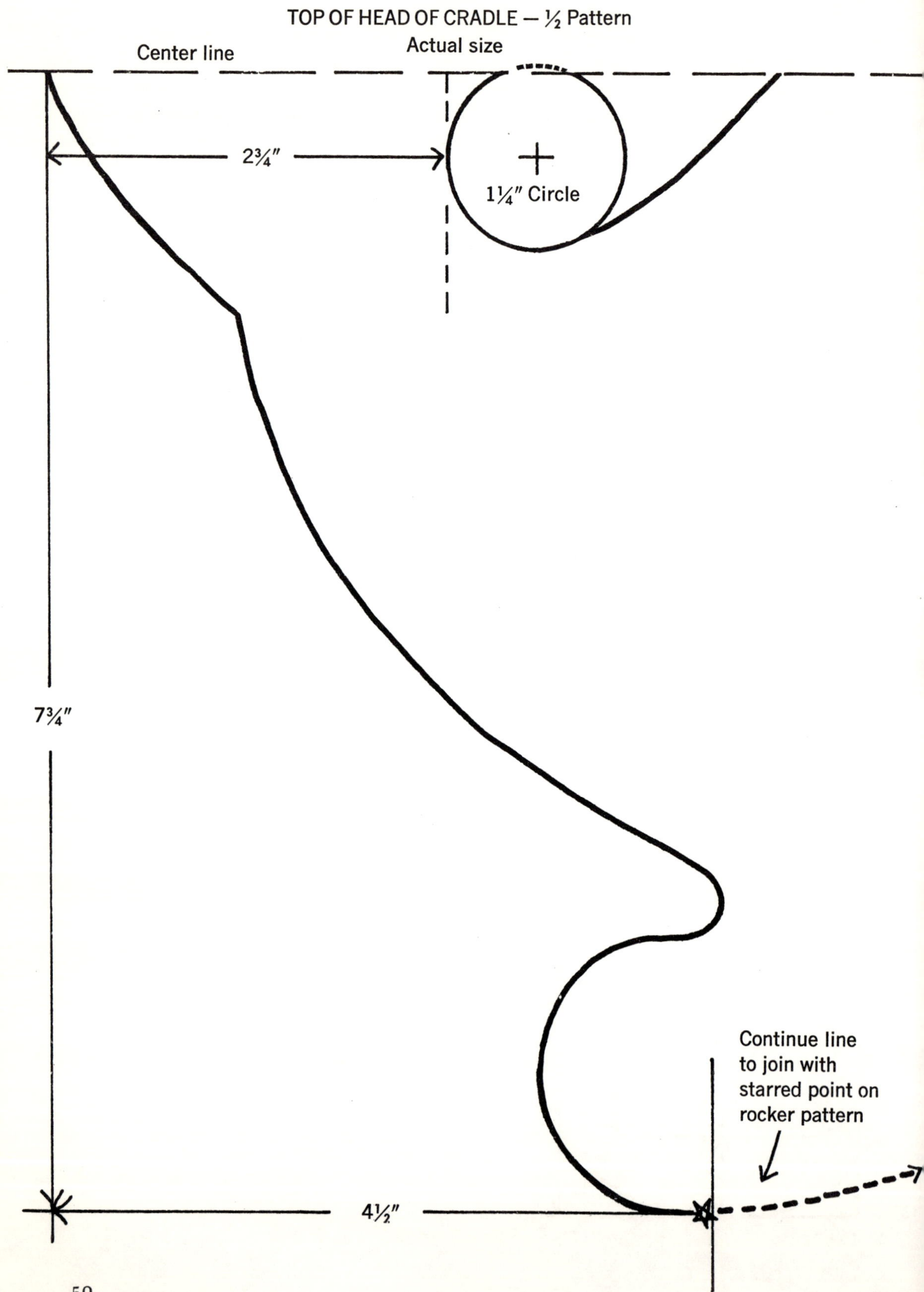
TOP OF HEAD OF CRADLE — ½ Pattern
Actual size
Center line
2¾"
1¼" Circle
7¾"
4½"
5º
Continue line
to join with
starred point on
rocker pattern

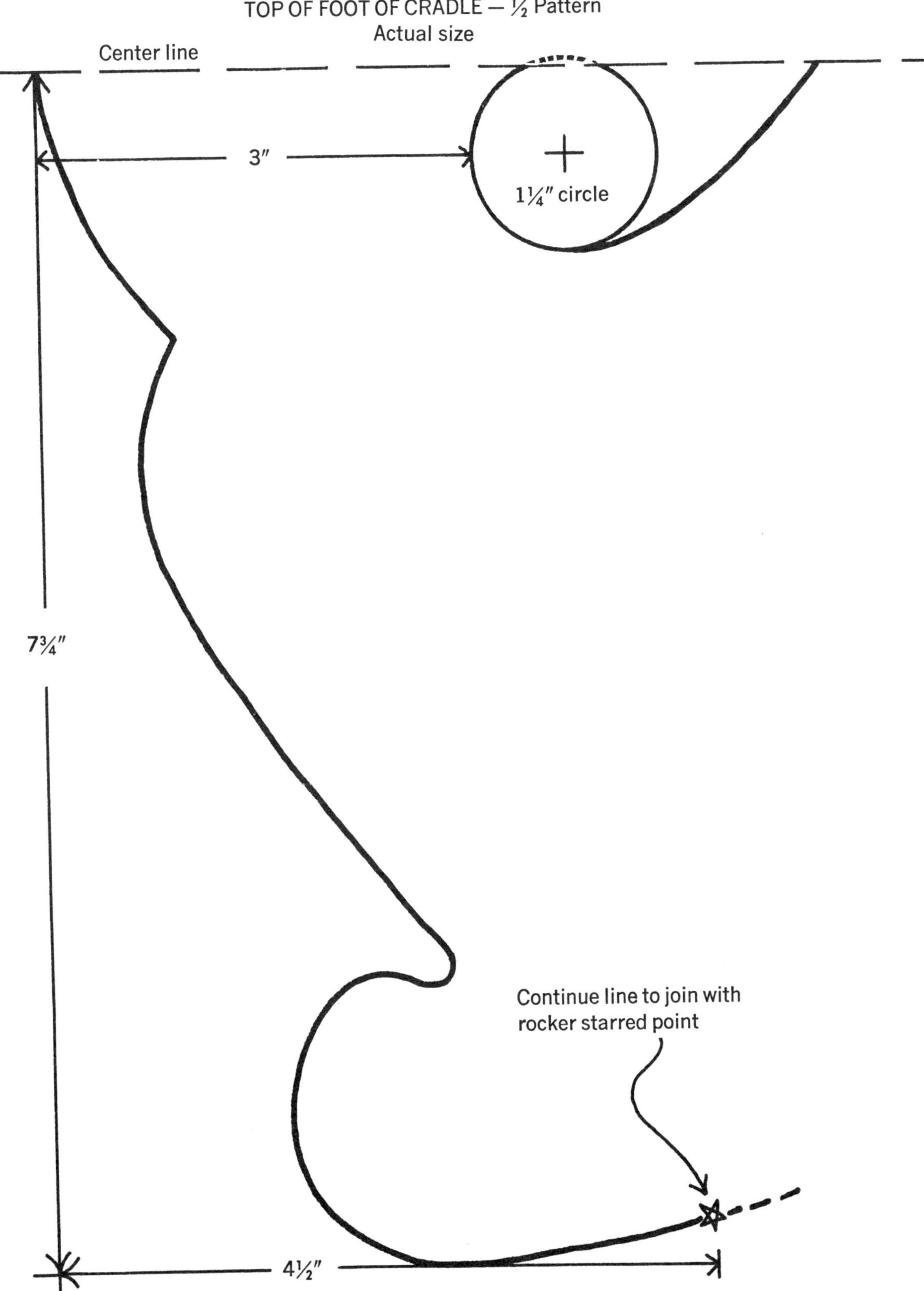

TOP OF FOOT OF CRADLE — ½ Pattern
Actual size
Center line
3"
1¼" circle
7¾"
Continue line to join with
rocker starred point
4½"

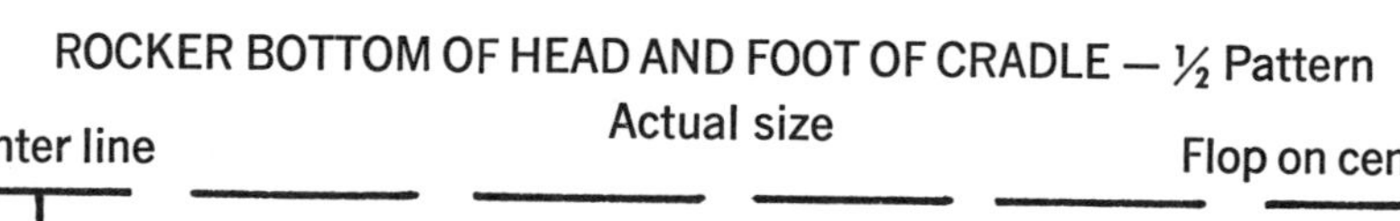

PATTERN C

ROCKER BOTTOM OF HEAD AND FOOT OF CRADLE — ½ Pattern
Actual size

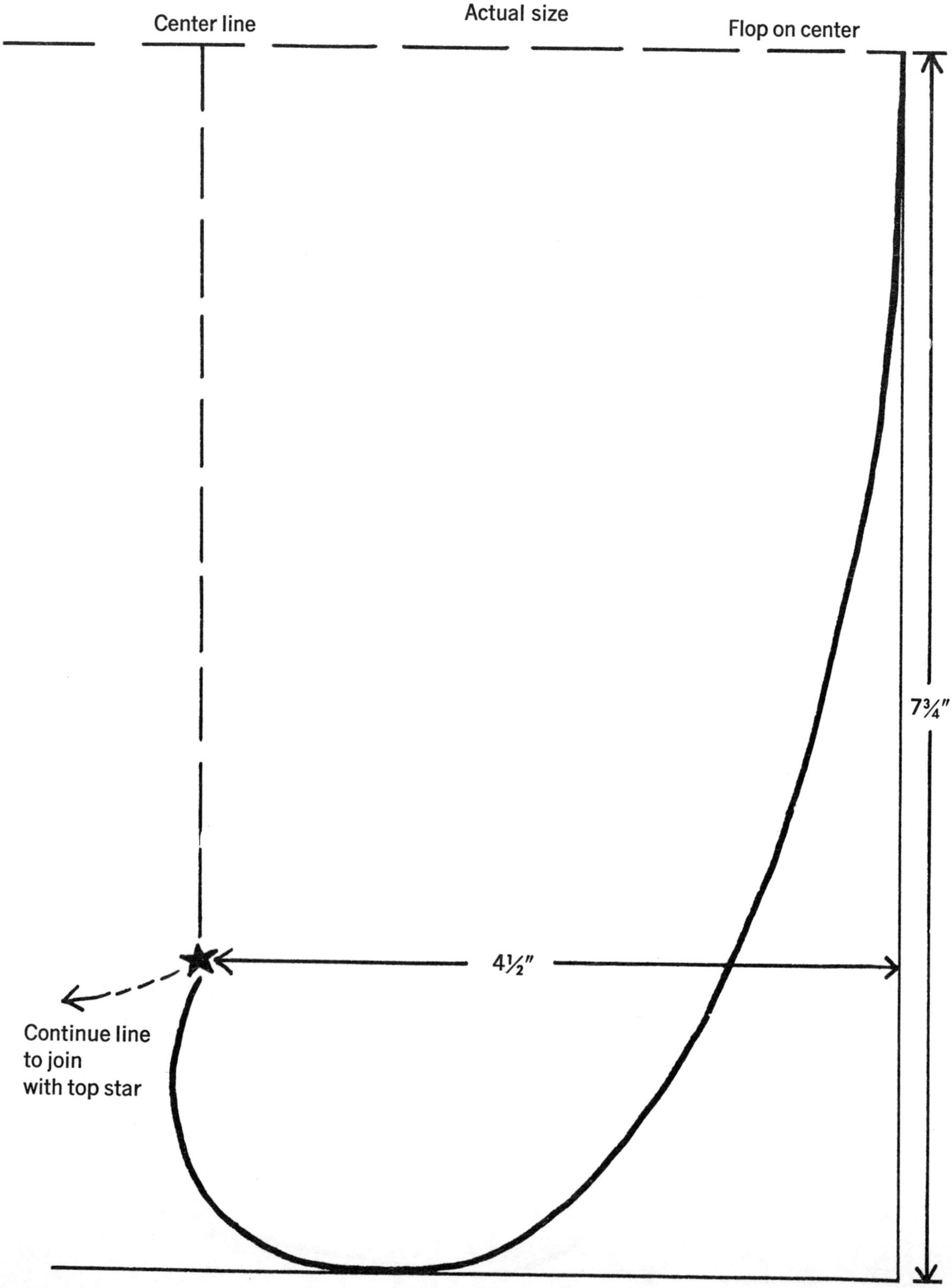

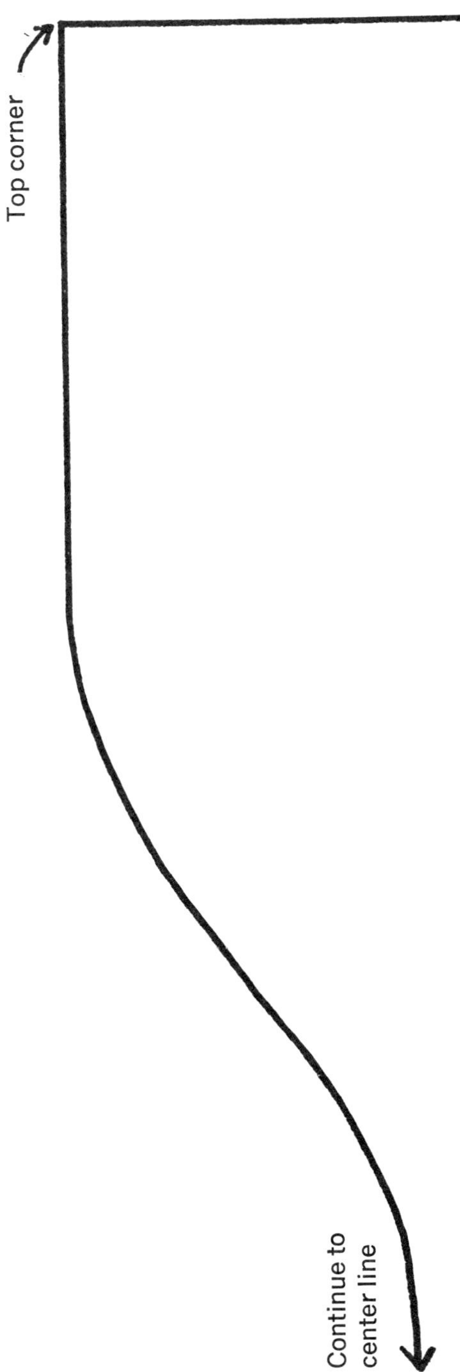

Place one side piece on the foot of the cradle in the location shown in Diagram A. Glue and nail through the foot into the end of side piece using four finishing nails. Now nail the other side piece into position in the same manner. Glue and nail the head piece on the other end of the side pieces in the same location as shown in Diagram A.

Now the head, foot, and side pieces are in place. Measure the inside bottom of the cradle which should be about $16\frac{1}{4}'' \times 9\frac{1}{4}''$. Cut the bottom piece to fit. Apply glue to the edges of the bottom piece and fit it into the cradle, flush with the bottom edges of the head, foot, and sides of the cradle. Drive about five nails along the outside lower edges of the side pieces and three nails through the head and foot of the cradle to secure the bottom piece.

DIAGRAM A

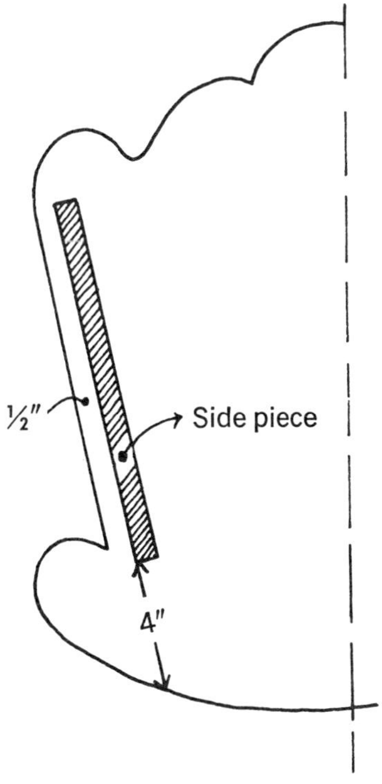

Placement of side pieces on head and foot of cradle

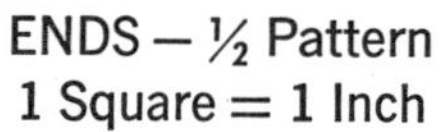

PAINTING PATTERNS

ENDS — ½ Pattern
1 Square = 1 Inch

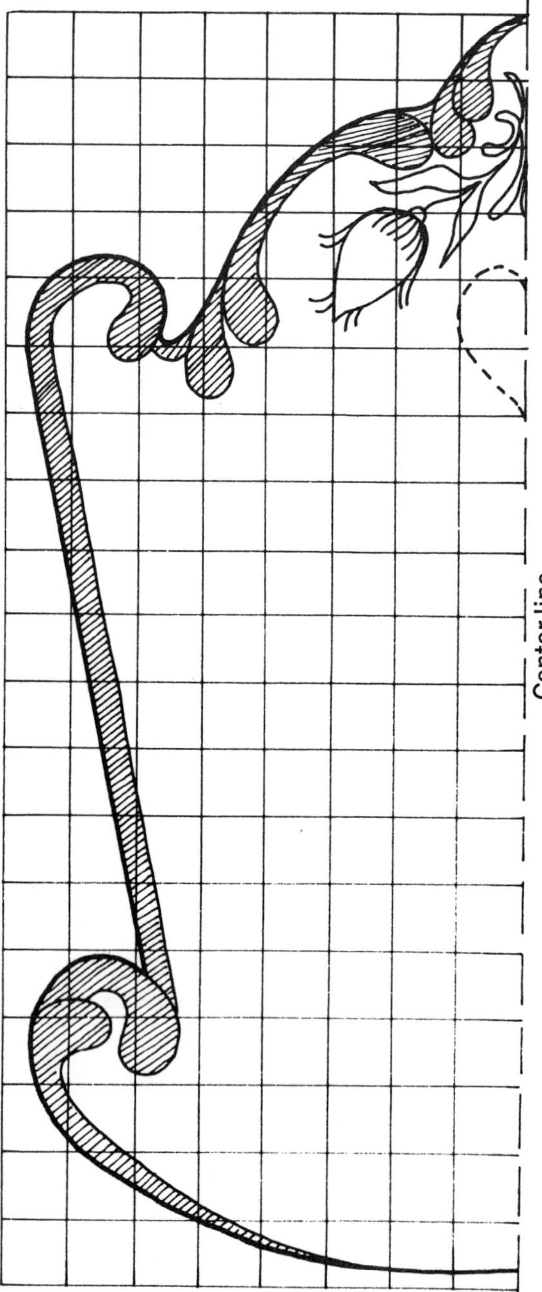

SIDES — ½ Pattern
1 Square = 1 Inch

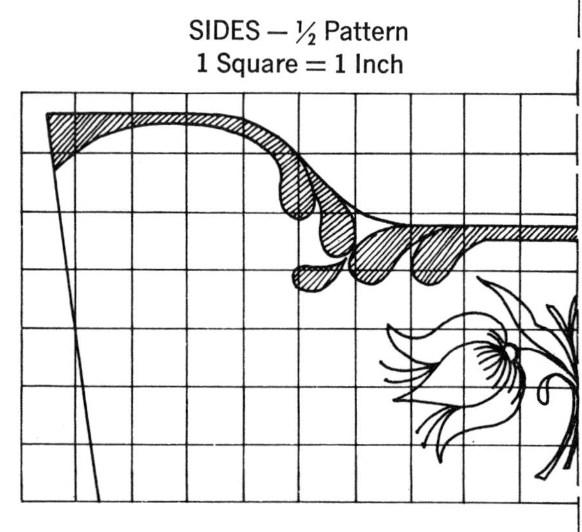

COLOR GUIDE (See color print 6)
Tulips: pink with red accents
Leaves and stems: green
Scrolls: light blue

Doll Trunk

The little doll trunk was inspired by an old antique trunk that was made of metal and outfitted with fancy trim and hardware. These miniature trunks are almost impossible to come by these days, so here is our interpretation in wood. We have painted the trunk gray and for effect, have painted the decorative trim with acrylic artists' paints. For the interior, use a contrasting color or line with a small-print paper or calico cloth. You will also find this treasure chest handy for other things such as recipes, jewelry, or a chess set.

MATERIALS:

1″×12″ white pine shelving—4 feet long
3 dozen 1½″ finishing nails
2 ornamental hinges—½″ to 1″ wide
1 catch or hasp—about 1½″ size

STEP ONE: CUTTING

Measure and cut the following pieces:

Sides: Cut two pieces—11″×5½″
Ends: Cut two pieces—5½″×5½″
Top: Cut one piece—11″×7″
Bottom: Cut one piece—11″×7″

STEP TWO: ASSEMBLY

Sand all pieces thoroughly before assembling. Start about three nails into each end of the side pieces about ⅜″ in from the edge. Glue and nail through the side pieces into the edges of the end pieces forming a four-sided box (Diagram A on page 56). Now glue and nail the top and bottom pieces to the box using two nails on each end and four nails on each side. You have now nailed the box completely closed. Countersink all nails and fill with spackling paste.

Going around the four sides of the box,

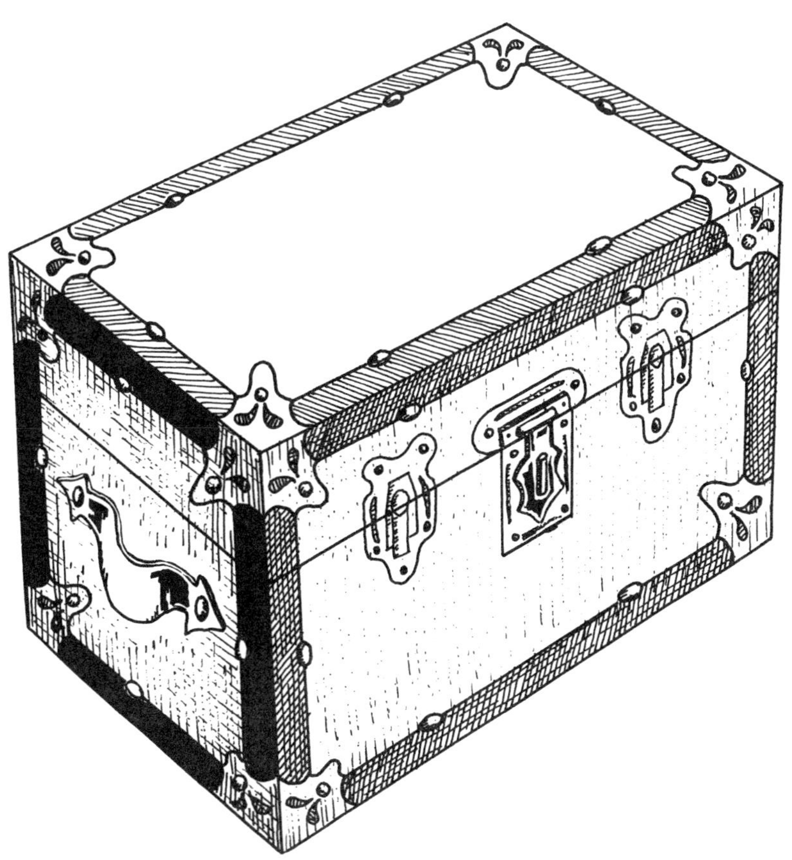

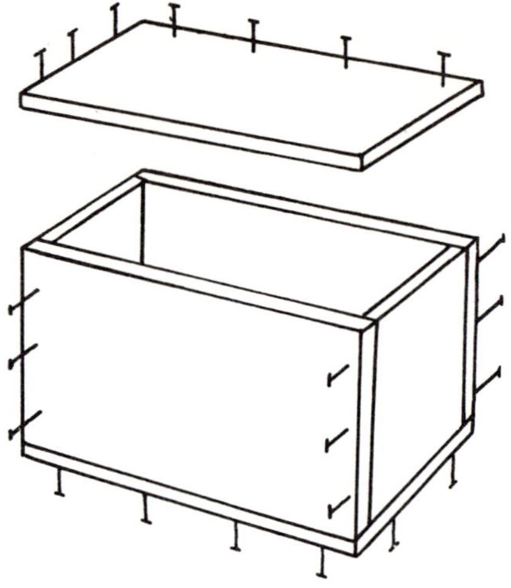

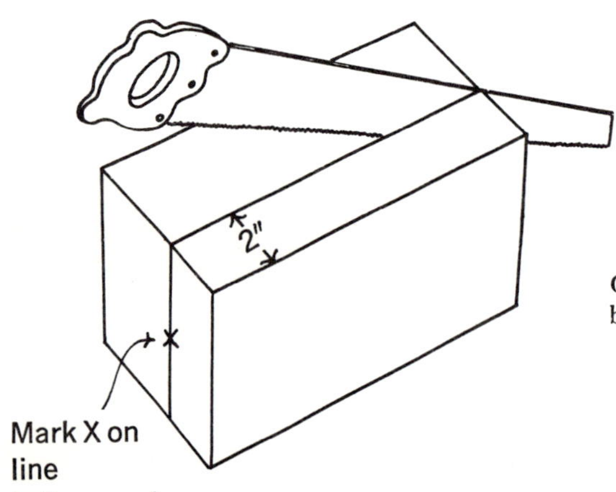

On four sides, carefully mark off 2″ from top of box. Then saw box into two pieces

measure 2″ down from the top of the box and draw a line. Draw an X on the line at some point for future reference (Diagram B). Following the line, cut the box into two pieces using a jig saw or hand saw. Sand all edges.

Using the X as a guide, place the two pieces back into their original position. Tape to hold the box together at the corners.

Position the hinges about 2″ from the ends and attach the screws (Diagram C).

Attach the hasp on the center line of the opposite side of the box. Remove the tape, and the trunk is ready to paint and decorate. After the trunk has been decorated, you may want to attach leather handles on each end of the trunk as shown on our sample in the book. You will need a soft leather, which could be cut from an old leather handbag. Cut two handles from the pattern in Diagram D and tack into place with upholstery tacks, as in Diagram E.

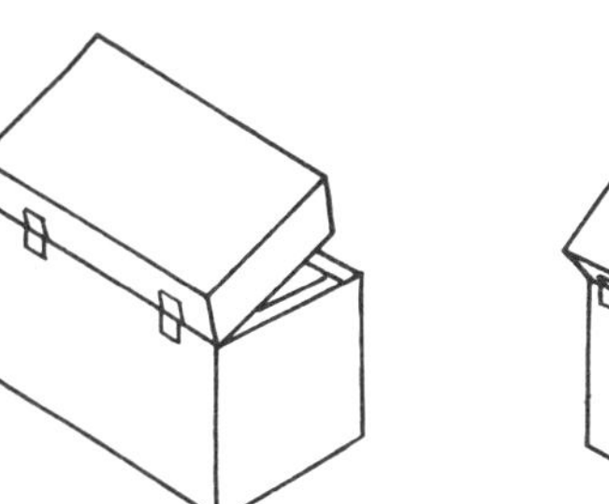
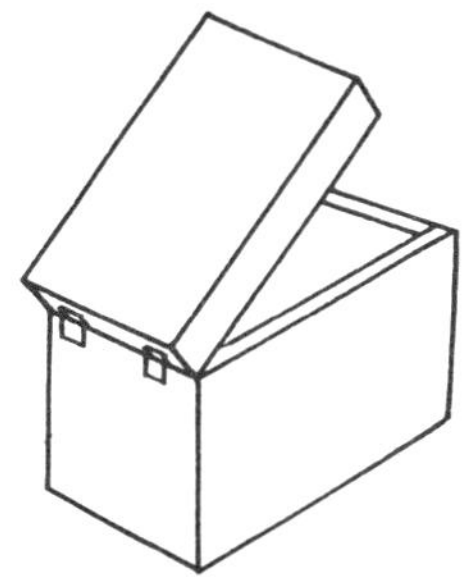

Place hinges on side for trunk, or on end piece to use as a recipe box

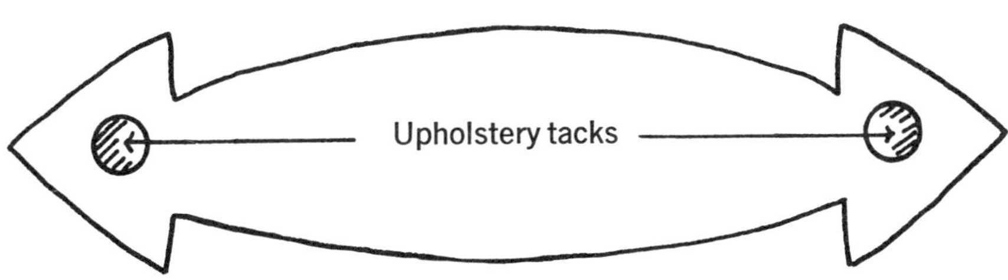

Cut two handles and attach them to the ends of the trunk with upholstery tracks

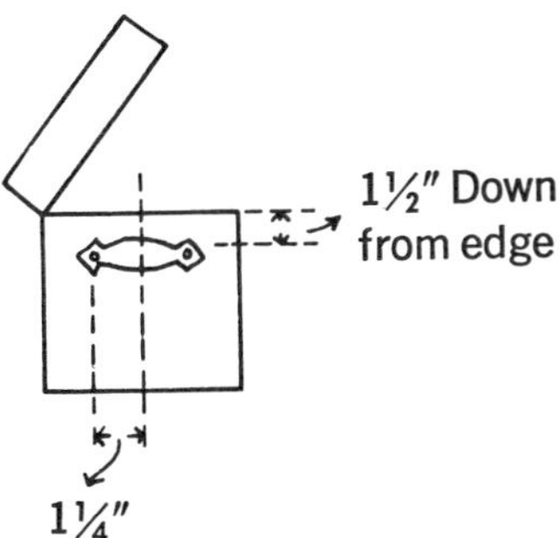

To allow slack in the handles, tacks should be placed 1¼″ each side of the center line

Actual size

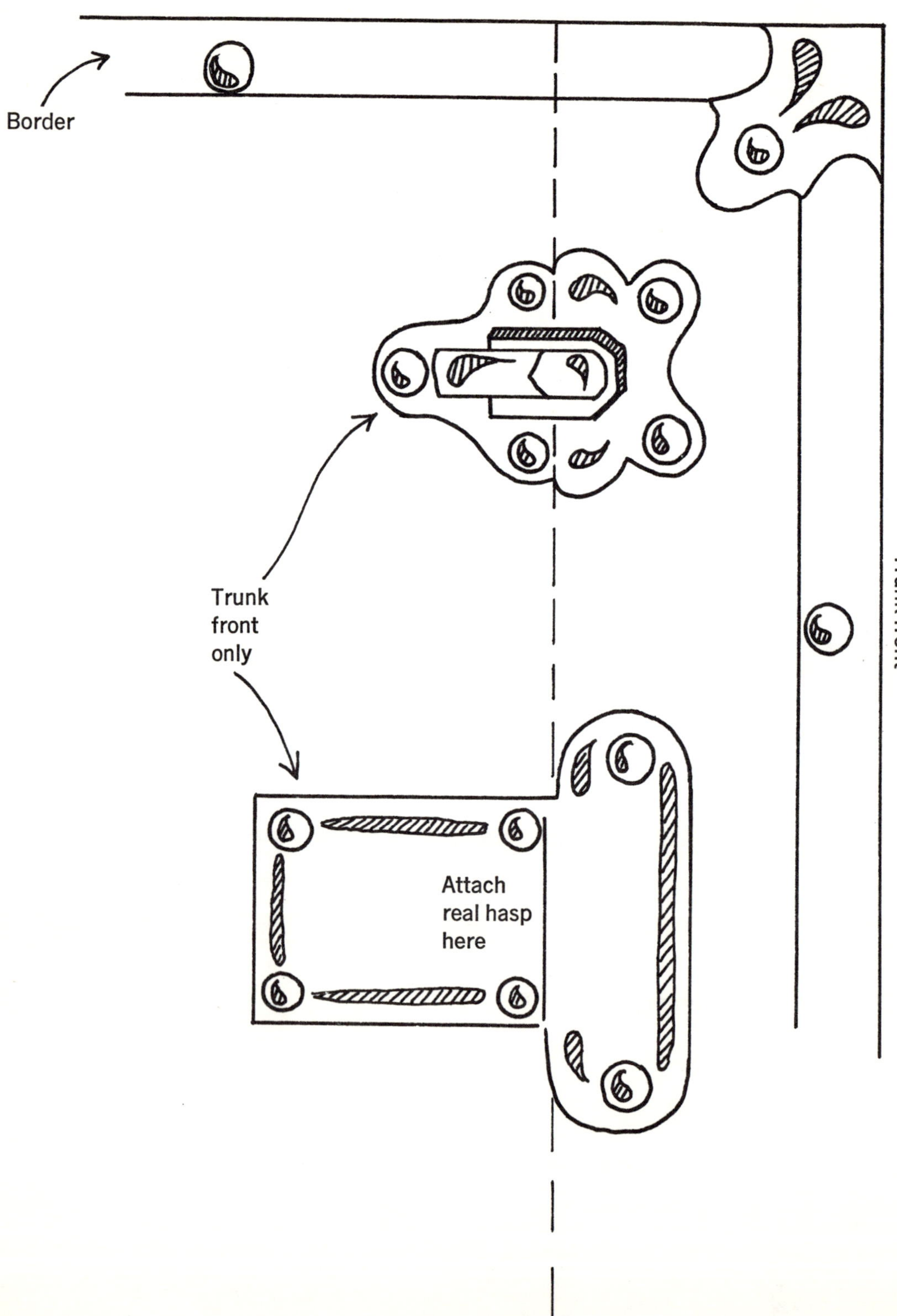

PAINT DESIGNS AS SHOWN

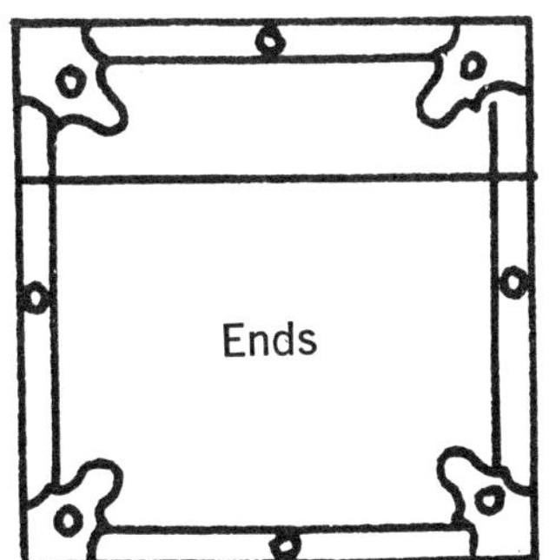

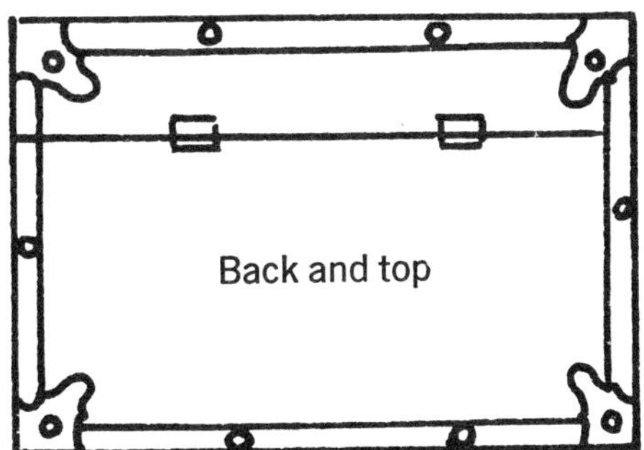

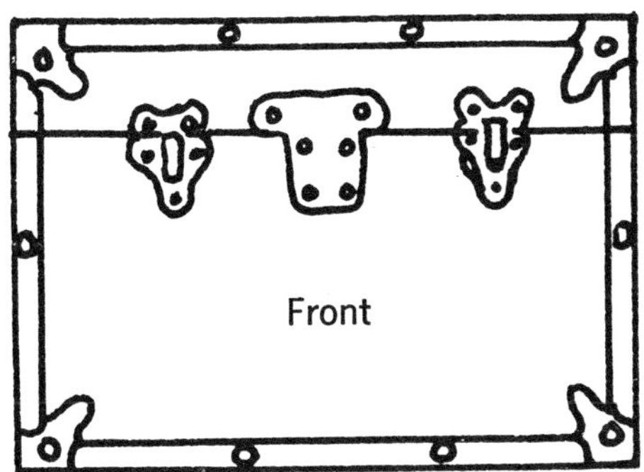

COLOR GUIDE (See color print 6)
Border: dark blue
Brass trim: gold
Accents (shaded) on brass: gold with a little
    black to darken

Stable

If you know a child who is crazy about horses, this little stable should be under his Christmas tree next December. Add a horse or two from the local toy emporium and it will be complete. The hayrack is screwed to the wall and is an optional feature. In the seventeenth and eighteenth centuries, a stable was featured as part of the doll house, but in the nineteenth century it came into its own and became a separate toy. It can also double as a crèche at Christmas time. We have painted ours bright red on the outside, sparkling white inside, with a gold floor and rich brown roof. A simple line border and a good luck hex sign complete the picture.

MATERIALS:

One piece ⅜″ plywood—2′×4′
5 feet of white pine shelving—1″×12″
Fifty finishing nails—1½″ long
3 feet of ¼″-diameter dowel (for hayrack, optional)

STEP ONE: CUTTING

Measure and cut the following pieces:

Floor: Cut one piece of plywood—16″×22″

Back: Cut one piece of plywood—14⅛″×22″ (Taper top edge from 14⅛″ at center line to 11¼″ on each side. See Diagram A.)

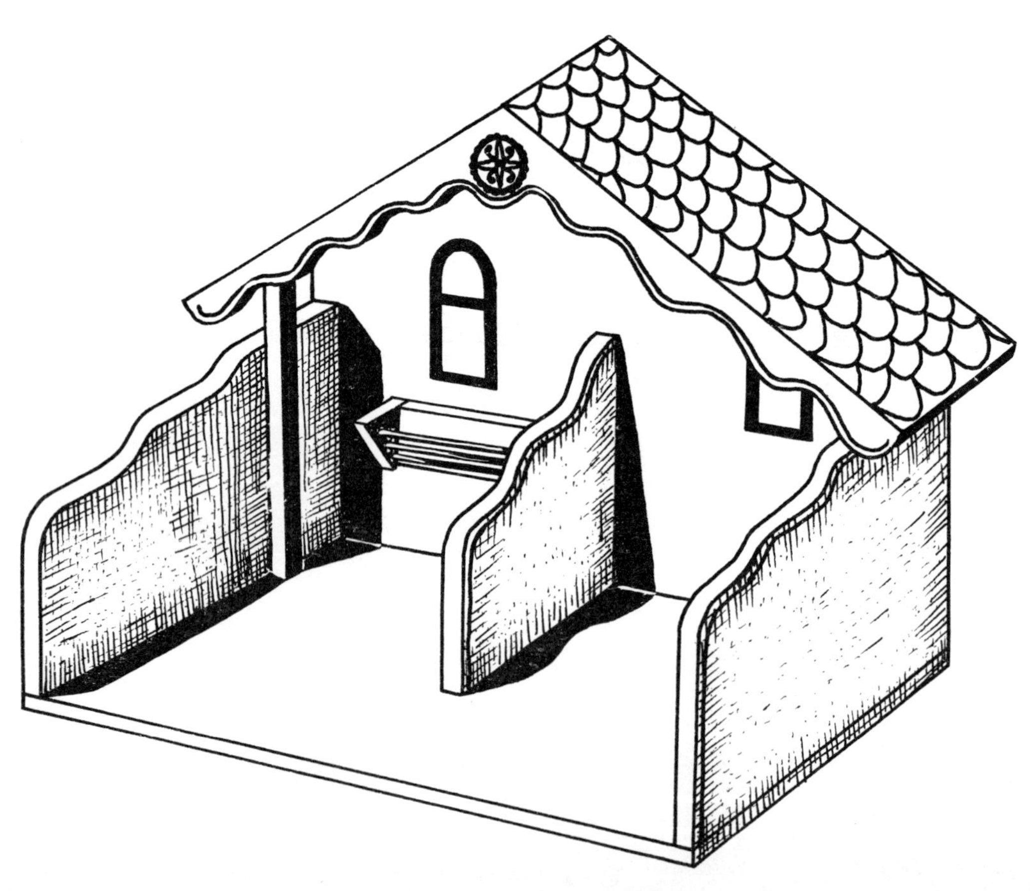

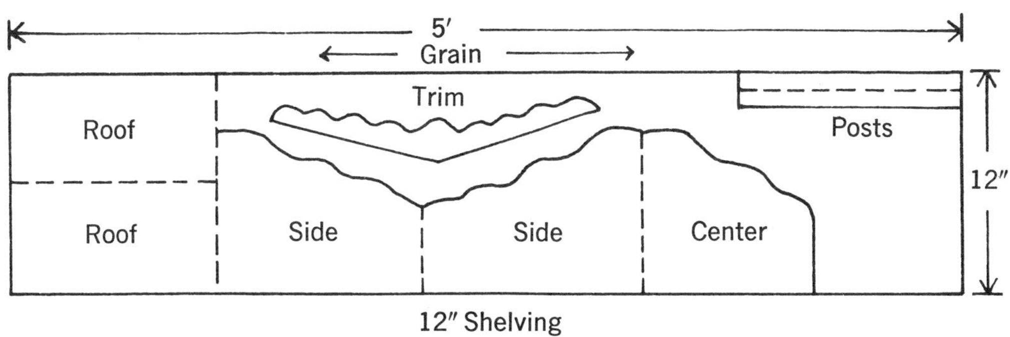

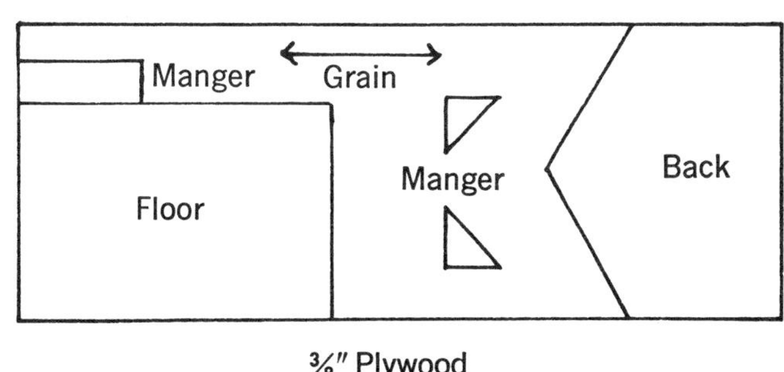

CUTTING PATTERN A

SIDES — Cut 2
1 Square = 1 Inch

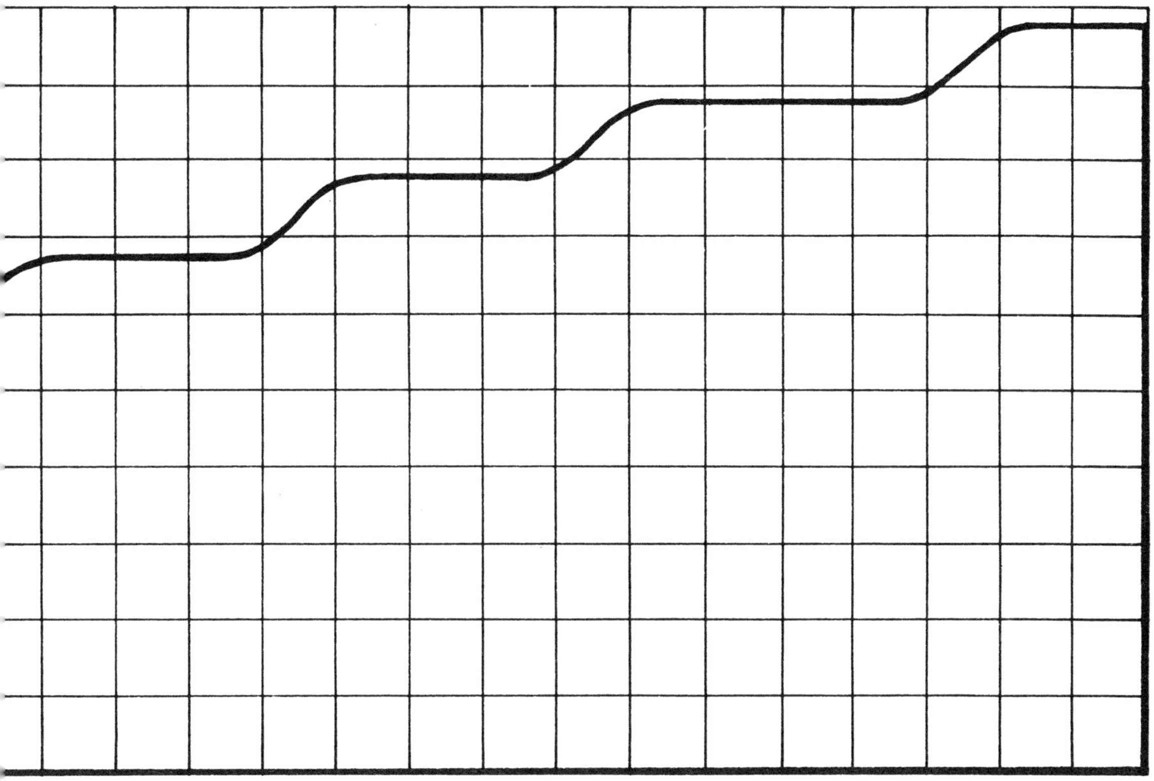

DIVIDER — Cut 1
1 Square = 1 Inch

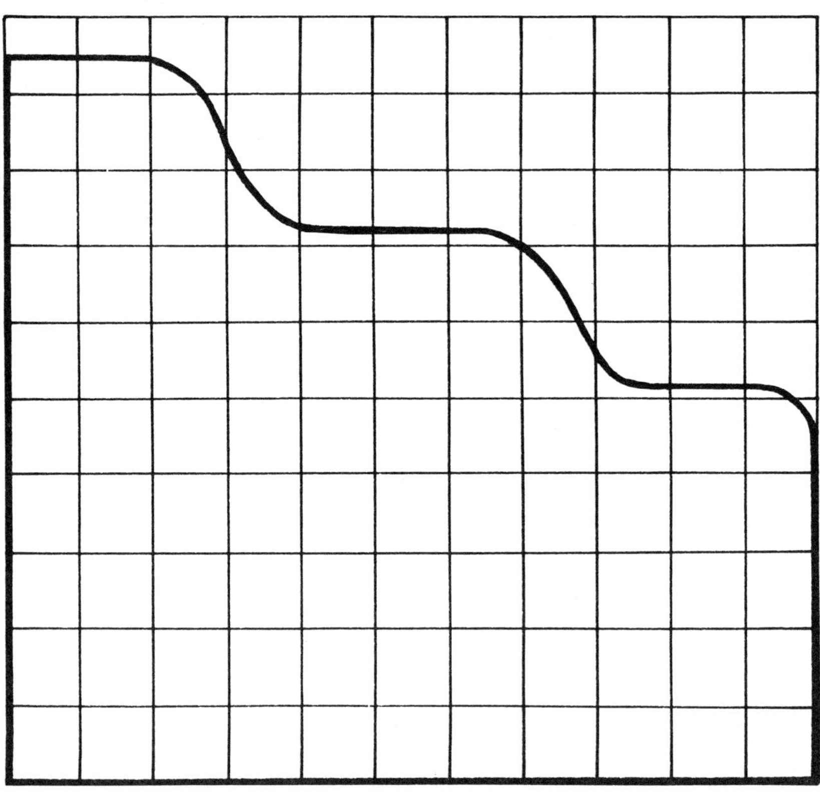

Sides: Cut two pieces from shelving—
9⅝″×16″ (These two pieces can be
cut separately or clamped together so
that the fancy Pattern A at the top edge
can be cut out at the same time with
a jig saw or saber saw.)

Divider: Cut one piece from shelving—
9½″×11″ (Follow Pattern B for the
top contour line.)

Roof pieces: Cut two pieces from shelving
—6″×13″ (Taper the two edges that
will be joined to form the roof peak—
³⁄₁₆″. See Diagram B.)

Roof facing: Cut one piece from shelving
—4″×25″ (Use the stable back piece
as a pattern to draw the top roof line
on the board. Then with Pattern C,
complete the cutting design of the bottom contour. See Diagram C on page
64.)

DIAGRAM A

CUTTING PATTERN C

ROOF FACING
½ PATTERN — Cut 1
1 Square = 1 Inch

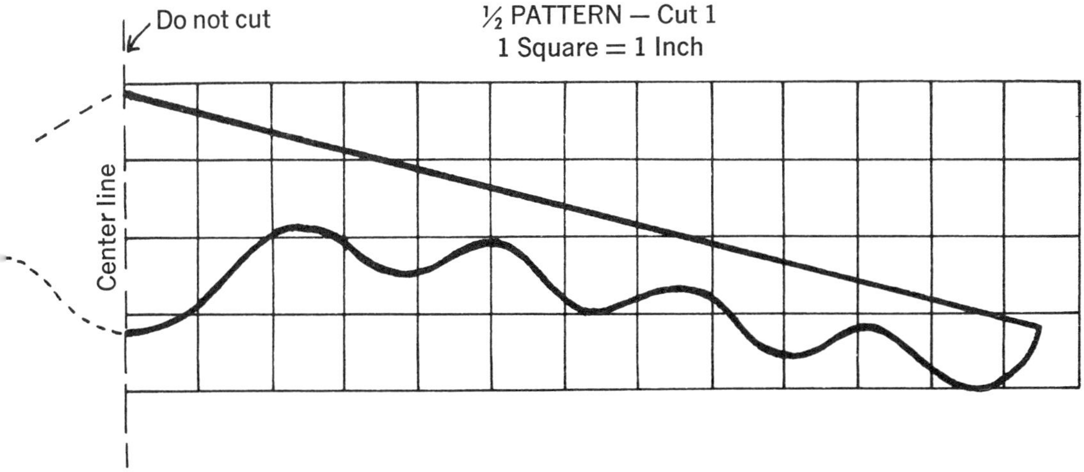

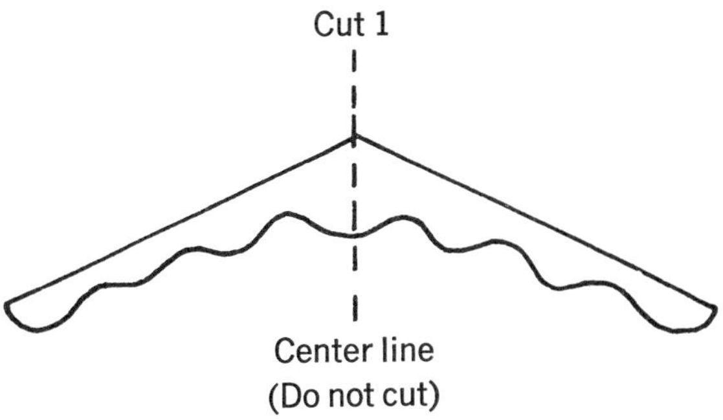

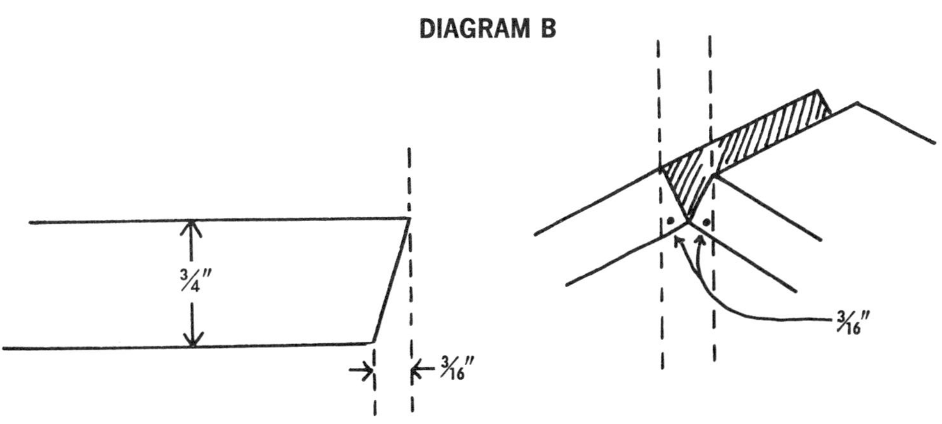

DIAGRAM C

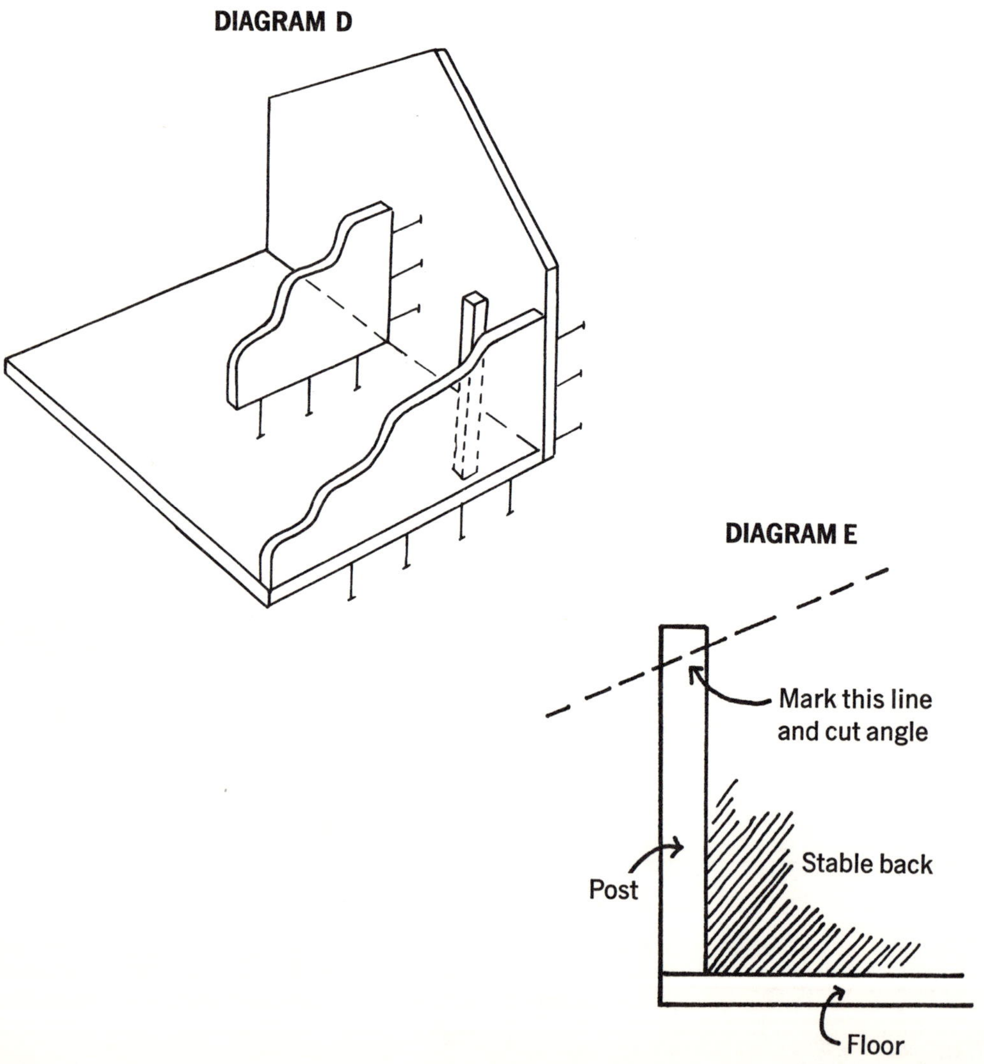

Use stable back as a pattern for the top line of the roof to ensure exact roof peak

With the floor piece flat in front of you, join the back piece to the floor by nailing through the back piece into the back edge of the floor using five or six nails. Make sure that the edges are flush on the sides and bottom.

Place the side pieces into position on top of the floor and nail through the floor and back into the edges of the side pieces (Diagram D). Again, make sure that the sides are flush with the floor and back piece.

Place the divider at the center line of both the floor and back, apply glue and nail through the floor and back piece to secure the divider.

DIAGRAM D

Before assembling the roof, cut two support posts—$\frac{3}{4}'' \times \frac{3}{4}'' \times 11\frac{1}{2}''$ long. Get the proper roof angle for the top of each post by placing them in the back corners of the stable and marking the angle to match the slope of the top edge of the back piece. Mark the pitch of the roof and saw the correct angle (Diagram E).

Now, line up one side of the roof trim with one edge of one roof piece, making sure that the tapered peak is flush at the center. Nail through the bottom edge of the trim into the roof. Use glue and four nails. Then nail the remaining roof piece to the trim in the same manner.

Now place the roof on the top of the back piece and nail into place with six or eight nails. Next, place the support posts under the roof behind the roof trim and nail through the posts into the side pieces, using three nails for each post and one nail through the roof into the top of each post.

HAYRACK

Cutting:

Ends: Cut two pieces from plywood—see Diagram F

Back: Cut one piece from plywood— $5'' \times 1\frac{7}{8}''$

Dowel: Cut six pieces—each 6″ long

Assembly:

Clamp the two end pieces together and drill five $\frac{1}{4}''$-diameter holes as indicated on the pattern. With a little glue, fit the dowels into the holes so that they are flush with the outsides of the end pieces (Diagram F). Nail the back piece between the end pieces and flush with the top edges of the end pieces. Use two nails through each end.

Center the hayrack in the left-hand section of the stable, measuring 6″ from the floor to the top of the rack. Nail into place.

DIAGRAM F

HAYRACK

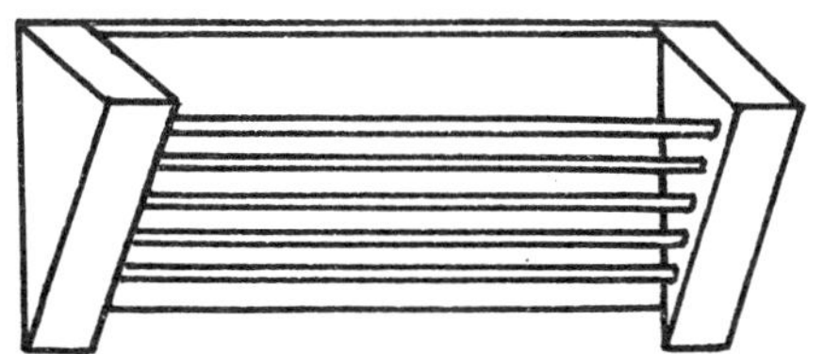

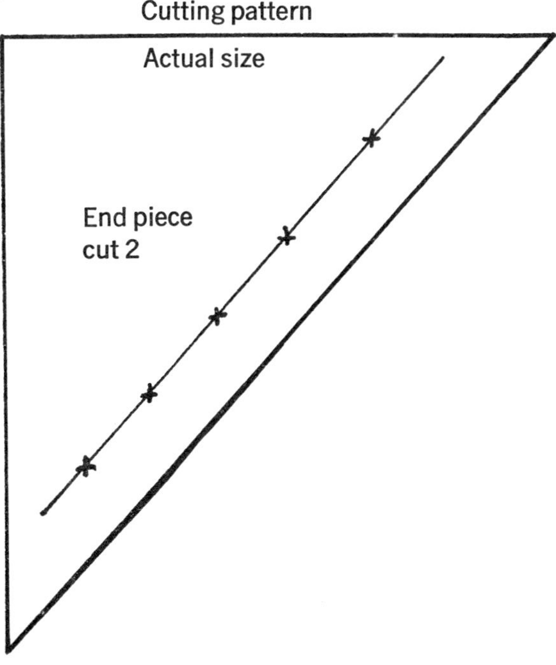

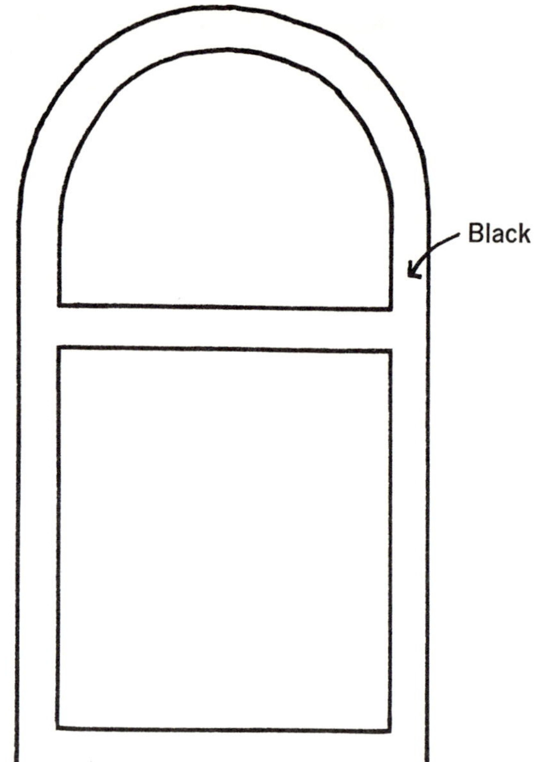

PAINTING PATTERNS

Actual size

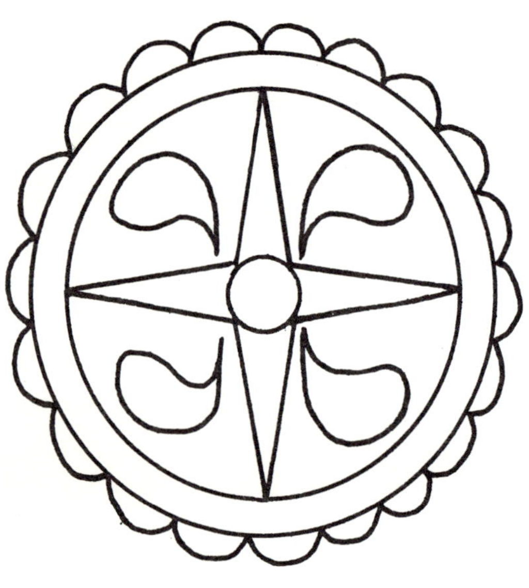

Hex sign

COLOR GUIDE (See color print 1)
Four-pointed star: light blue
Star center and straight border: gold
Raindrops and scalloped border: black

Roof shingles

Black lines — repeat design to cover roof

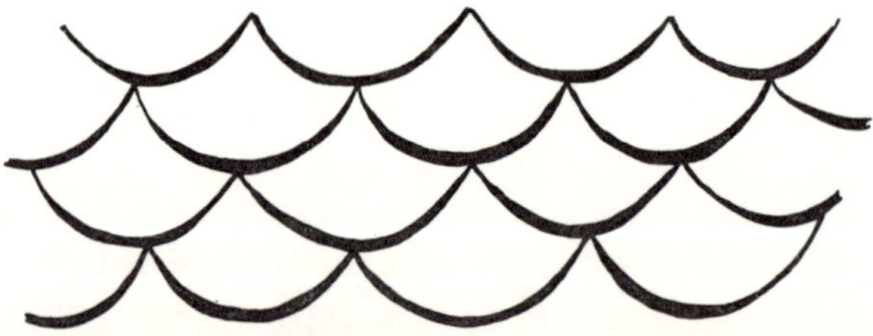

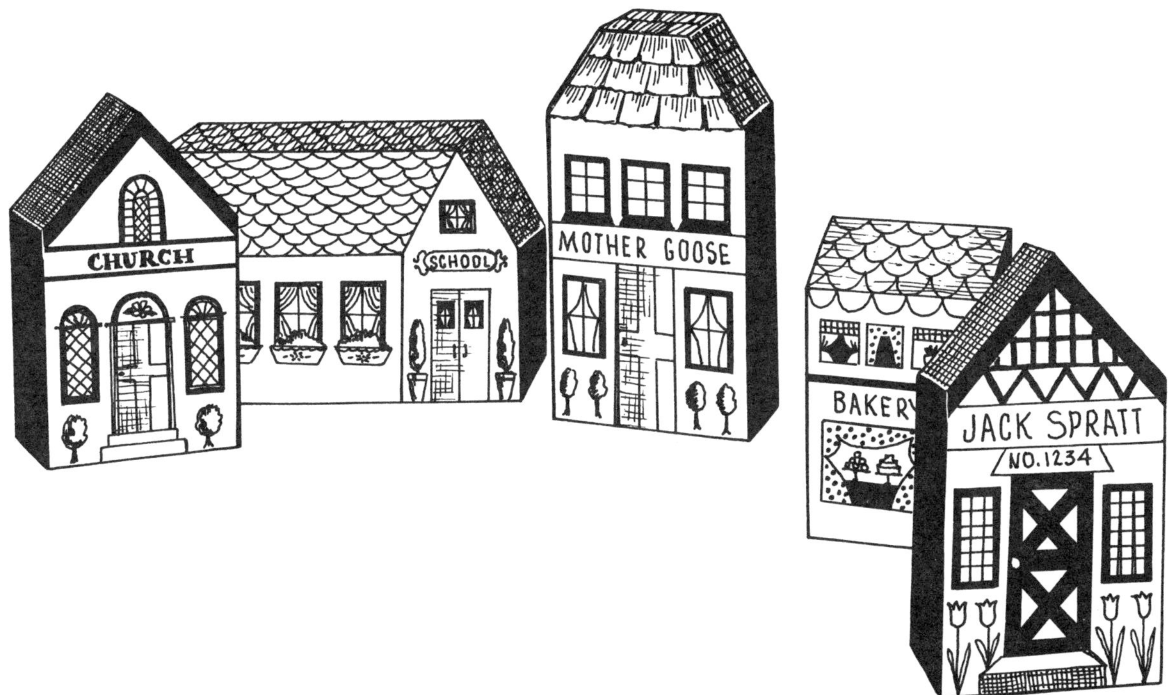

Village Blocks

While in Oslo, Norway, we came across a charming idea for using odds and ends of scrap lumber. A local folk artist had taken little blocks of wood, sanded them smooth, and painted them to look like houses, shops, and schools. We suggest you paint some village blocks for a child who is going through the building phase. These colorful little houses are fun to combine with miniature trains, cars, animals, and people.

MATERIALS:

Any odd pieces of shelving left over from your toy projects, or any others, are suitable if the wood is at least 3/4″ in thickness . . . this is necessary for balance. Cut rectangles in the general dimensions of 4″ × 2½″ to 3″. Vary the size and shape to create visual interest; cut some with sloping roofs. About four to six houses will make an interesting village grouping.

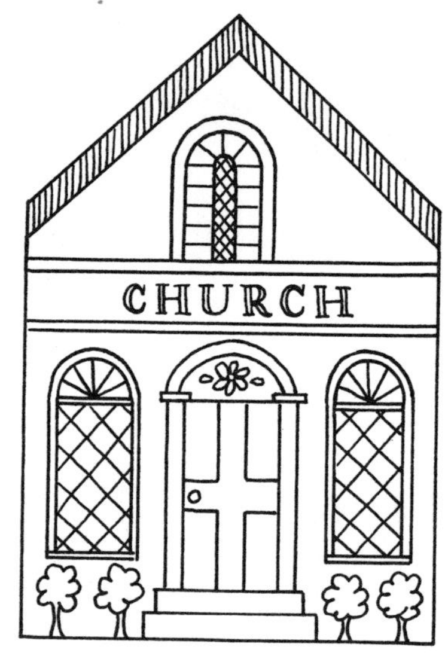

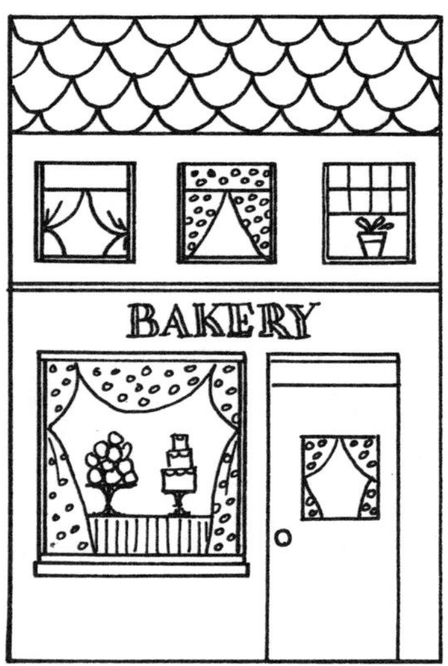

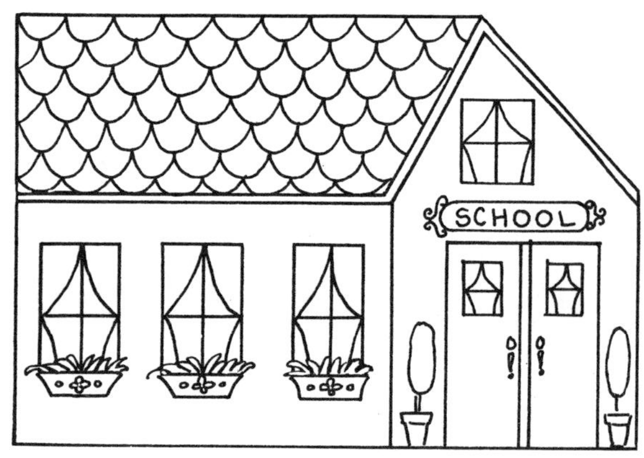

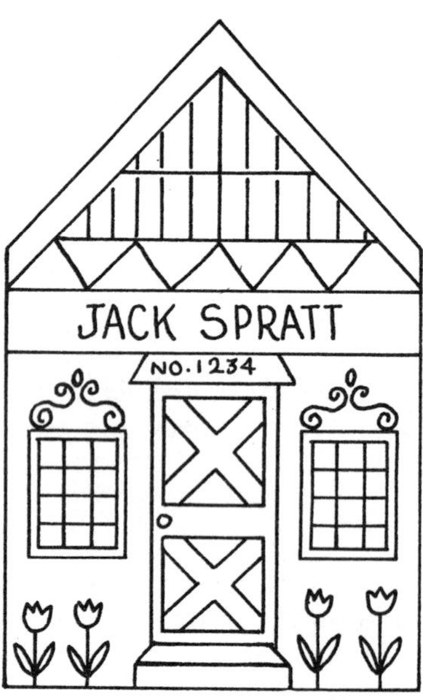

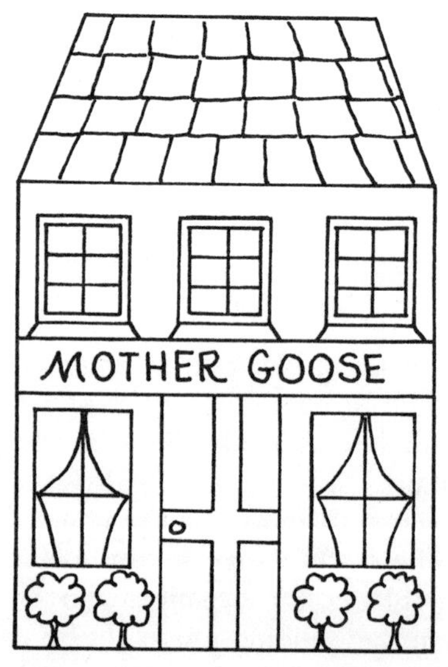

Paint the blocks any color that suits your fancy, using your imagination to make them bright and fun.

68

Noah's Ark

Noah's ark originated as a folk toy, and by the nineteenth century had become one of the most desirable toys a child could possess. Although some toy arks of the past have had as many as two hundred pairs of exotic and domestic animals, we have included only a small group to be cut out and stored in the cabin of the ark. The roof is hinged and the concealed wheels under the ark allow it to be pulled about.

MATERIALS:

1"×12" white pine shelving—8' long
½"-diameter dowel—18¼" long
2 butt hinges with screws—1½" size
1 wooden doorknob—¾" diameter
⅛" nylon clothes line—36" long
8 washers with ⁹⁄₁₆" hole
3 dozen finishing nails—1½" long
4 cotter keys—³⁄₃₂" diameter, about 1¼" long

STEP ONE: CUTTING

Measure and cut the following pieces:

Ark sides: Cut two pieces—4½"×16½"
Ark ends: Cut two pieces—5½"×7½"
Deck: Cut one piece—7½"×14⅜"
Cabin sides: Cut two pieces—4½"×9"
Cabin ends: Cut two pieces—4½"×6½"
Cabin roof: Cut one piece—4¾"×11"
     Cut one piece—4"×11"
Wheels: Cut four circles—3" diameter with ⁹⁄₁₆"-diameter hole in the center of each circle
Chimney: Cut two pieces—1½"×2"
Axles: Cut two pieces of dowel—each 9⅛" long

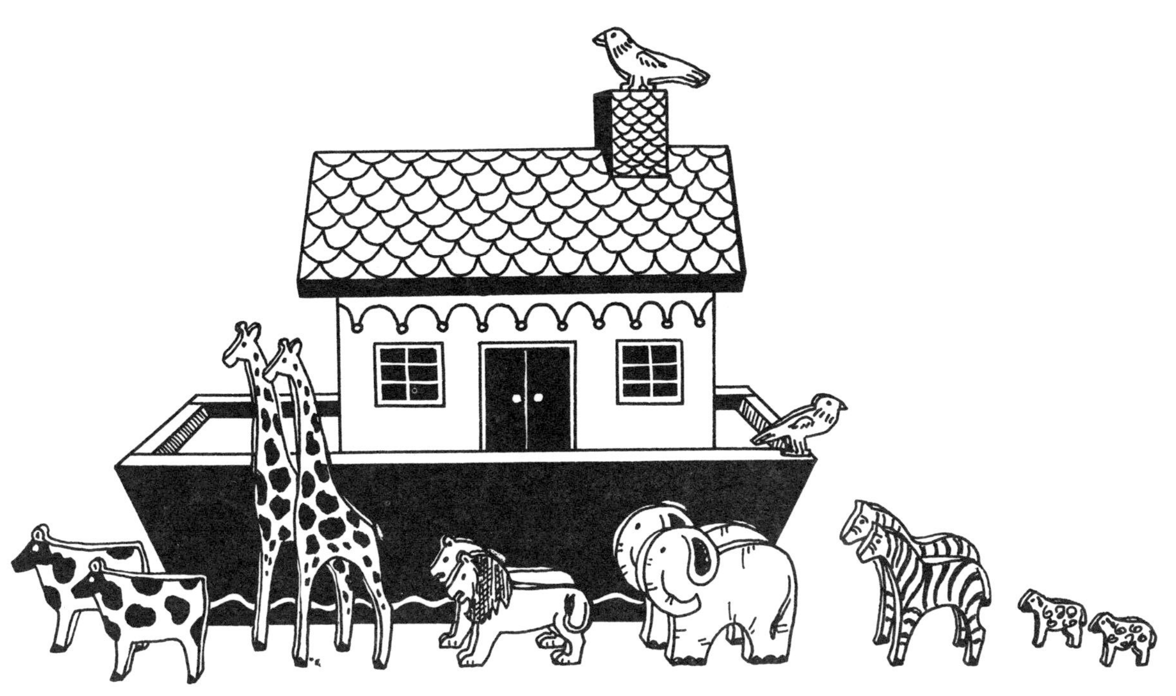

To cut the proper angle on the sides of the ark, measure 2" in from each lower corner and mark. Connect this mark and the upper corner with a straight line and cut (Diagram A). Now place both sides together with all edges matching, and holding them firmly together, drill the two holes for the axles as shown in the diagram. Drill through both side pieces at the same time.

Place the ends of the ark into position on a side piece in order to mark and cut the top and bottom edges at the proper angle shown in Diagram B. Also use the side piece as a template to mark the angles of the front and back edges of the deck and cut these angles as shown in Diagram C.

Following the measurements in Diagram D, cut the proper shape of the cabin ends and the angles on the top edge of the cabin sides. On one end of each chimney piece, cut the angle shown in Diagram E. The pieces of the ark are now ready for assembly.

STEP TWO: ASSEMBLY

Begin assembly by gluing and nailing one end piece to a side piece of the ark. Drive three finishing nails through the side piece into the end piece. Glue and nail the other end of the ark to the same side piece. Turn the assembly over and nail the other side of the ark to the ends in the same manner.

The next step is to assemble the cabin. Apply glue to the edge of a cabin end piece and, using two nails, nail through the cabin side into the end piece. Nail the other cabin side to the opposite end of the end piece. Then apply glue to both edges of the remaining end piece and fit it between

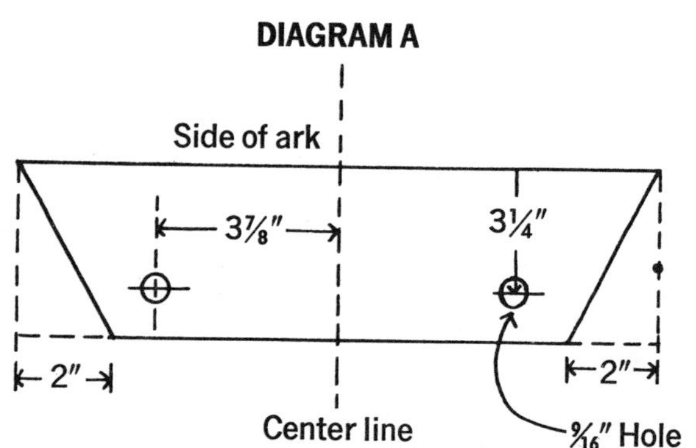

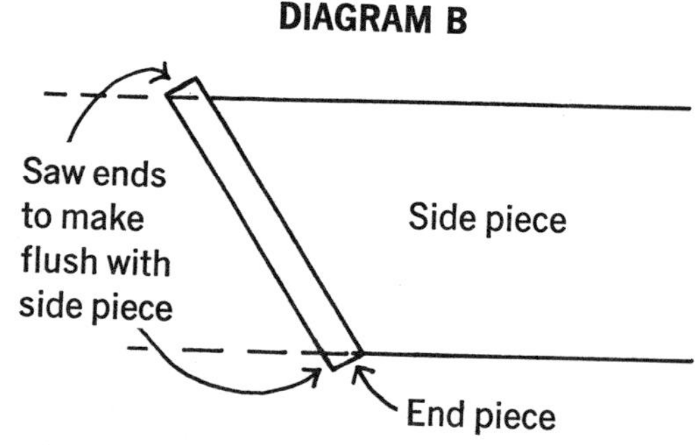

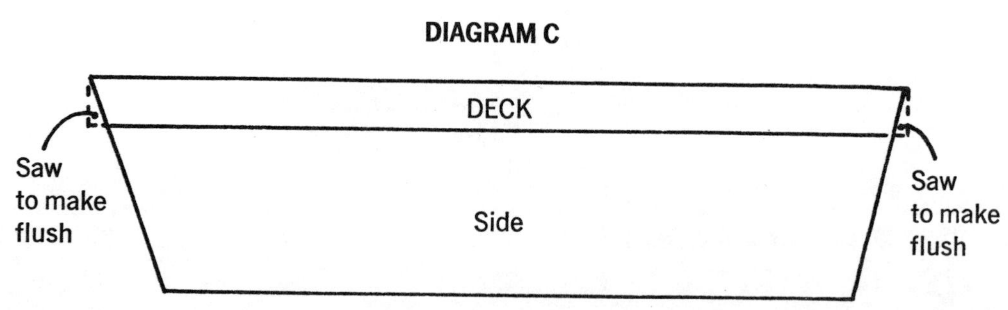

DIAGRAM D 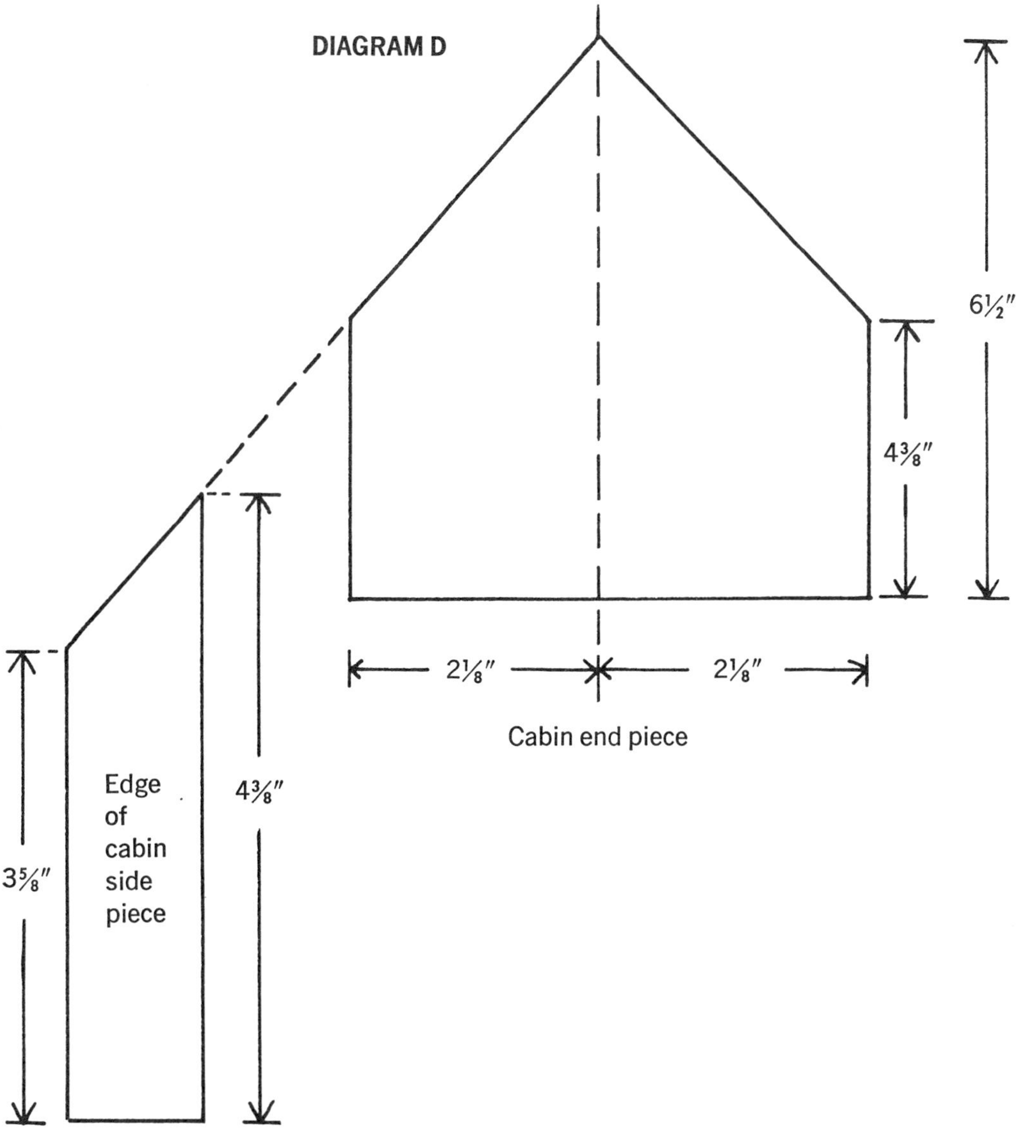
6½"
4⅜"
4⅜"
3⅝"
Edge
of
cabin
side
piece
2⅛"
2⅛"
Cabin end piece

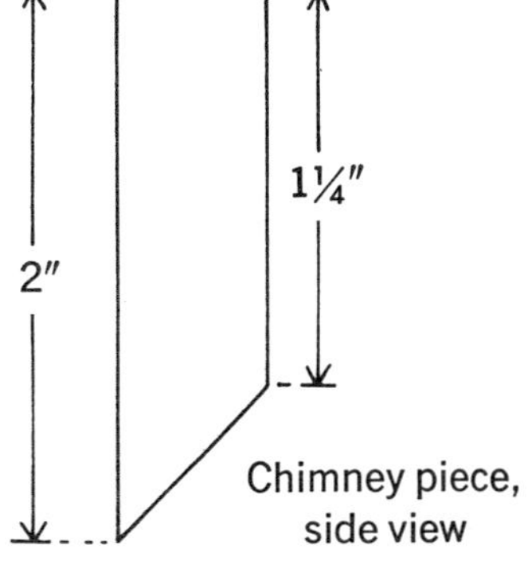

DIAGRAM E
1¼"
2"
Chimney piece,
side view

the sides at the other end of the cabin. Drive two nails through each side into the end piece.

Now place the deck flat on your bench with the angled edges on the underside and draw a center line lengthwise ($3\frac{3}{4}''$ from each side). Draw vertical center lines on both ends of the cabin ($2\frac{7}{8}''$ from each side). Apply glue to the bottom edges of the cabin and place it on the deck $2''$ from one end with center lines matching. After allowing the glue to dry thoroughly, turn the cabin and deck upside down and nail through the deck into the bottom edges of the cabin using two nails for each side and one nail for each end of the cabin.

Assemble the roof by gluing and nailing the two roof pieces together as shown in Diagram F, using three finishing nails. Glue the two chimney pieces together and secure with a nail as shown in Diagram G. Then glue the chimney onto the roof, $1\frac{3}{4}''$ from one end of the roof edge and allow to dry. Then place the roof on the cabin with the chimney at the short end of the deck and the roof extending $1''$ beyond each end of the cabin. Following Diagram H, attach two butt hinges to the roof and cabin side.

Stack the four wheels on a piece of $\frac{1}{2}''$ dowel and sand the wheel edges, eliminating any bumps or rough spots to ensure smooth sailing for the ark. On both ends of each axle, drill $\frac{1}{8}''$-diameter holes, $1\frac{7}{8}''$ in from the ends as shown in Diagram I. To attach the wheels to the ark, turn the ark upside down and insert an axle through the hole in the side of the ark from the outside. On the end of the axle which is inside the ark, place a washer, then a wheel, two washers, a wheel, and finally a washer as shown in Diagram J. Insert two cotter keys to hold the wheels in place and secure the end of the axle in the opposite side of the ark. Install the other axle in the same manner.

Apply glue to the edges of the deck and place it into the ark, securing it by driving one nail through each end of the ark.

Drill a $\frac{3}{16}''$ hole in the front end of the ark just below the top edge of the ark and slightly above the deck. Insert the nylon

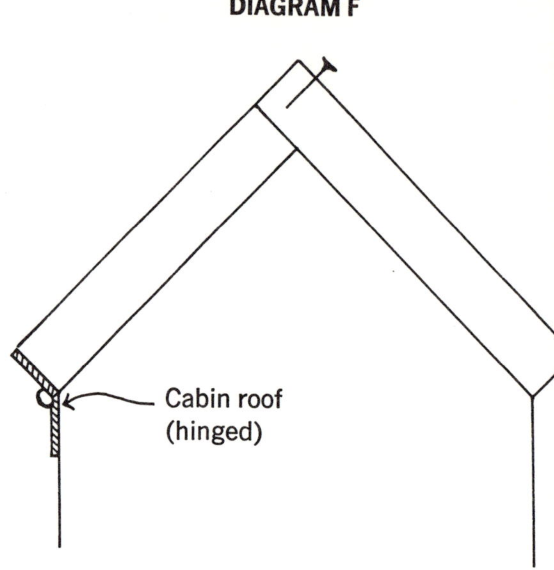

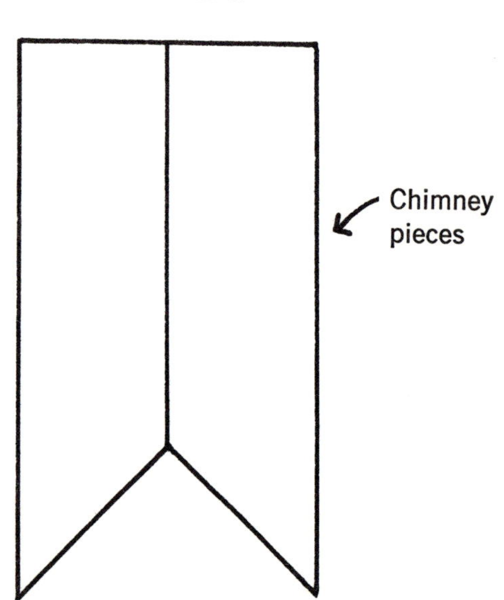

clothes line and tie a knot on the end. Slip a wooden drawer knob on the other end of the line and tie another knot to secure the knob.

The animals for the ark can be cut from white pine using a jig saw or saber saw. Trace the patterns onto the wood, drawing two of each animal to make the traditional pairs associated with Noah's ark.

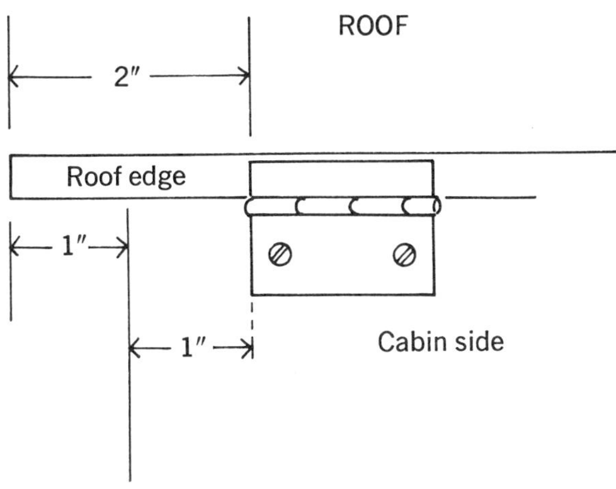

DIAGRAM H
ROOF
2"
Roof edge
1"
1"
Cabin side

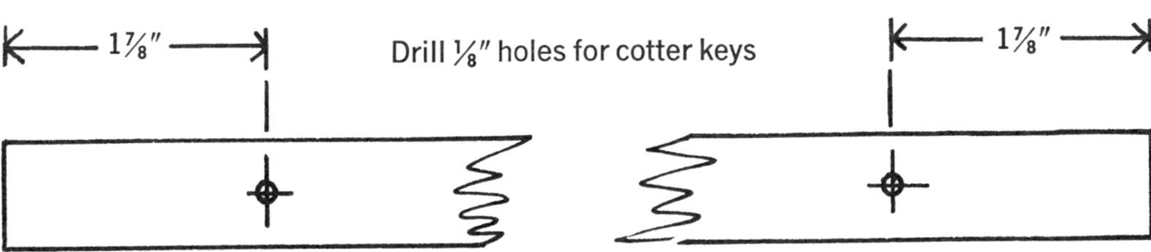

DIAGRAM I
1⅞"
1⅞"
Drill ⅛" holes for cotter keys
Axle — ½" Dowel

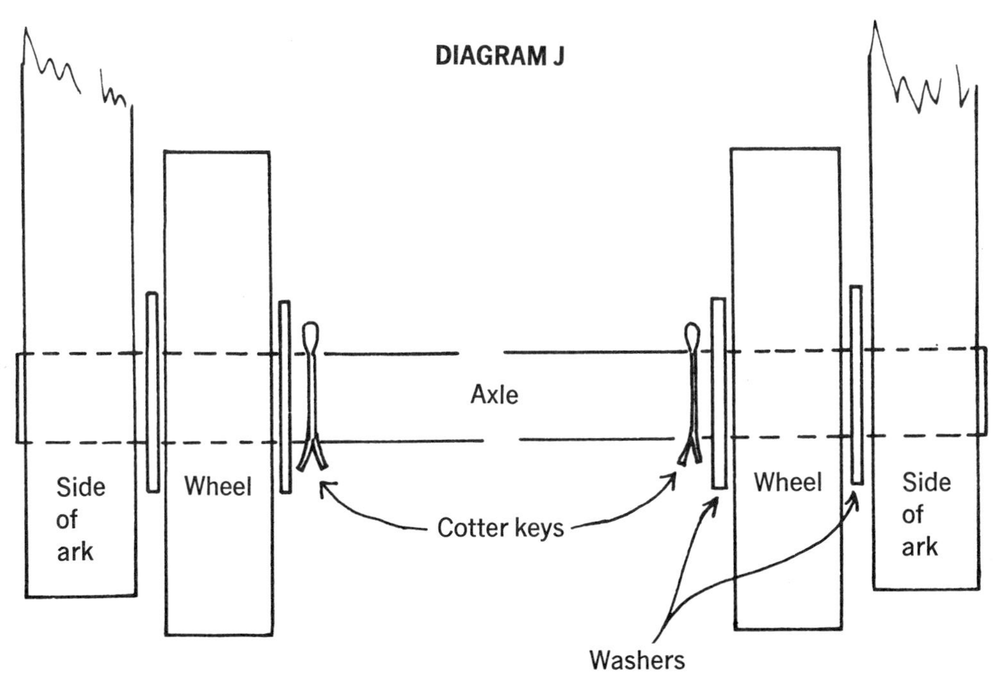

DIAGRAM J
Axle
Side
of
ark
Wheel
Cotter keys
Wheel
Side
of
ark
Washers

ANIMAL PATTERNS

Cut in pairs — Actual size

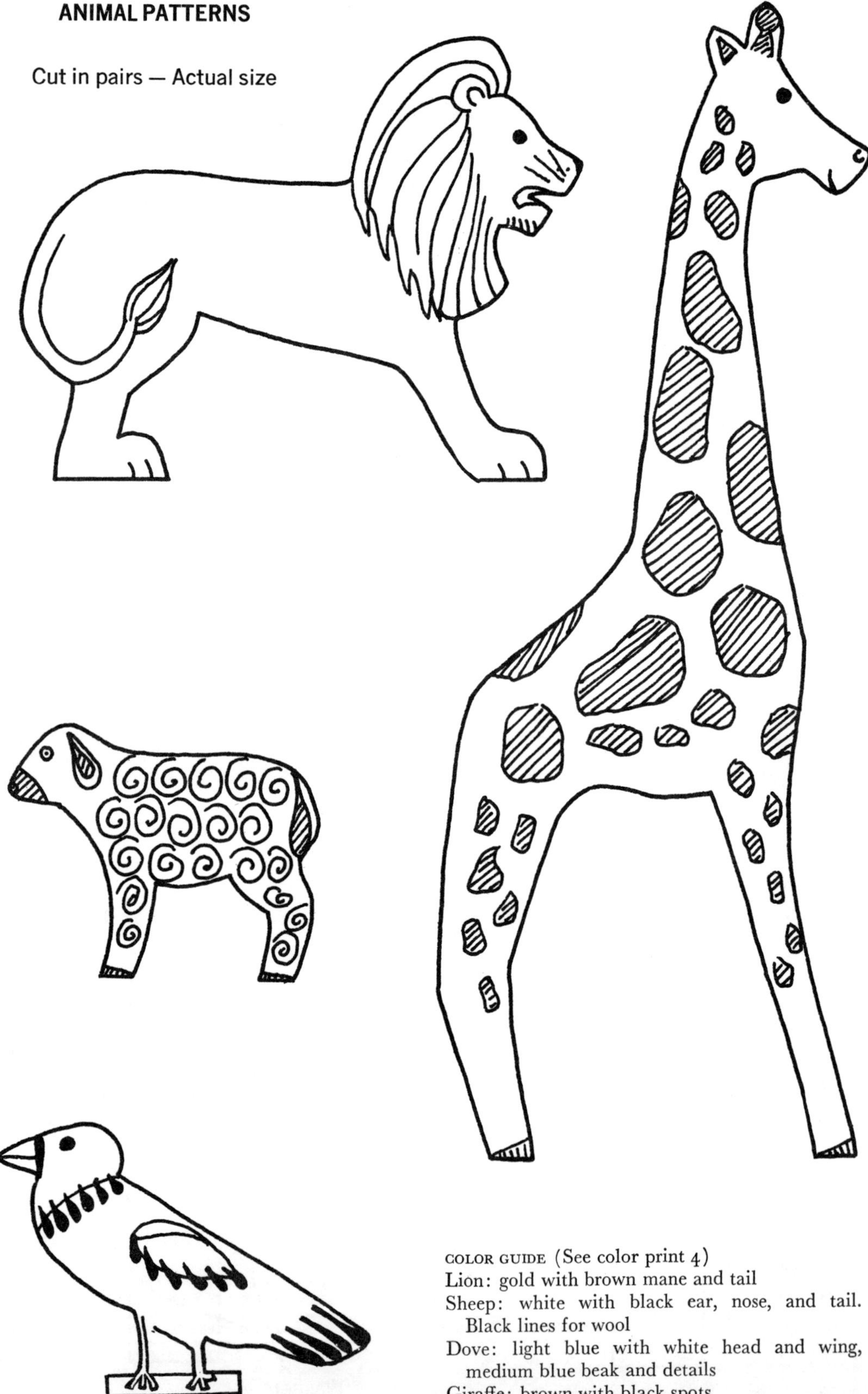

COLOR GUIDE (See color print 4)
Lion: gold with brown mane and tail
Sheep: white with black ear, nose, and tail.
   Black lines for wool
Dove: light blue with white head and wing,
   medium blue beak and details
Giraffe: brown with black spots

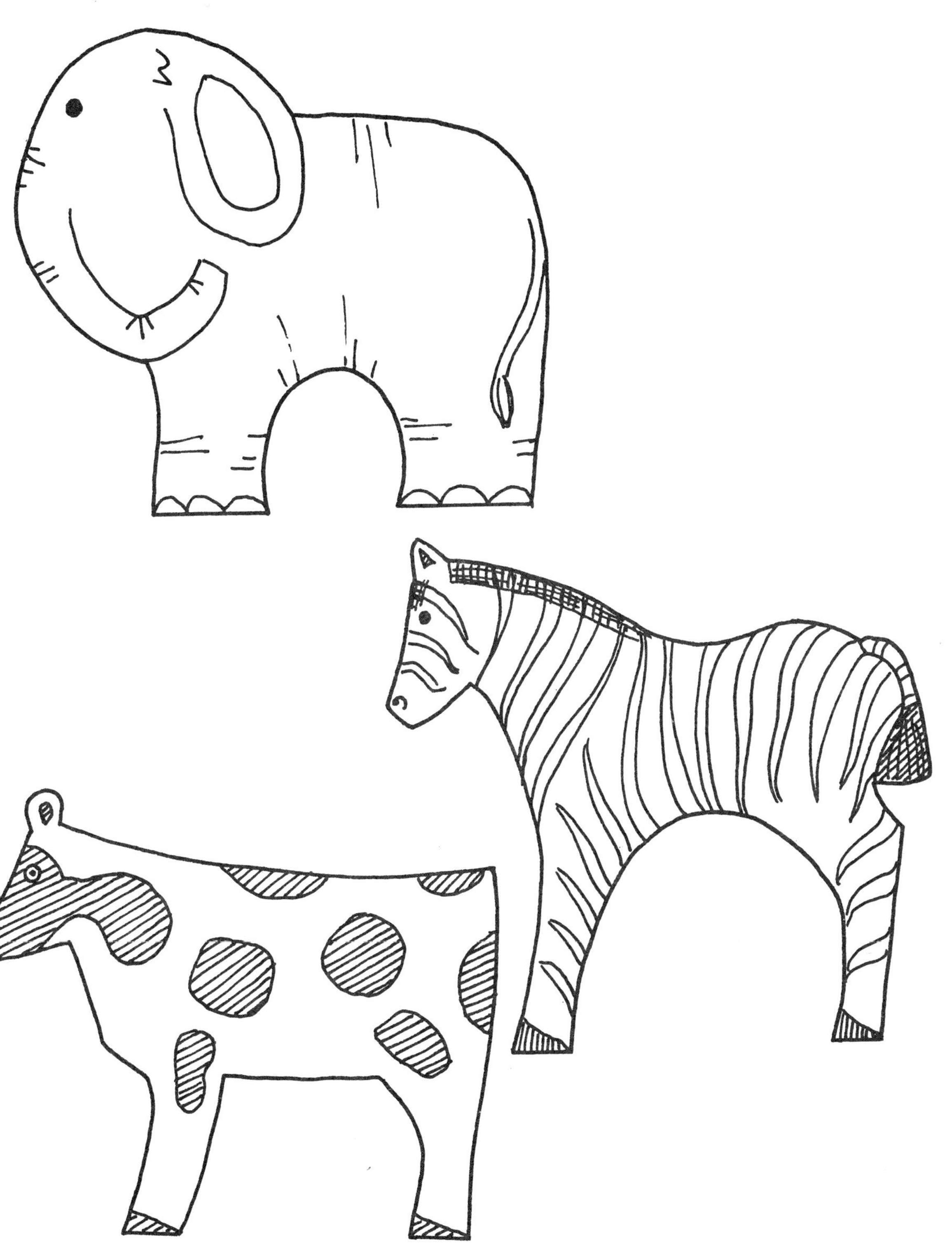

COLOR GUIDE (See color print 4)
Elephant: gray with pink ear, black details
Zebra: yellow with brown stripes, black mane
   and tail
Cow: white with black spots

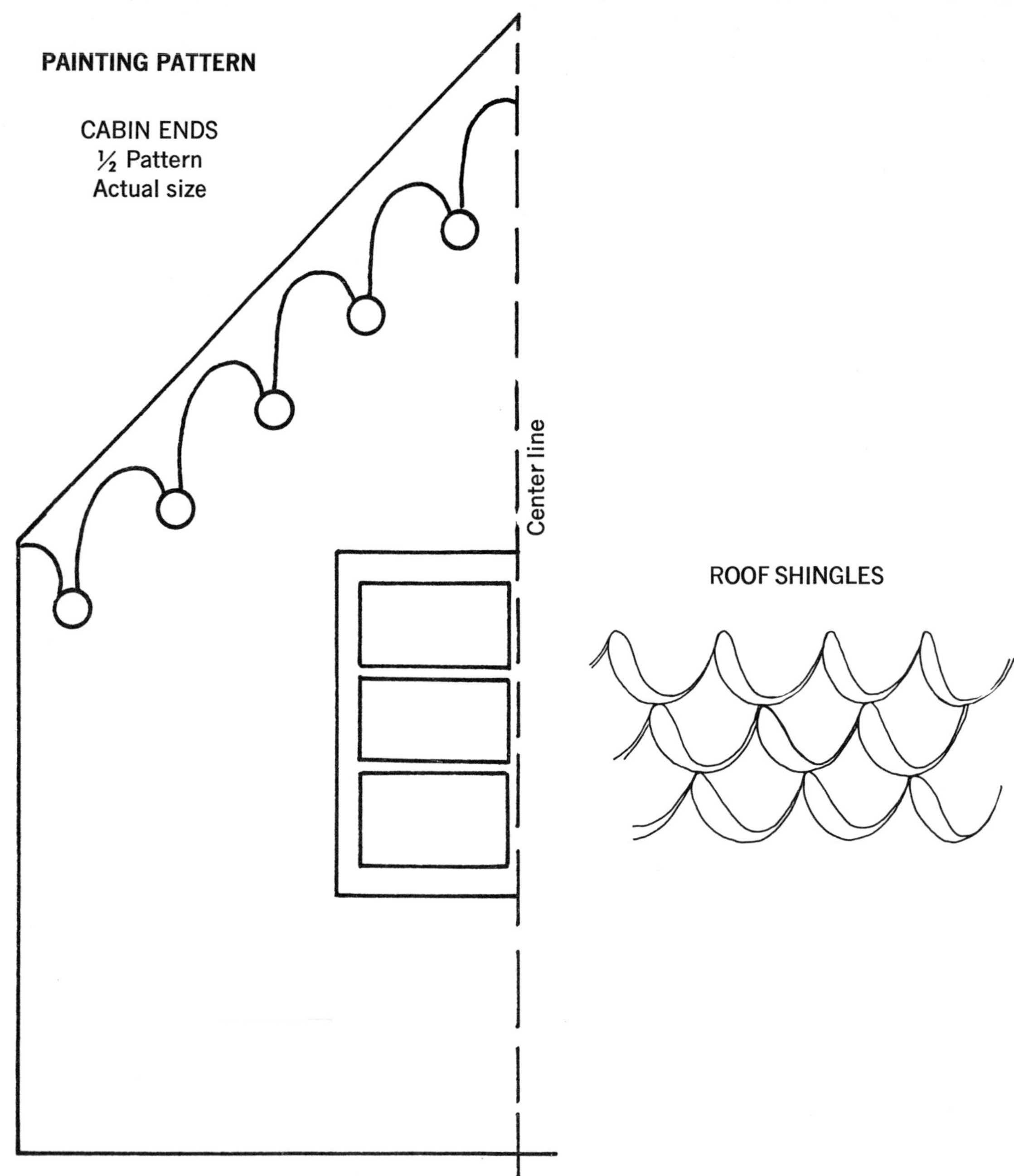

COLOR GUIDE (See color print 4)
Roof and chimney: red
Cabin and deck: medium blue
Ark hull: black
Windows: black with green dividers, outlined in
    red
Roof line swag on cabin: white
Roof: shingles in black strokes
Door: green, outline in red
Water line on hull: medium blue wavy line

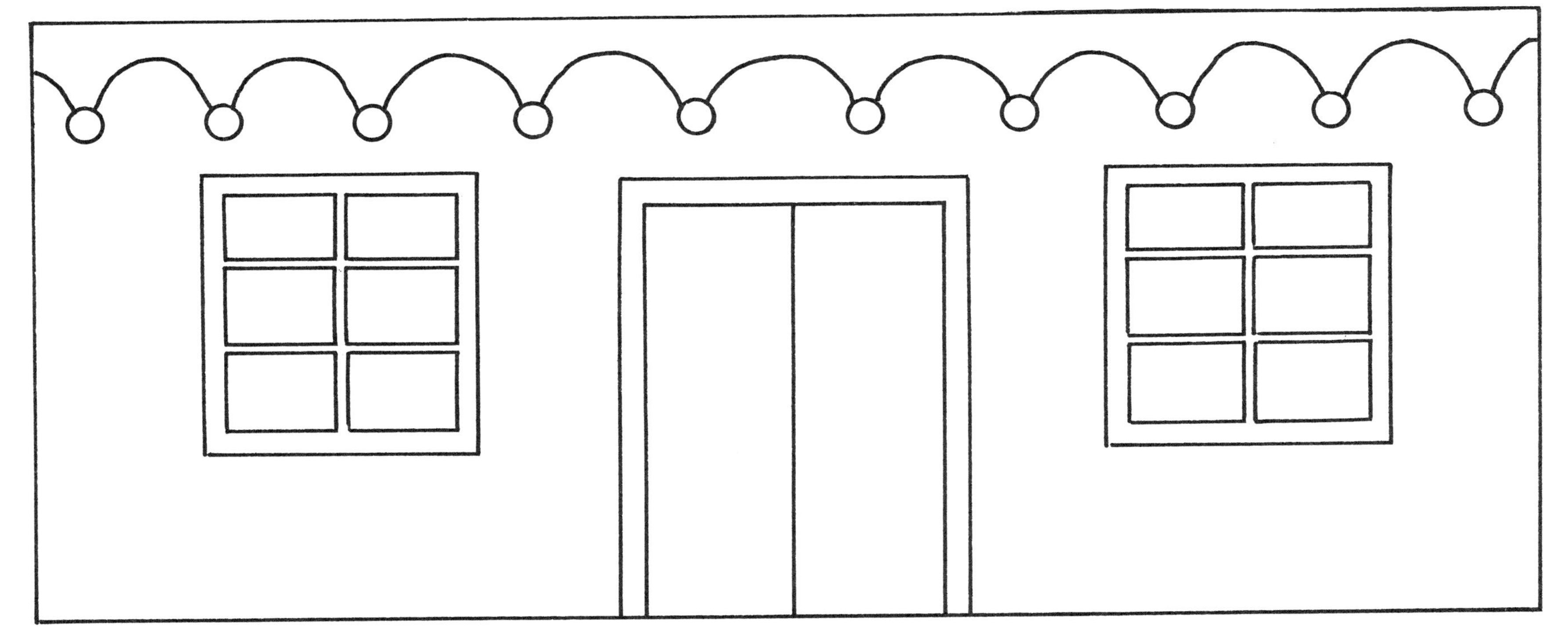

PAINTING PATTERN
CABIN SIDES
Actual size

Folk Art Wagon

This nubby little red wagon is fun for the children to pull around, and it can also serve as a portable toy chest. The 18″ handle shown on the model is a suitable length for small children, but you may want to use a longer handle for a tall or older child.

MATERIALS:

1″×12″ white pine shelving—96″ long
⅞″-diameter dowel—18″ long
⅝″-diameter dowel—30½″ long
¼″-diameter dowel—9″ long
³⁄₁₆″-diameter dowel—6″ long
Five steel washers—⅝″ diameter
One ¼″-diameter carriage bolt—5″ long
Two nuts and a washer (to fit carriage bolt)

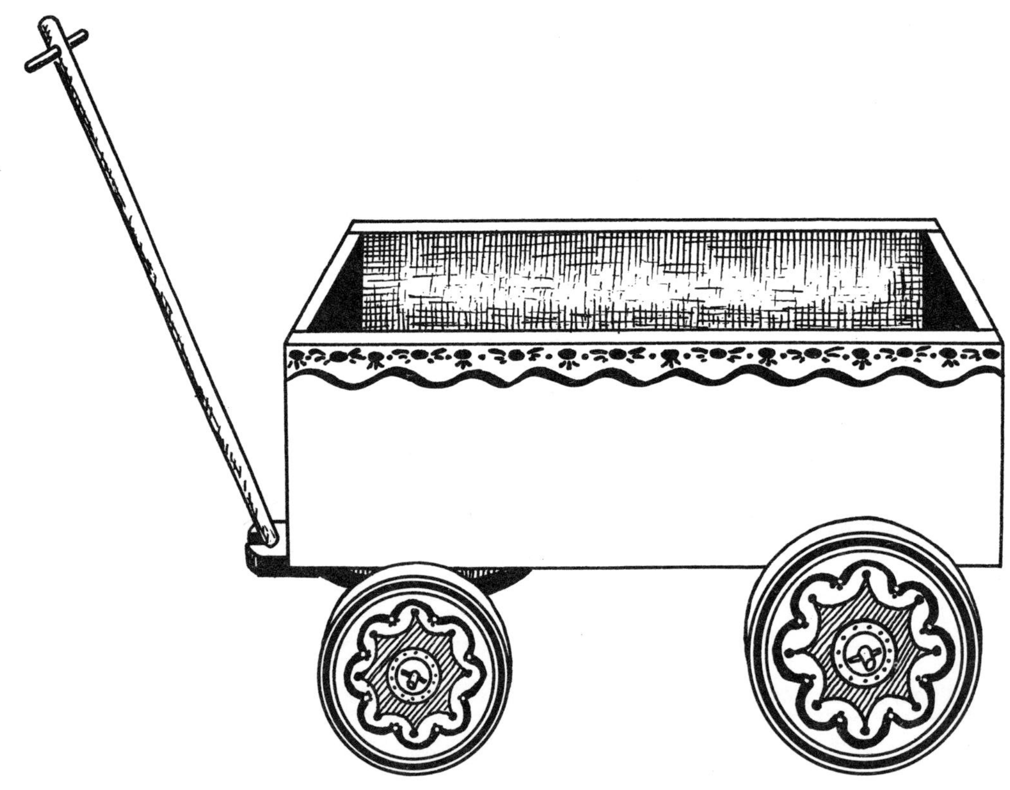

SUGGESTED LAYOUT FOR CUTTING

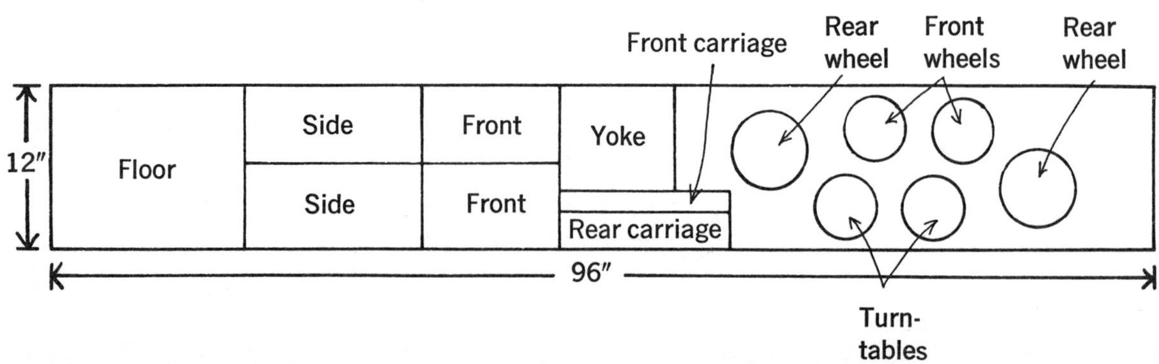

Actual size — ½ Pattern

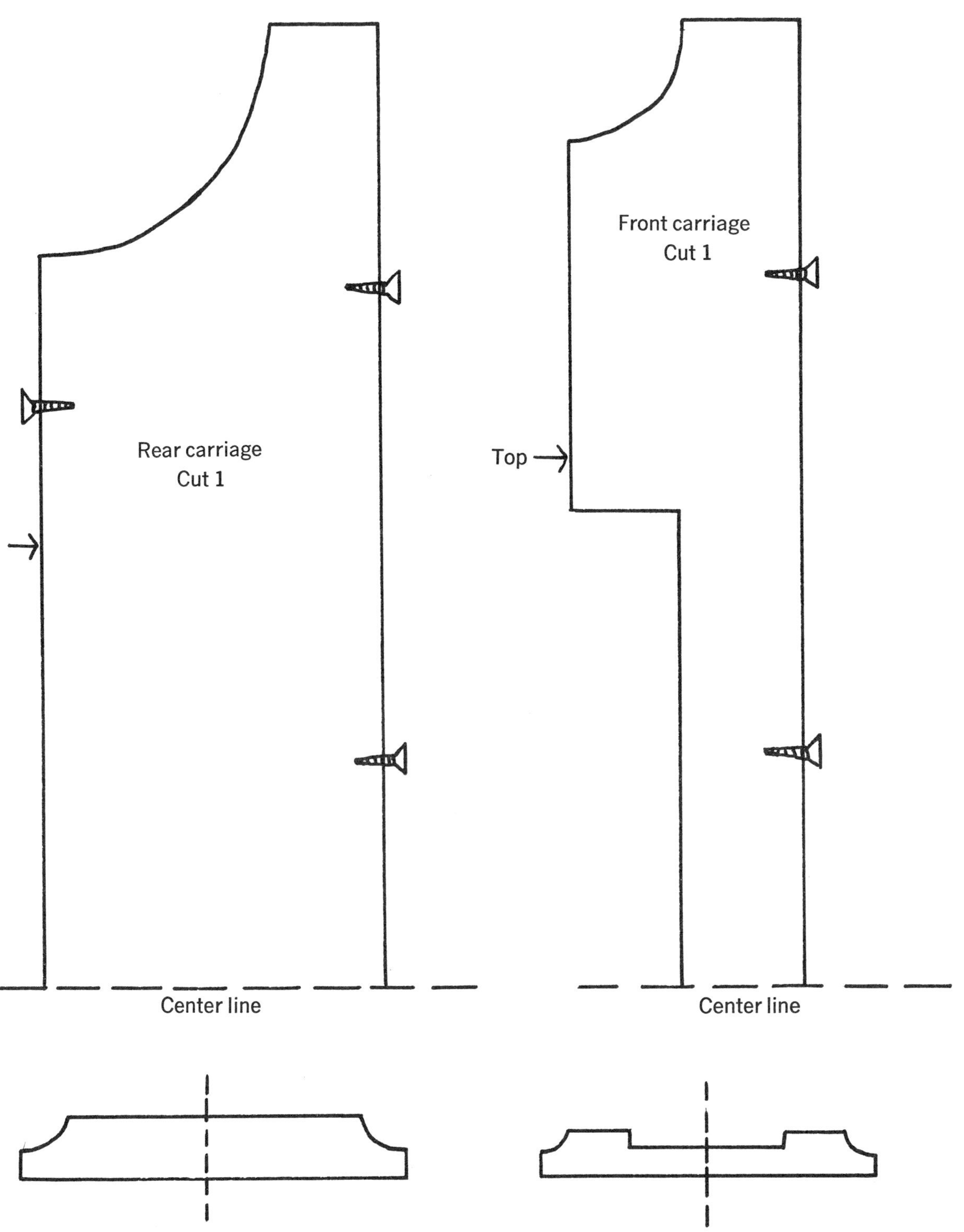

CUTTING PATTERN B

YOKE — Actual size

Wood grain

⁹⁄₃₂″ Hole

1″

¼″-Diameter hole

For handle retainer

Side view

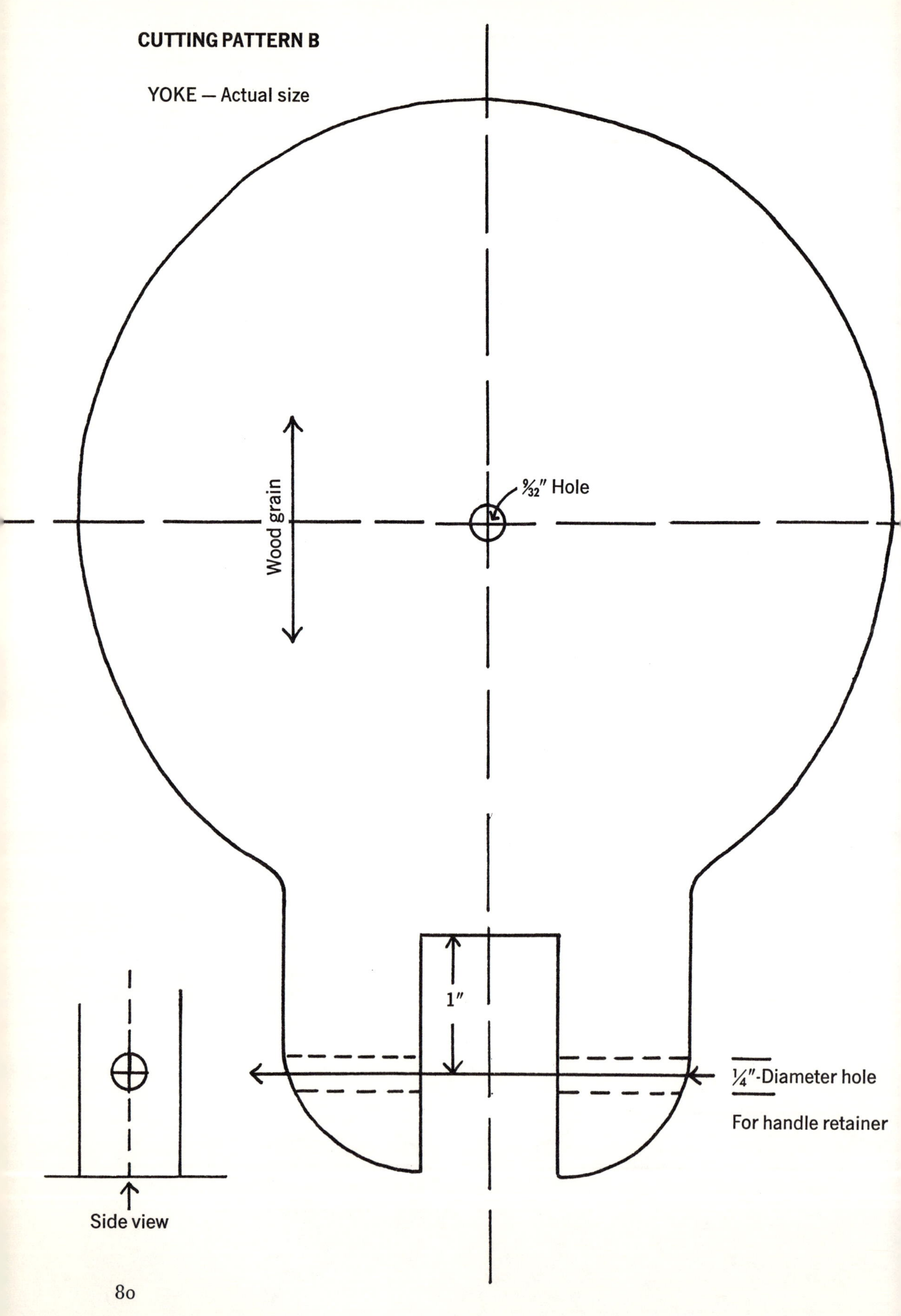

Three dozen finishing nails—1¾″ long
One dozen standard nails—1¼″ long
One dozen flat-head screws—1½″ long

STEP ONE: CUTTING

Following the Suggested Layout for Cutting, measure, and lay out the following pieces on white pine shelving:

Floor: Cut one piece—11¼″×20″

Sides: Cut two pieces—5⅞″×20″

Front and back: Cut two pieces—5⅞″× 9¾″

Rear carriage: Cut one piece—2¼″× 12¼″

Front carriage: Cut one piece—1½″× 12¼″

Turntables: Cut two circles—6″ diameter

Yoke: Cut one piece—6″×8″

Rear wheels: Cut two circles—7″ diameter

Front wheels: Cut two circles—5⅝″ diameter

Axles: Cut two pieces of ⅝″ dowel—15¼″ long

Axle pins: Cut four pieces of 3⁄16″ dowel —1⅜″ long

Handle retainer: Cut one piece of ¼″ dowel—3¾″ long

Handle crosspiece: Cut one piece of ¼″ dowel—5″ long

Handle: Cut one piece of 1″ dowel—18″ long

Trace the cutting patterns for the yoke, front carriage, and rear carriage onto the wood and cut with a jig saw or saber saw. Drill a 9⁄32″-diameter hole in the exact centers of the two turntable circles.

Drill a ⅝″-diameter hole in the exact center of the four wheels. Through the yoke, from side to side, drill a ¼″ hole for the handle retainer as indicated on the cutting pattern.

STEP TWO: ASSEMBLY

The first step is to assemble the body of the wagon by applying glue to the bottom edges of the side pieces and nailing through the floor into the side pieces. Use four 1¾″ finishing nails for each side, making sure that the sides are flush with the floor edge.

Glue and nail the front and back pieces between the sides, flush with the floor edge, using three 1¾″ nails for each joint. Turn the assembly upside down and draw a center line the full length of the floor. Next, measure 3⅞″ from the back edge and draw a line across the floor. A third line should be located and drawn 3″ back from the front edge (Diagram A). These lines locate the wheel assemblies.

Following Diagram A, drill one 9⁄32″-diameter hole for the carriage bolt. Next, drill three pilot holes for the 1½″ screws (slightly smaller than the diameter of the screw) through the floor. On the top edge of the rear carriage, drill three holes to match the holes in the floor. Glue and

DIAGRAM A

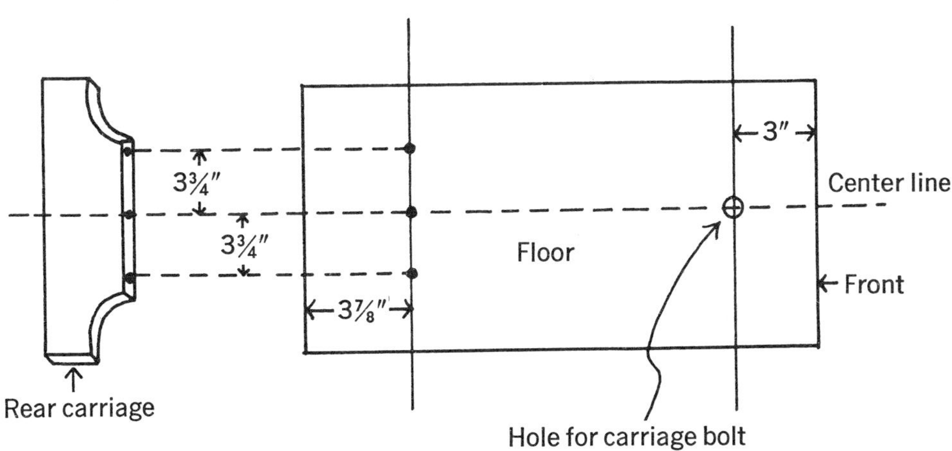

screw the rear carriage to the floor by inserting screws through the floor and into the rear carriage using three 1½″ screws.

Now, with the body upside down, insert the carriage bolt up through the inside of the wagon floor. Apply glue to one turntable circle and slip it over the carriage bolt. Nail it to the floor with four 1¼″ nails. Glue and nail the second turntable circle on top of the first in the same manner (Diagram B). The body can now be set aside until the front carriage and yoke are assembled.

To attach the front carriage to the yoke, draw center lines on the yoke and front carriage. Place the yoke on the front carriage and match center lines, making sure that the carriage is at right angles with the yoke. Glue and nail into place, through the yoke, with four 1¼″ nails (Diagram C).

To assemble the axles, locate and mark the center line of each 15¼″ piece of ⅝″ dowel. On each of these axles drill four pilot holes for the 1½″ screws through the axle rod; drill one hole 1½″ on each side of the center line and one hole 3″ past the first hole toward the ends (Diagram D).

Place the axles on the front and back carriages with center lines matching in both directions. Using the axle as a template, continue drilling the pilot holes through the axles into the front and rear carriages. Apply glue and place the axles into position and screw into place with four 1½″ flat-head screws on each axle.

Now place the yoke and front carriage with the axle side down and use the yoke as a template to drill a ⁹⁄₃₂″-diameter hole through the carriage and axle for the carriage bolt.

Drill two ³⁄₁₆″ holes in each axle, ½″ in from each end for the axle pins (Diagram E).

Following Diagram B, assemble by first placing one ⅝″ washer over the bolt, followed by the yoke and axle assembly and a ¼″ washer. Finally, place two ¼″ nuts over the bolt and draw the first nut up until it is firm against the washer. Then back

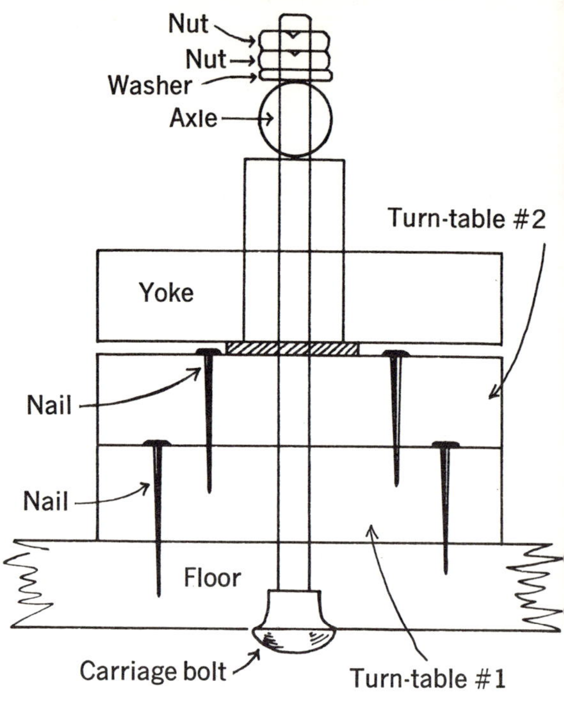

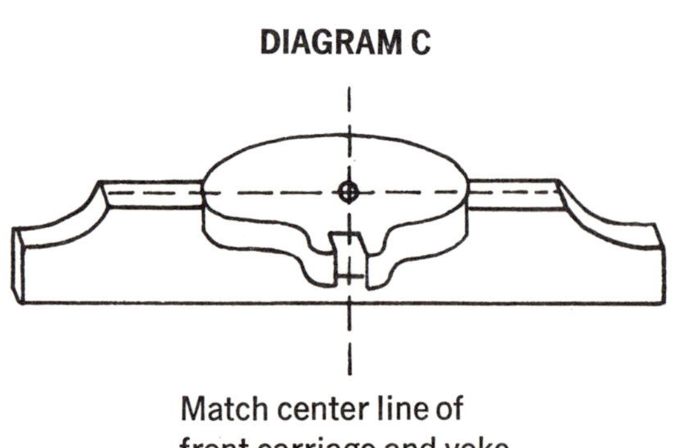

Match center line of
front carriage and yoke

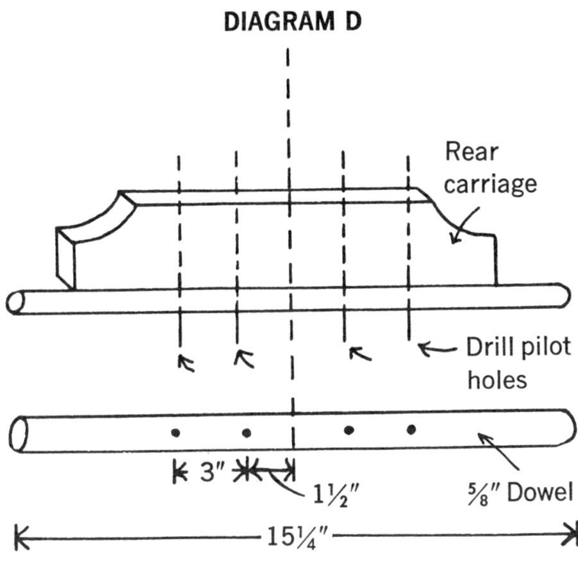

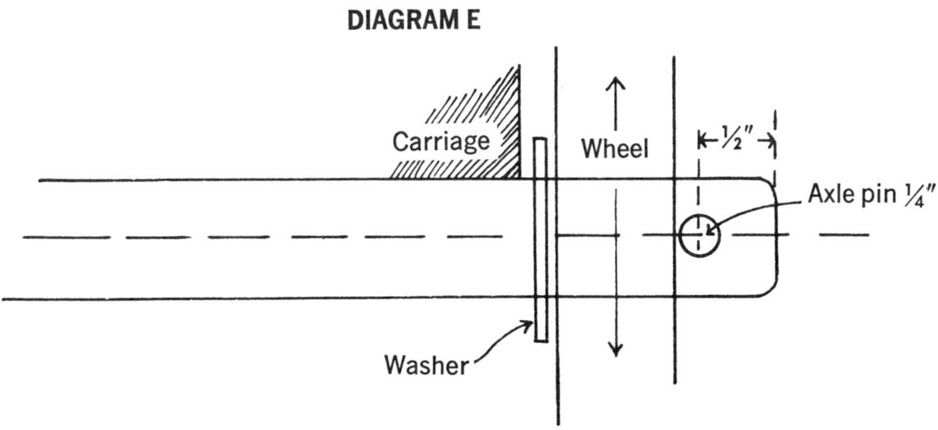

it off until the front carriage assembly moves or turns smoothly. Now run the second nut up into place and tighten it against the first nut to lock it in place.

Using sandpaper, lightly sand the ends of both axles until the wheels turn freely but not loosely. Place a ⅝" washer on the axle and then a wheel, driving an axle pin into place to secure the wheel (Diagram E).

The last step is to attach the wagon handle. Drill one ¼"-diameter hole through the 1" dowel, ½" from one end. At the opposite end of the dowel, drill a 9/32" hole ⅝" from the end (Diagram F). Smooth the ends of the handle with sandpaper and insert the crosspiece into the end of the handle as shown in the diagram. Place the other end of the handle in the slot of the yoke, lining up the holes so that the retainer can be inserted through the three thicknesses of wood. Tap the retainer into place to secure the handle.

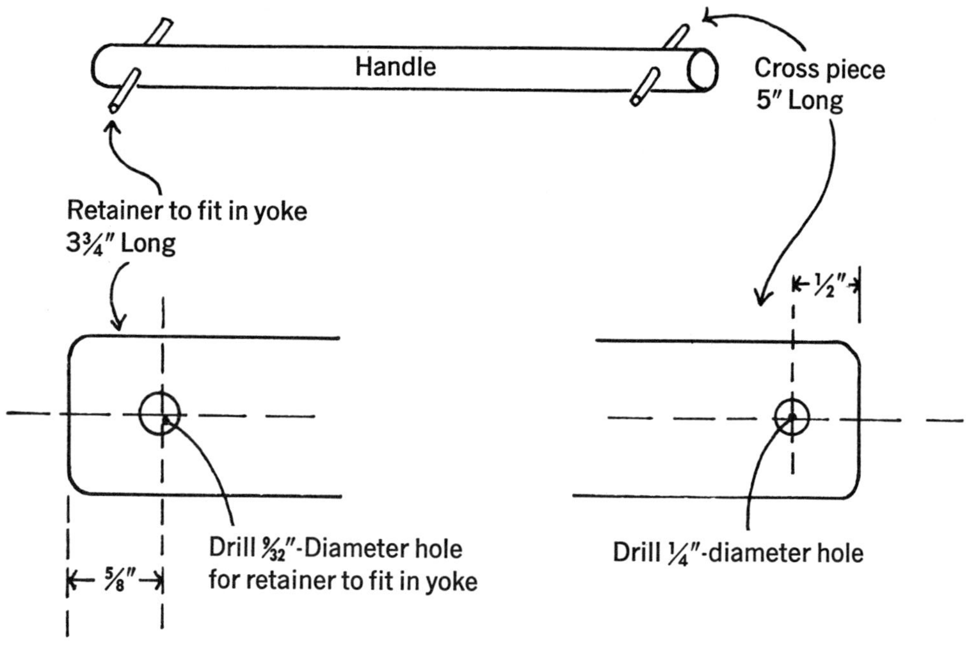

PAINTING PATTERNS

TOP BORDER — Actual size

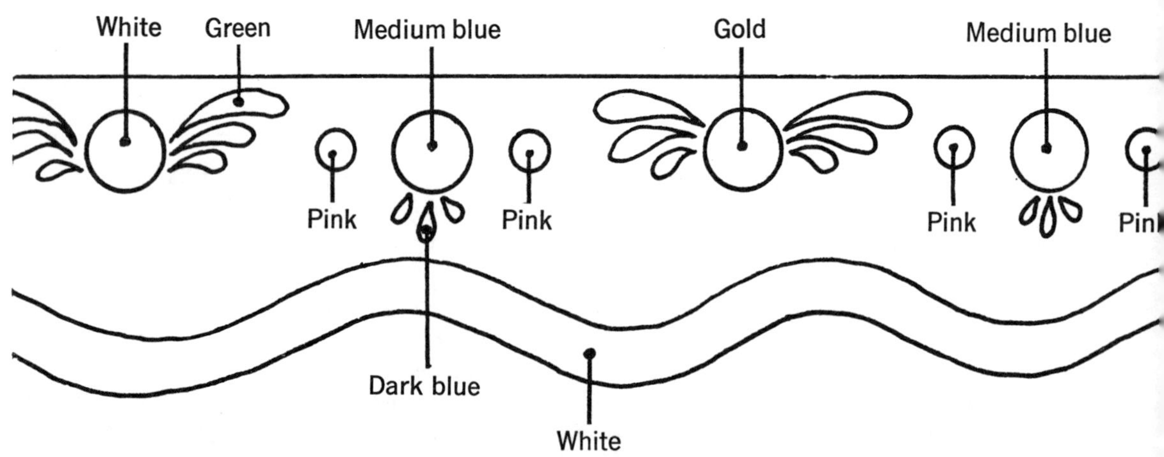

Repeat design around top edge of wagon body

FRONT WHEELS
Actual size
COLOR GUIDE
White
Red
White
Red
Gold
Medium blue
Dark blue
Gold
Red
White
Dark blue
Red
White
Center line

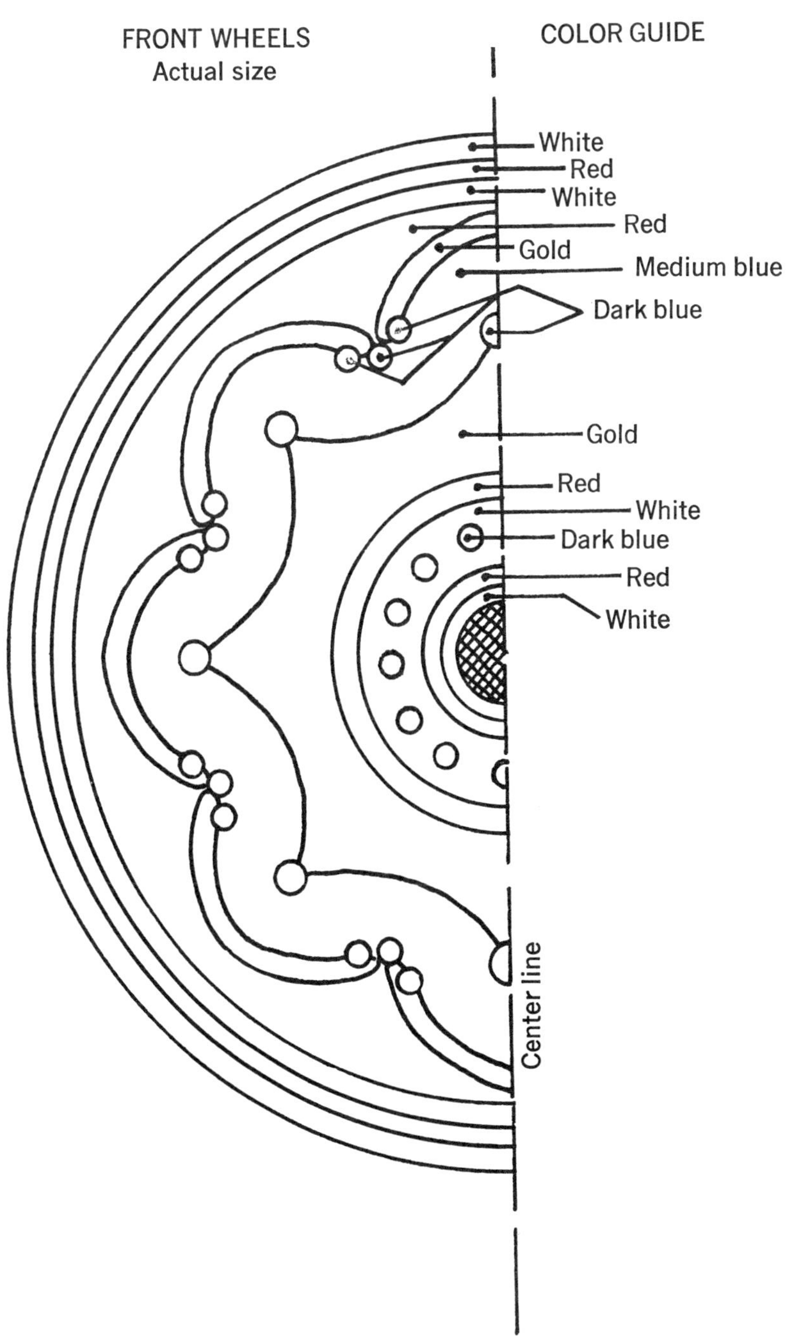

BACK WHEELS
Actual size
COLOR GUIDE
White
Red
White
Red
Gold
Dark blue
Dark blue
Medium blue
Gold
Red
White
Dark blue
Red
White
Center line

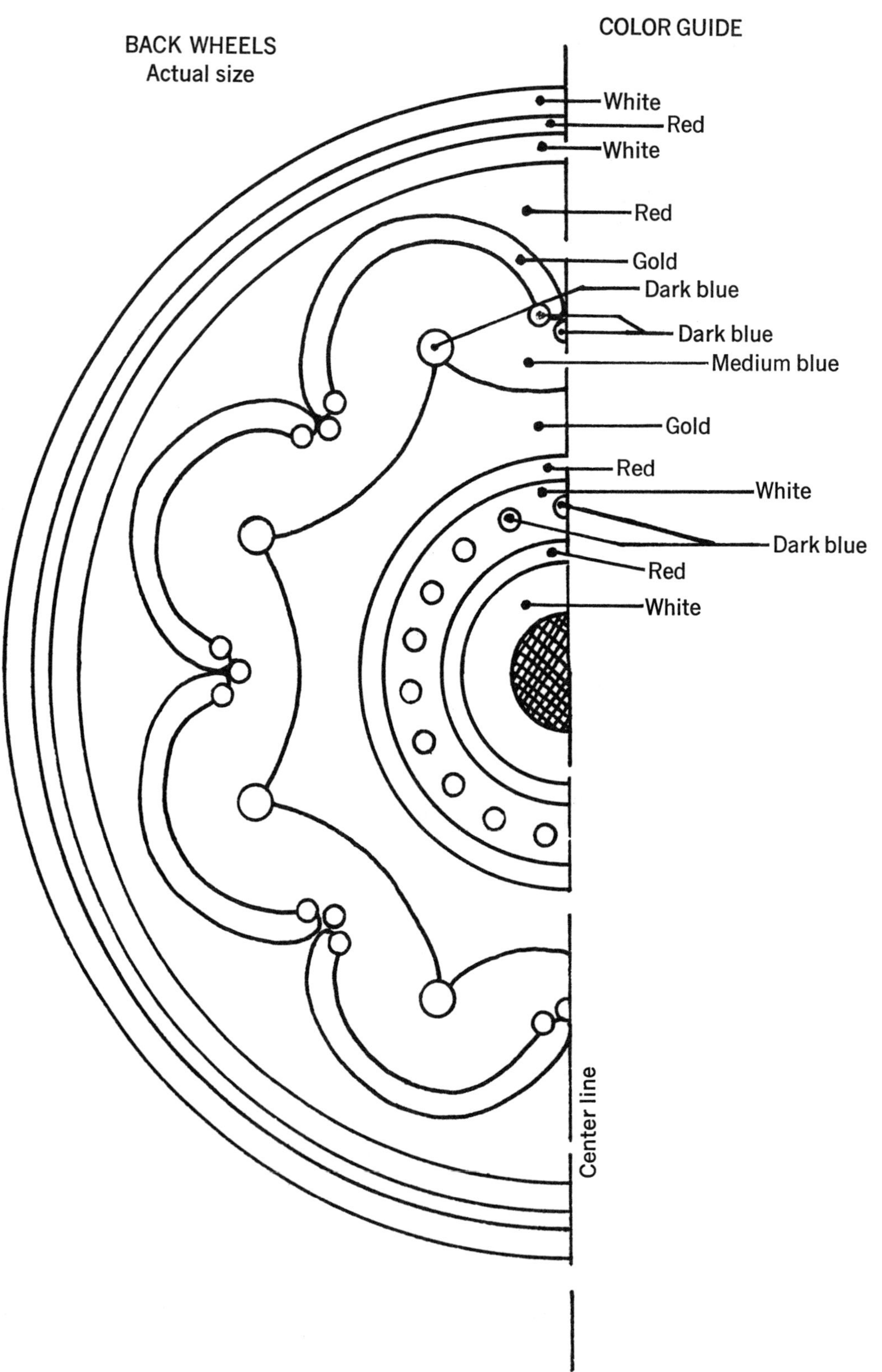

Folk Art Sled

The folk art museum in Innsbruck, Austria, has a most wonderful collection of sleighs, all richly painted in warm, mellow colors. Alpine designs being one of our favorites, we found it impossible to resist designing a sled of our own. It is hoped that many toddlers will enjoy being pulled about in this quaint little box sled.

MATERIALS:

1″×12″ white pine shelving—60″ long
1″×8″ white pine shelving—36″ long
⅜″ plywood—13¼″×20⅜″
One dozen 2″ finishing nails
One dozen 1½″ finishing nails
Two dozen 1½″ common nails

STEP ONE: CUTTING

Using the Suggested Layout for Cutting as your guide, measure and lay out the following pieces on your wood:

Floor: Cut one piece—13¼″×20⅜″
Back: Cut one piece—11⅛″×11¾″
Front: Cut one piece—3″×11¾″
Sides: Cut two pieces—10″×22″
Runners: Cut two pieces—3¾″×34″

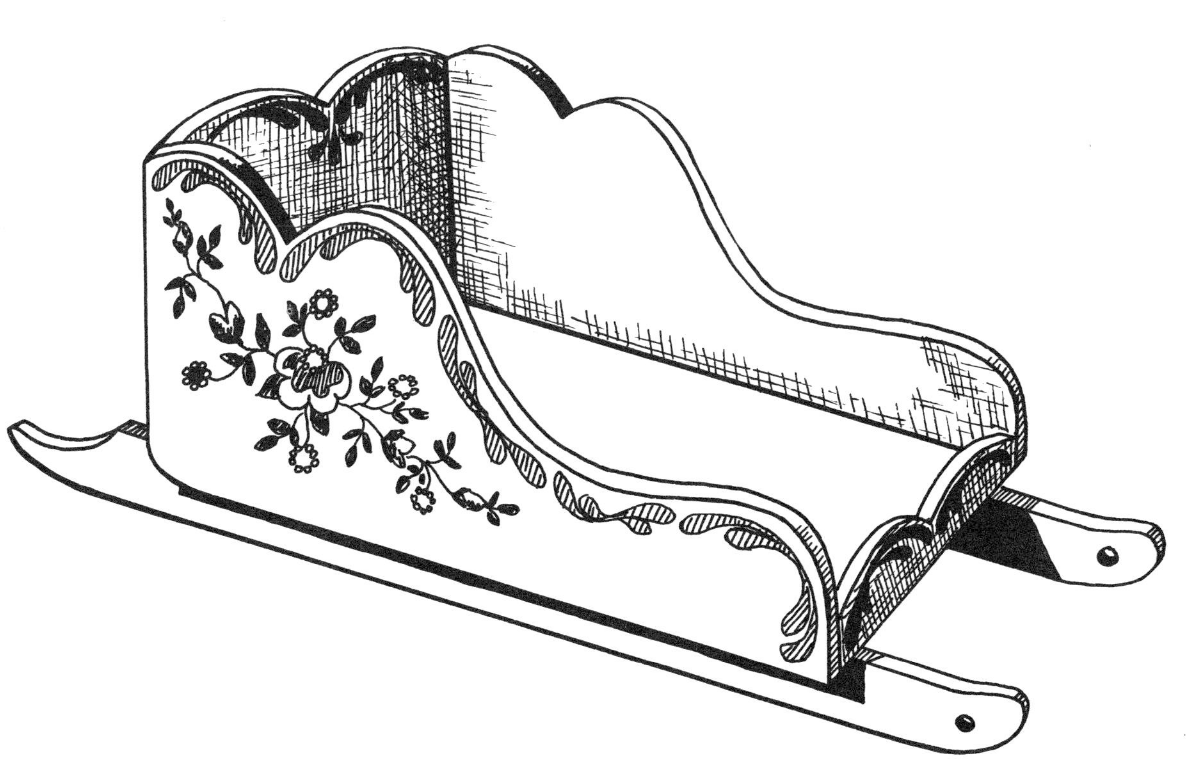

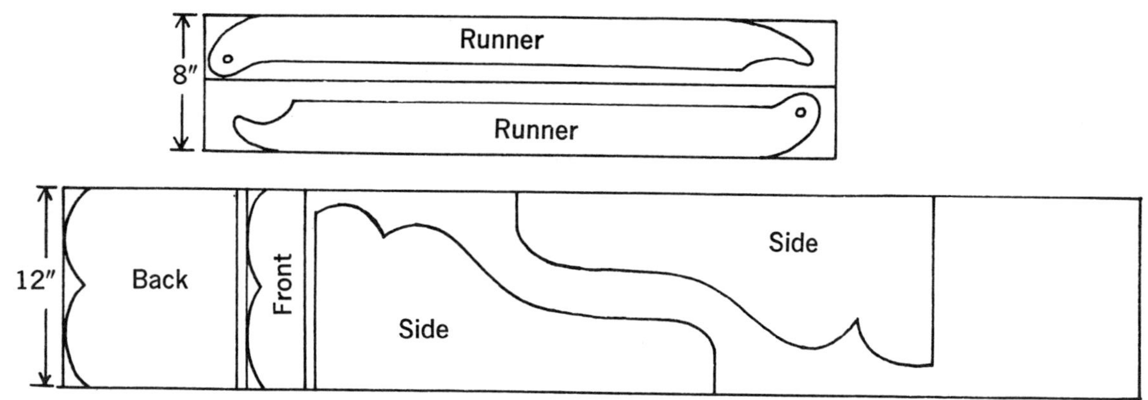

CUTTING PATTERN A

TOP DETAIL — FRONT AND BACK
Actual size — ½ Pattern

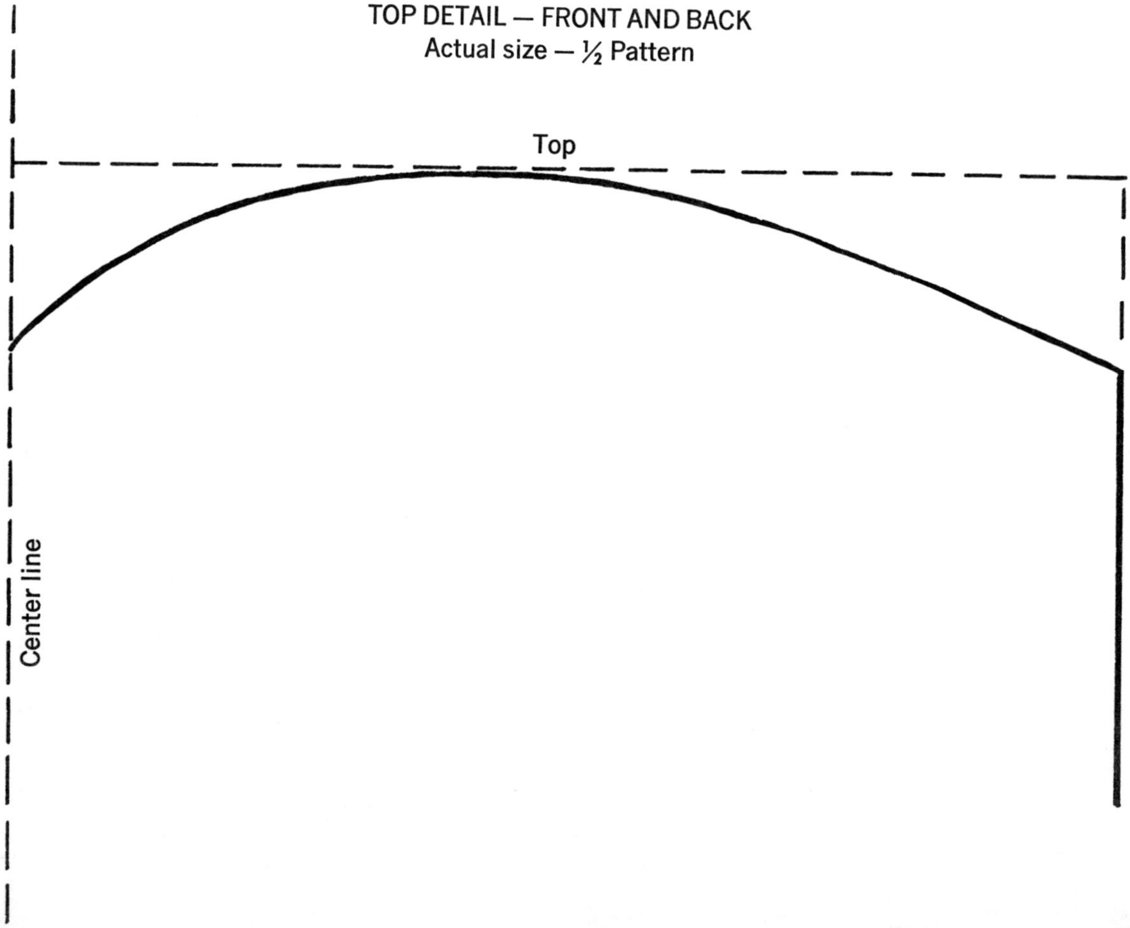

Trace the cutting patterns on the wood, being sure to enlarge the pattern for the sides. Cut the pieces with a jig saw or saber saw. Cut the bottom edge of the back piece at an angle by measuring $\frac{1}{8}''$ up on one side as shown in Diagram A on page 92.

STEP TWO: ASSEMBLY

Glue and nail the side pieces to the floor by nailing through the floor into the bottom edges of the side pieces. Use seven $1\frac{1}{2}''$ common nails for each side piece, making sure that the side pieces are flush with the edge of the floor.

Apply glue to the ends and bottom edge of the front piece and fit the front piece between the sides, flush with the floor, and secure by driving two $2''$ finishing nails through each side into the ends of the front piece.

Place the bottom edge of the back piece flush with the floor and the top edge flush with the top corner of the sides and nail into place using four $2''$ finishing nails through each side piece into the back piece. The sides at the lower edge will extend about $1\frac{1}{2}''$ beyond the back piece and floor piece.

The final step in assembling the sled is to attach the runners. Turn the sled upside down and draw two lines the full length of the floor from front to back. Draw these lines $1\frac{1}{2}''$ in from each of the two outside edges, parallel to the side pieces. The outside edges of the runners are to be located on these lines. Apply glue to the floor piece and place the runners into position on the lines with the front end of the runner $6''$ beyond the front edge of the sled. To hold the runners in place, drive one $1\frac{1}{2}''$ finishing nail at an angle through the side of the runner into the back and front pieces. Repeat with the other runner (Diagram B on page 92). Turn the sled upright and drive four or five nails through the floor into each runner.

After the sled has been painted, run a $\frac{3}{8}''$ hemp or clothes line rope through the holes in the front of the runners and knot the ends.

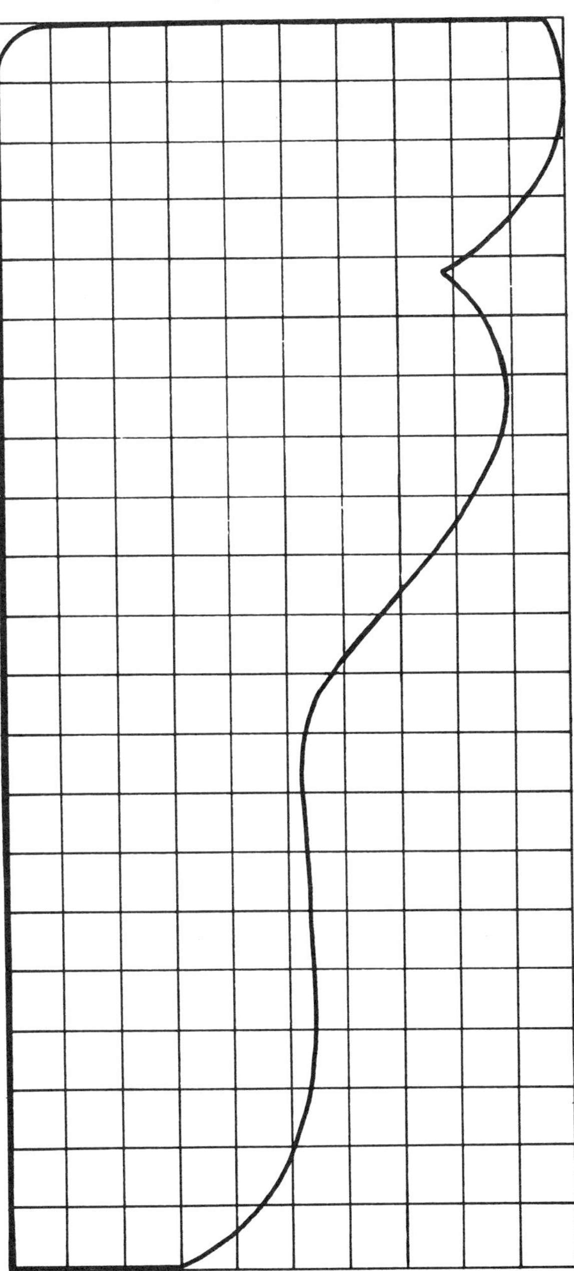

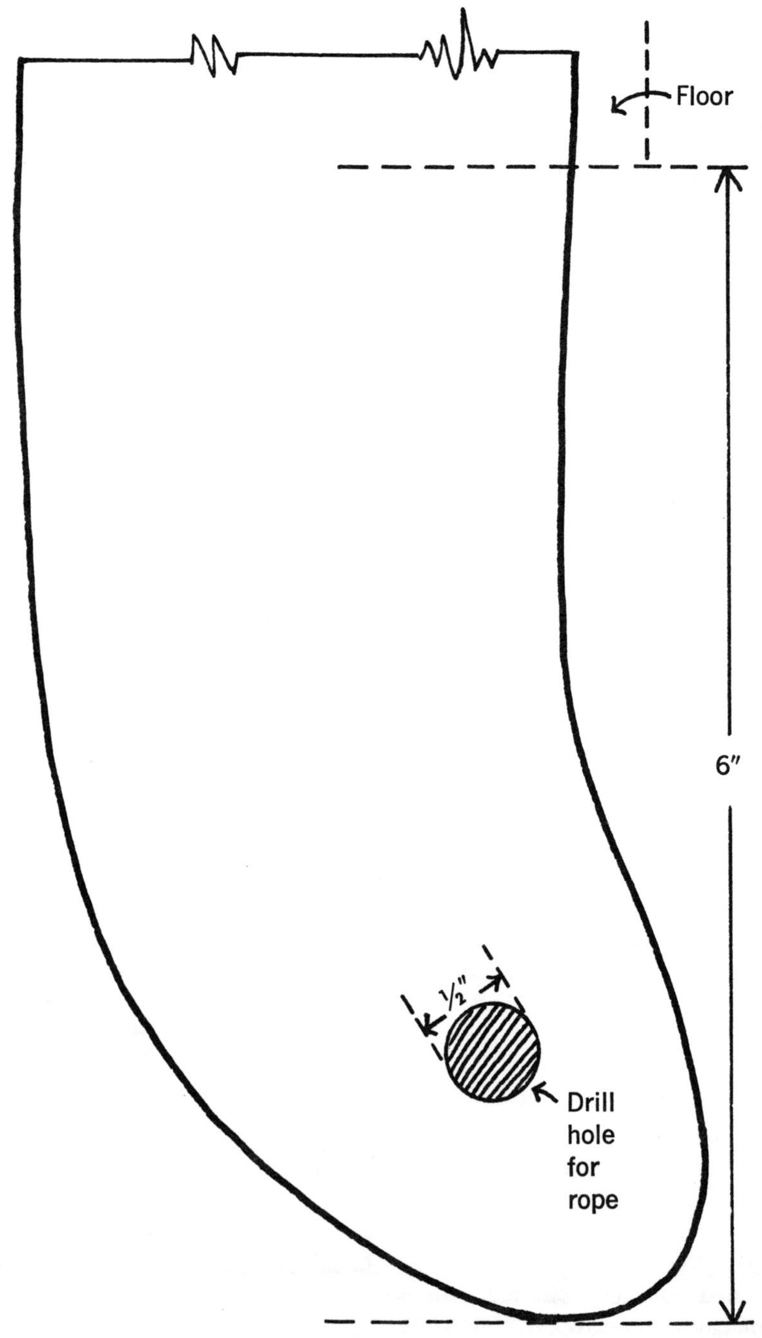

CUTTING PATTERN C

FRONT END OF RUNNER
Actual size

Floor

6"

½"

Drill
hole
for
rope

CUTTING PATTERN D

BACK END OF RUNNER
Actual size

34"

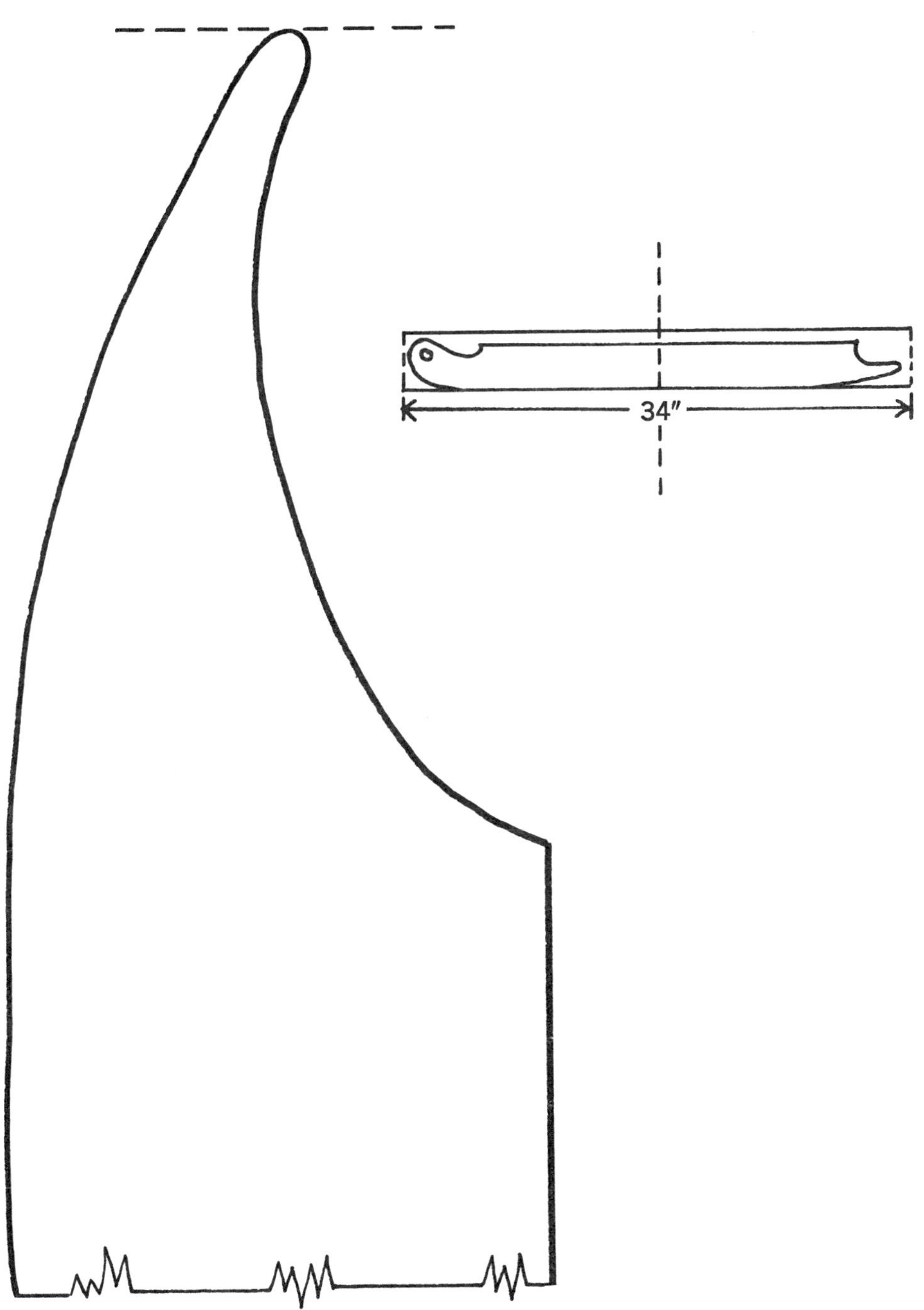

DIAGRAM A

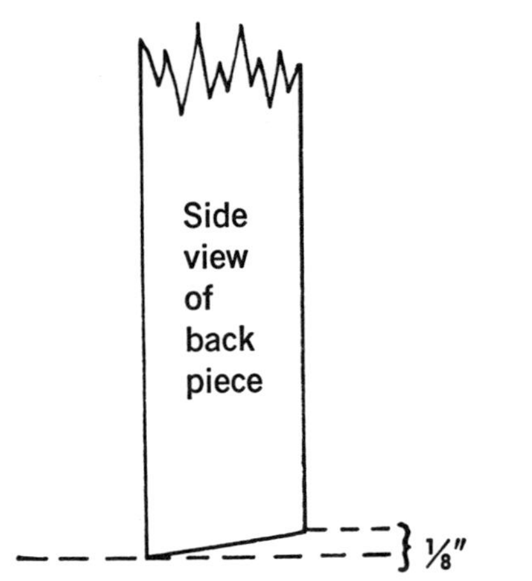

Cut the bottom edge of back piece at an angle

DIAGRAM B

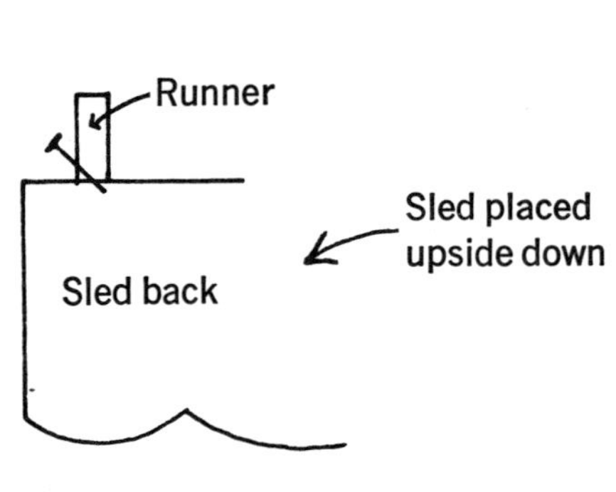

Drive nails through the runner at an angle

PAINTING PATTERNS

TOP DETAIL — FRONT AND BACK
Actual size — ½ Pattern

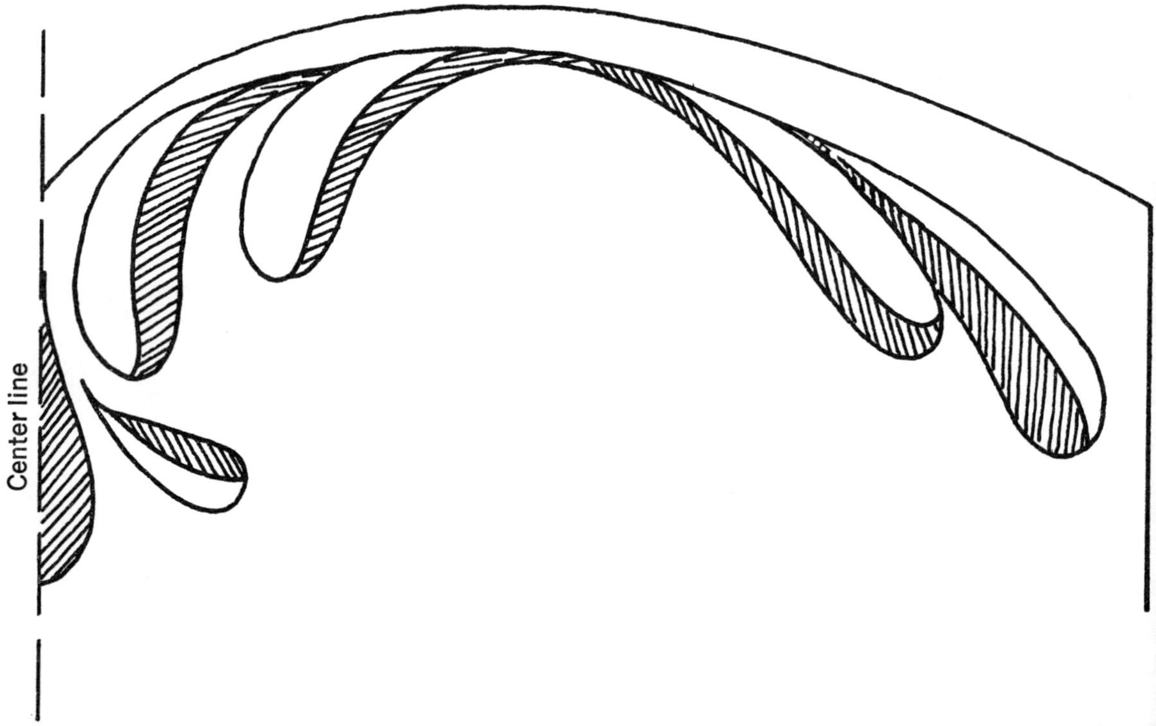

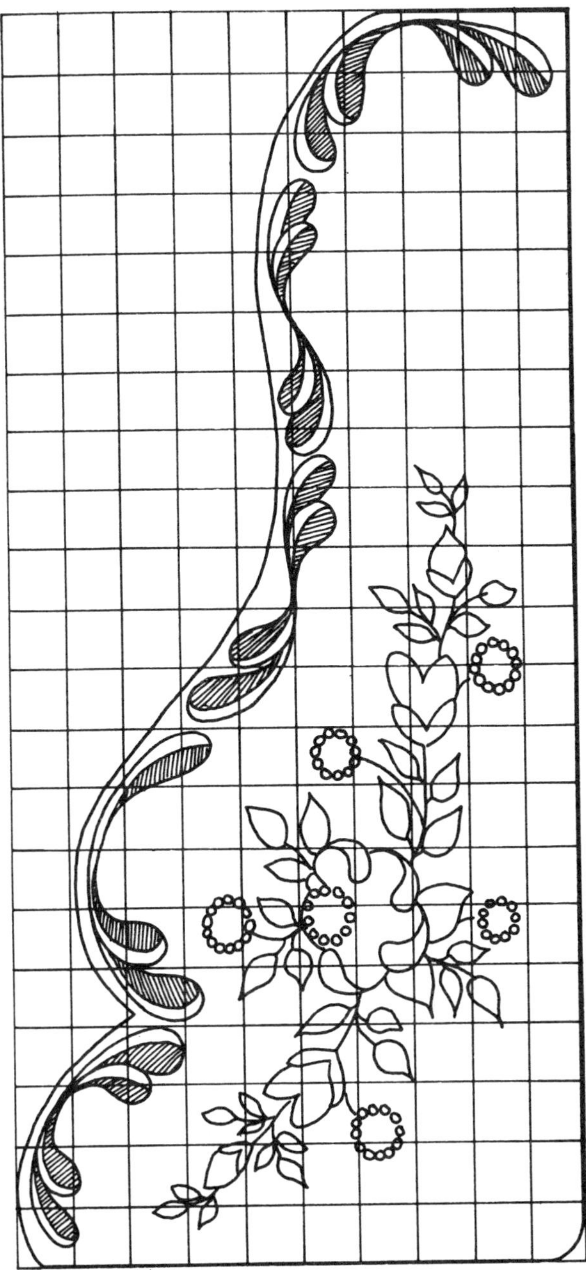

COLOR GUIDE (See color print 1)
Roses: red with pink detail, white dots at center
Leaves: green
Small round flowers: gold centers with a circle of
   white dots
Scrolls: gold with lighter gold accents

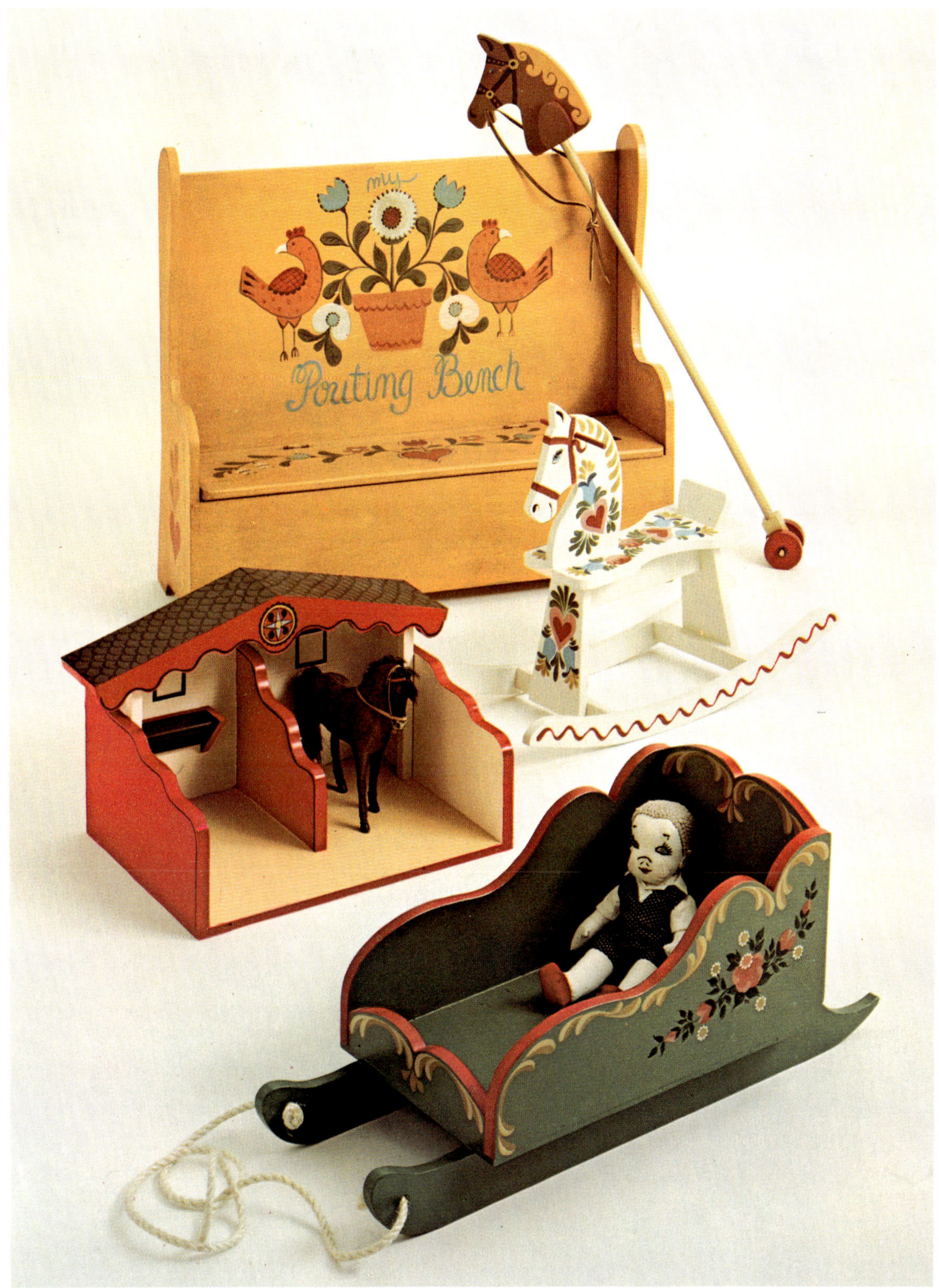
Pouting Bench

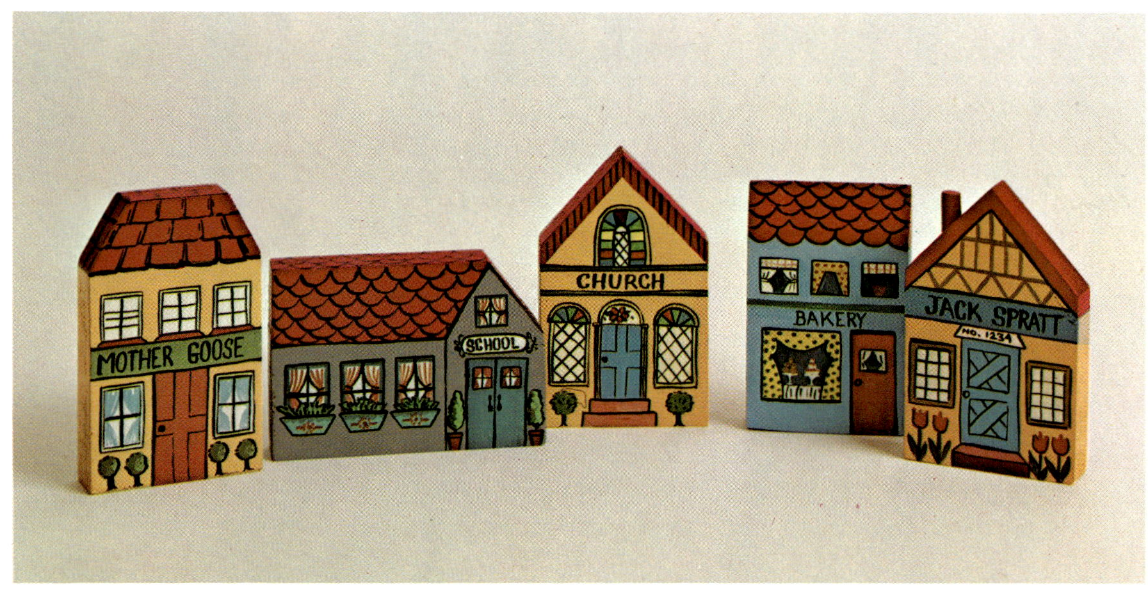

2

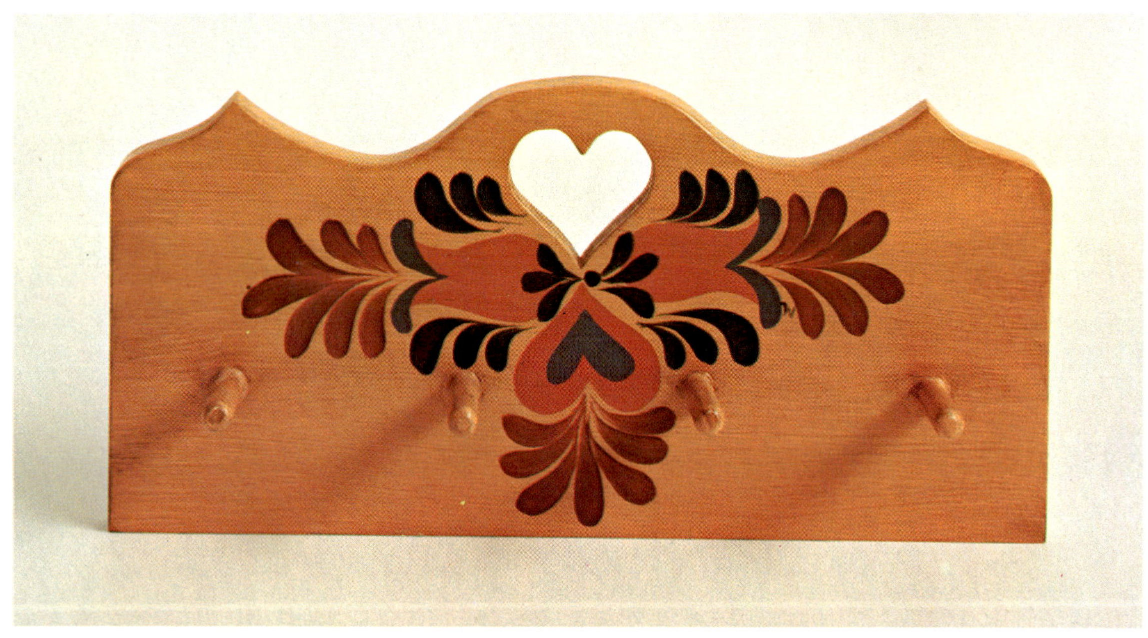

3

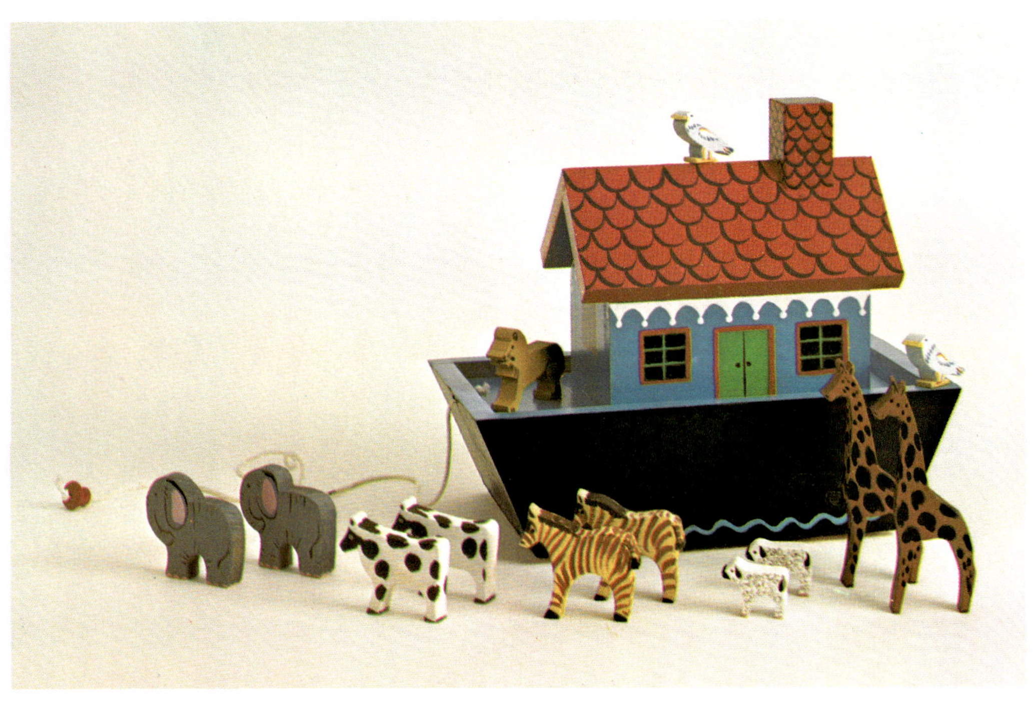

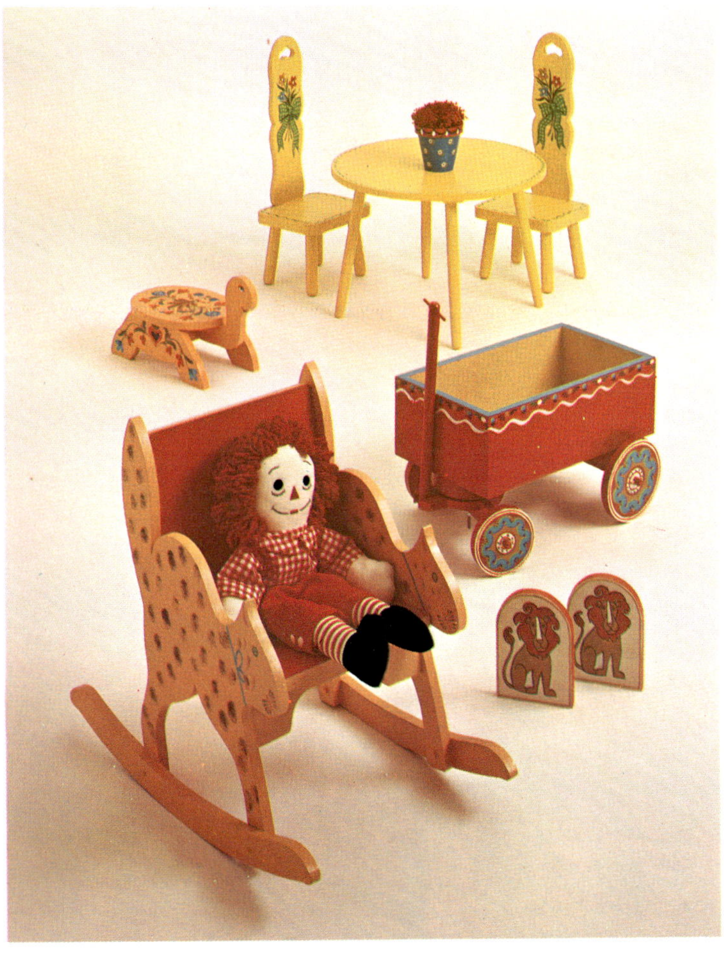

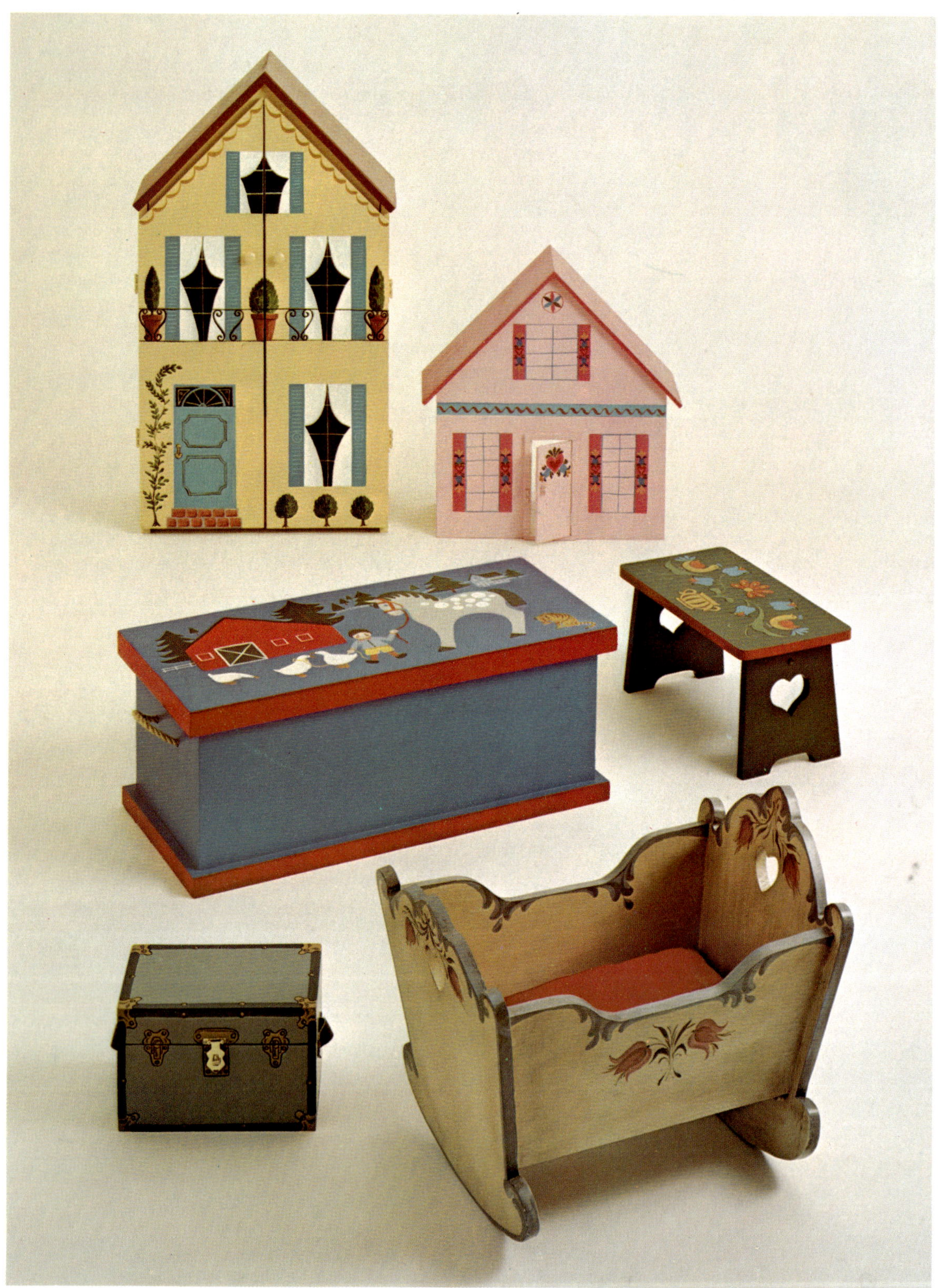

Chapter Six

Child-Size Furniture Patterns

Kit-Kat Rocker

The little kit-kat rocker was inspired by an antique rocking chair in the Shelburne Museum. The original is most likely one of a kind, built by a doting father for a child who was crazy about kittys. Our version is sturdy and not difficult to build.

MATERIALS:

¾″ plywood (good on both sides)—36″× 48″
1″ white pine shelving—¾″×44″ long

Four ³⁄₁₆″-diameter machine screws—1¼″ long
Nuts and washers to fit machine screws
Two dozen finishing nails—2″ long
1½ dozen finishing nails—1¼″ long

STEP ONE: CUTTING

Enlarge the patterns for the cat sides and rockers, and following the Suggested Layout for Cutting, measure and draw your patterns on plywood. Cut the pattern pieces with a jig saw or saber saw.

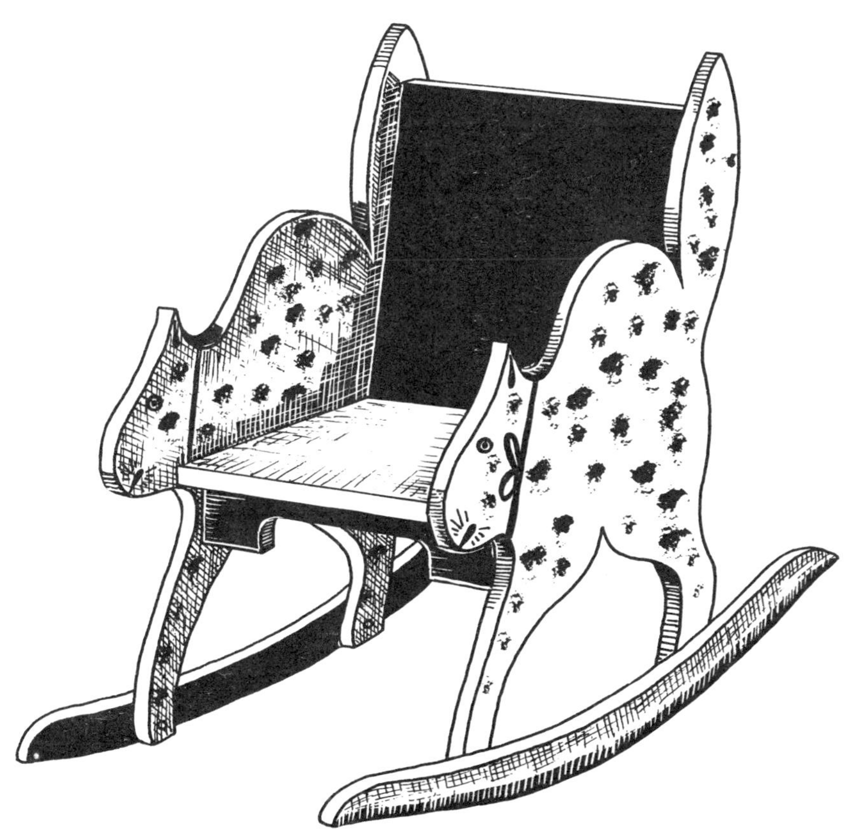

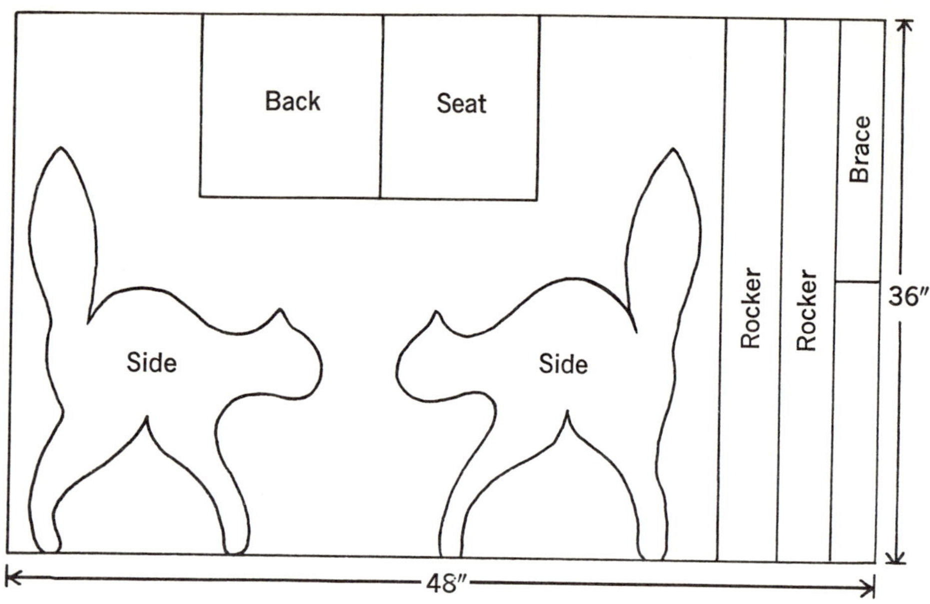

CUTTING PATTERN A

SIDE — Cut 2
1 Square = 2 Inches

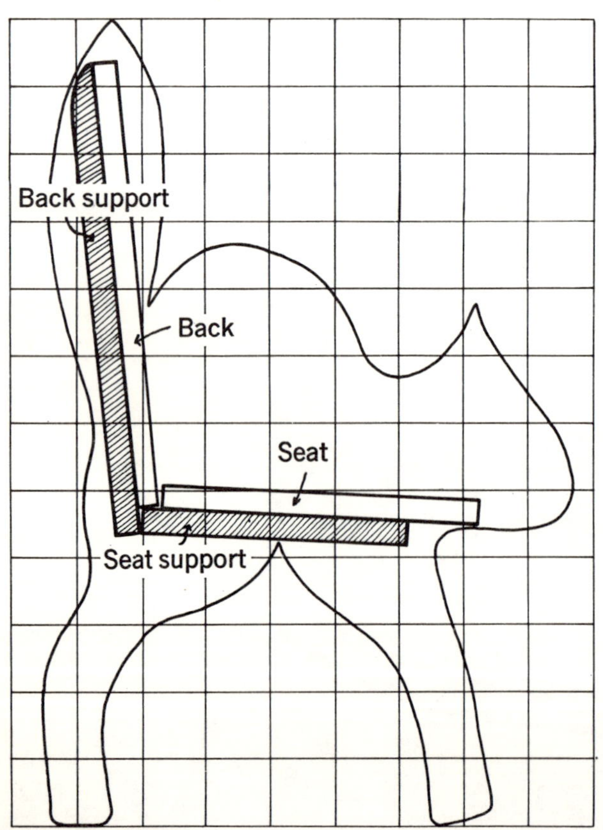

NOTE: When enlarging pattern, be sure to draw the back support and seat support as shown

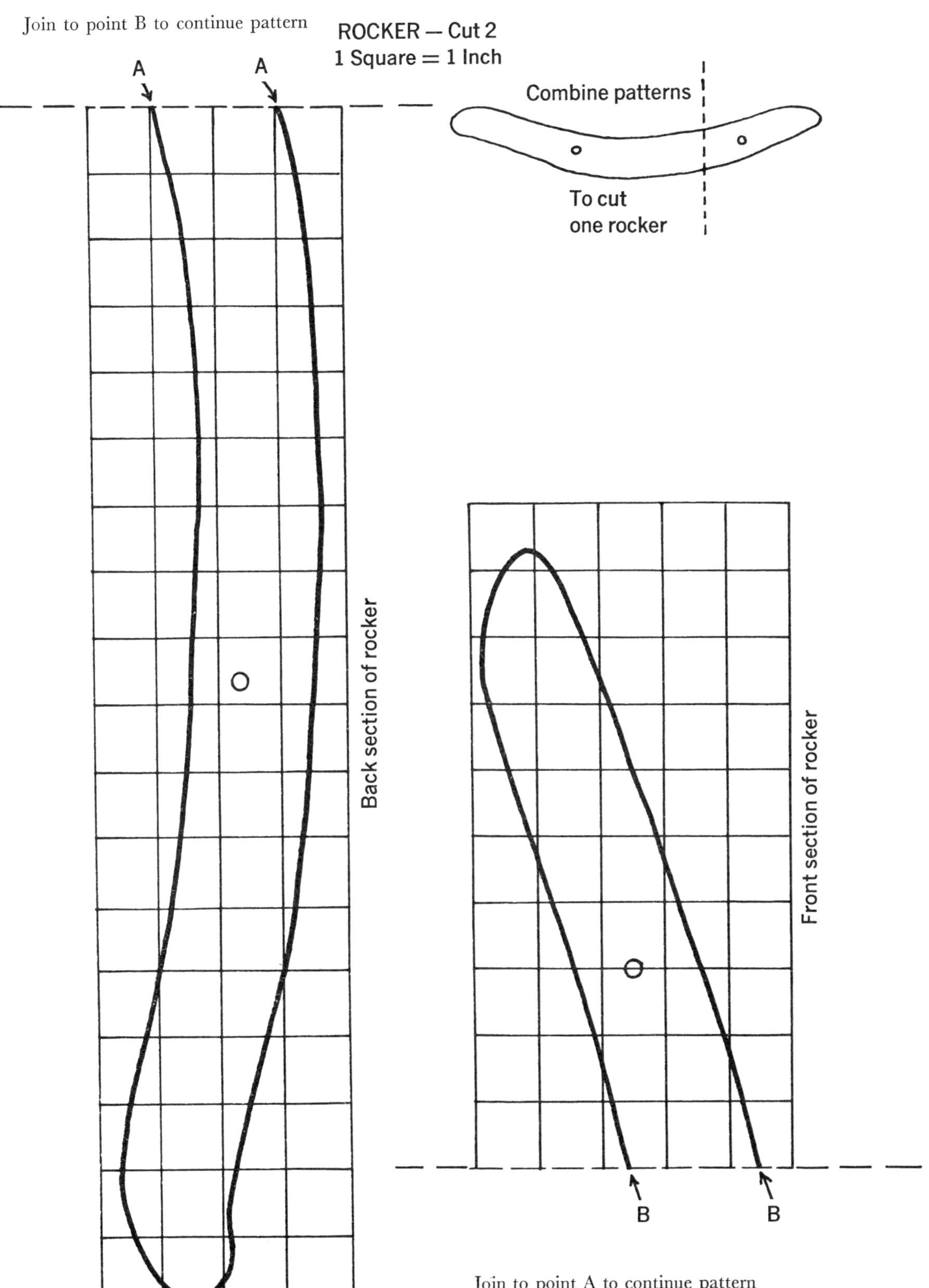
Join to point B to continue pattern
ROCKER — Cut 2
1 Square = 1 Inch
A
A
Combine patterns
To cut
one rocker
Back section of rocker
Front section of rocker
B
B
Join to point A to continue pattern

CUTTING PATTERN C

BRACE — Cut 1
Actual size — ½ Pattern

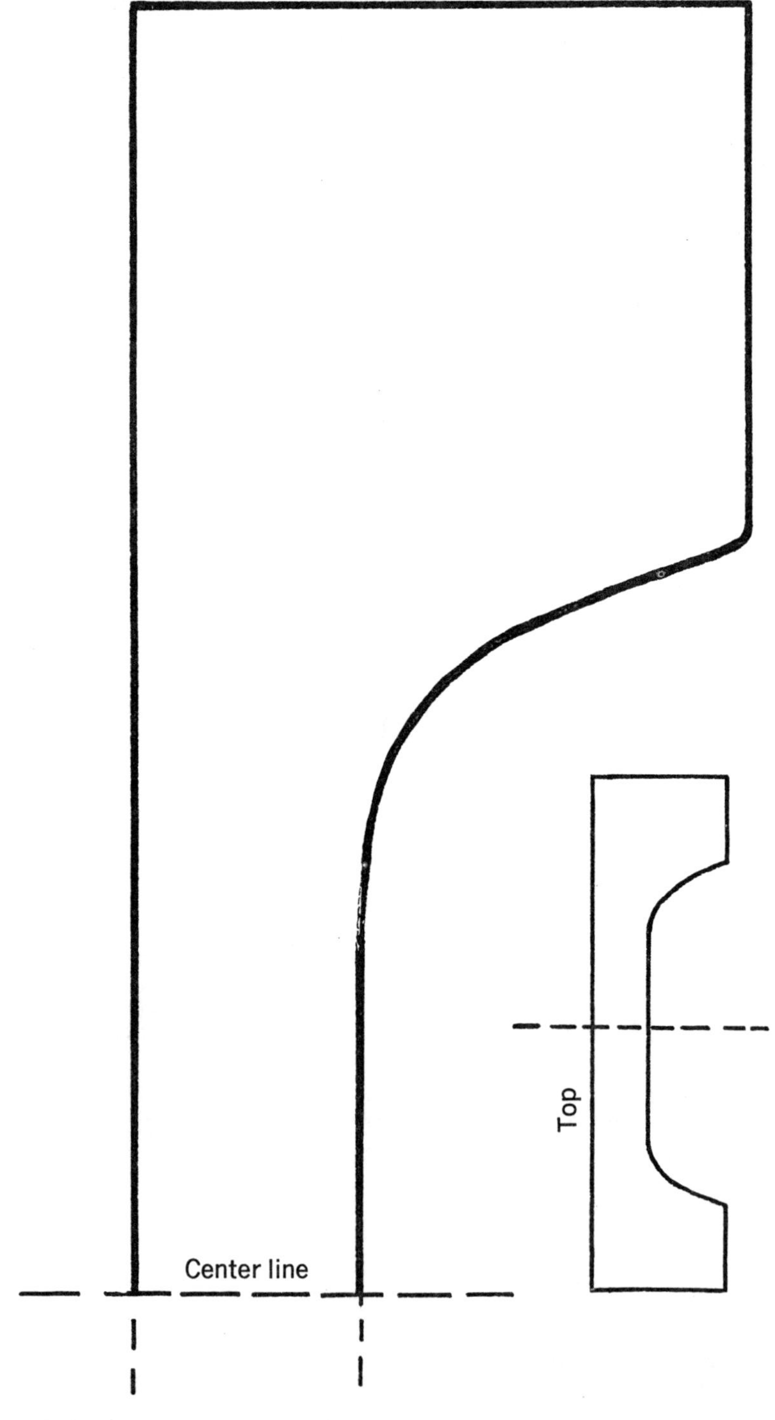

Sides: Cut two according to Pattern A
Rockers: Cut two according to Pattern B
Back: Cut one piece—13½″×13½″
Seat: Cut one piece—10″×13½″
Brace: Cut one piece 3½″×13½″ following Pattern C
Seat supports: Cut two pieces from pine—¾″×¾″×8¼″
Back supports: Cut two pieces from pine—¾″×¾″×13½″

STEP TWO: ASSEMBLY

With two or three small finishing nails, nail the two cutout sides together, matching outlines. Sand until the two pieces are identical. Do the same thing with the two rockers. Leave these parts nailed together until later in the assembly.

Drill two ³⁄₁₆″-diameter holes through the pair of side pieces, one at the bottom of each leg as shown in Diagram A. Center the holes ¹⁵⁄₁₆″ up from the bottom edges. After the holes have been drilled, separate the two side pieces and fill the nail holes with spackling paste.

With the side pieces flat in front of you (each cat facing in opposite directions), glue and nail the back supports and seat supports to the cat sides as shown on Cutting Pattern A. Drive four 1½″ nails through each support into the side pieces. Sand or file with wood rasp the top edge of the back supports until they are well rounded.

With the rockers still nailed together, lay them flat on your workbench and place one side piece on the rockers with the front leg located 6¼″ from the front end of the rocker to the center of the hole in the leg. With the bottom edge of the leg about ⅛″ above the bottom edge of the rocker, drill a ³⁄₁₆″-diameter hole through both rockers, using the side piece as a template (Diagram B).

Drop a ³⁄₁₆″ bolt through the leg and into the rockers to hold them in place while drilling the back holes in the rockers. Now move the back leg into place (⅛″ above the bottom edge of the rockers) and again, using the leg as a template, drill a ³⁄₁₆″-

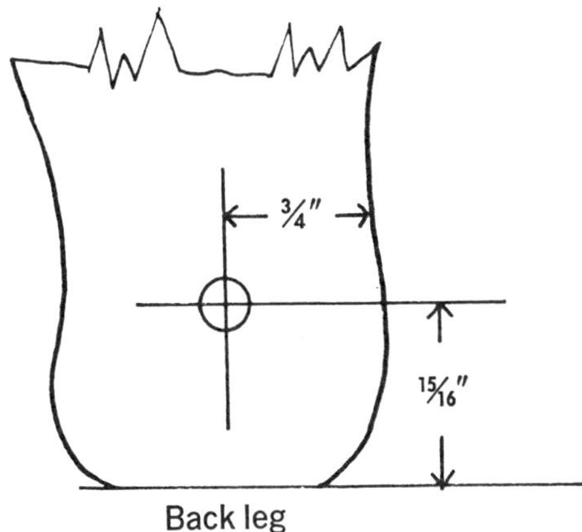

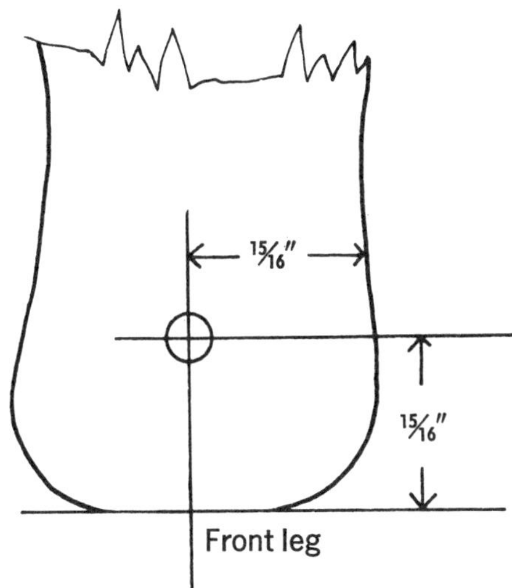

Drill holes through both side pieces when they are nailed together

diameter hole through the back part of the rockers.

Separate the rockers and fill the nail holes with spackling paste. Place the chair-back piece against the back brace with the bottom edge on the seat support and glue and nail into place by driving four 2″ nails through the side into the edges of the back piece. Turn this assembly over and nail the back piece to the other side piece in the same manner.

Stand the kit-kat on his feet and nail the

seat into place using four nails on each side, nailing through the sides into the seat edge.

Apply glue to the top edge and ends of the front brace and place it snugly against the bottom of the seat and the seat support ends. Drive a 2″ nail through each side into the brace. Then drive three nails through the top of the seat into the brace.

When attaching the rockers to the chair, keep in mind that the front legs are located 6¼″ from the front end of the rockers. Apply glue to the part of the leg that fits against the rocker and install a bolt from the outside of the rocker through the leg. Place a washer and nut on the bolt to secure the rocker to the leg. Insert the other three bolts to complete assembly.

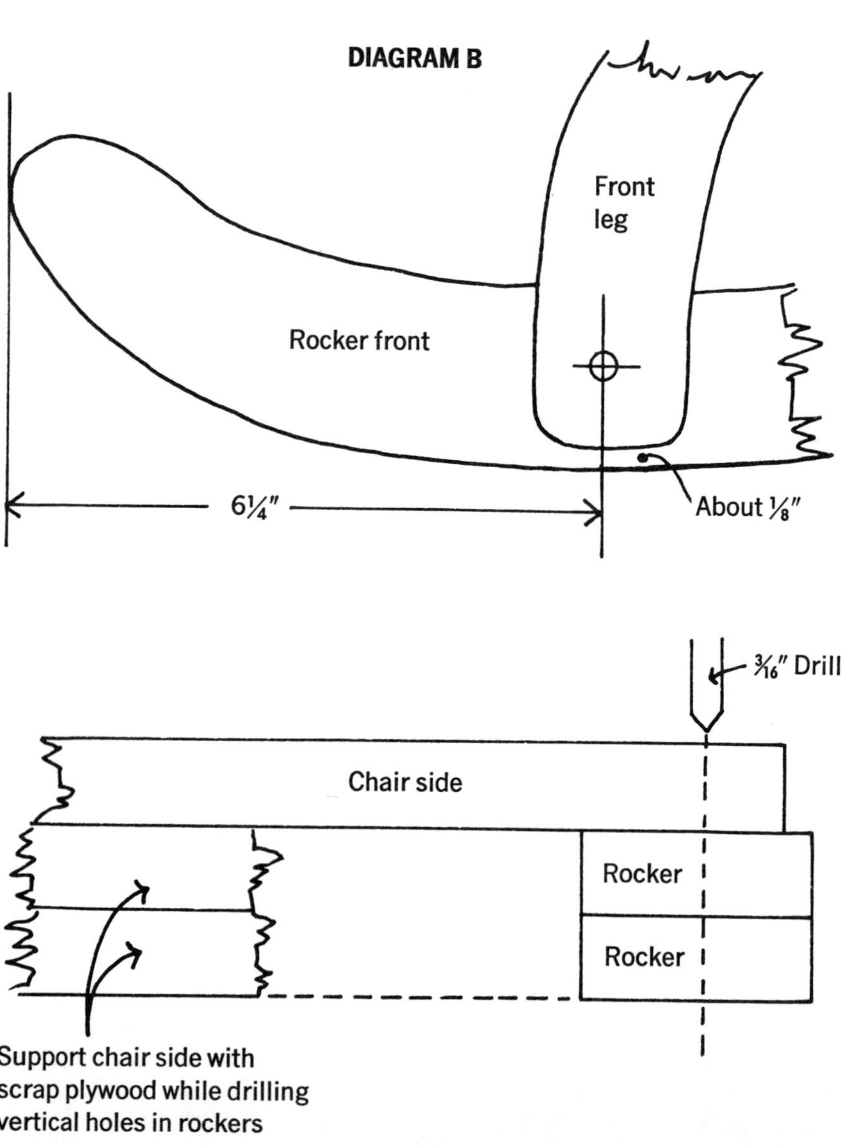

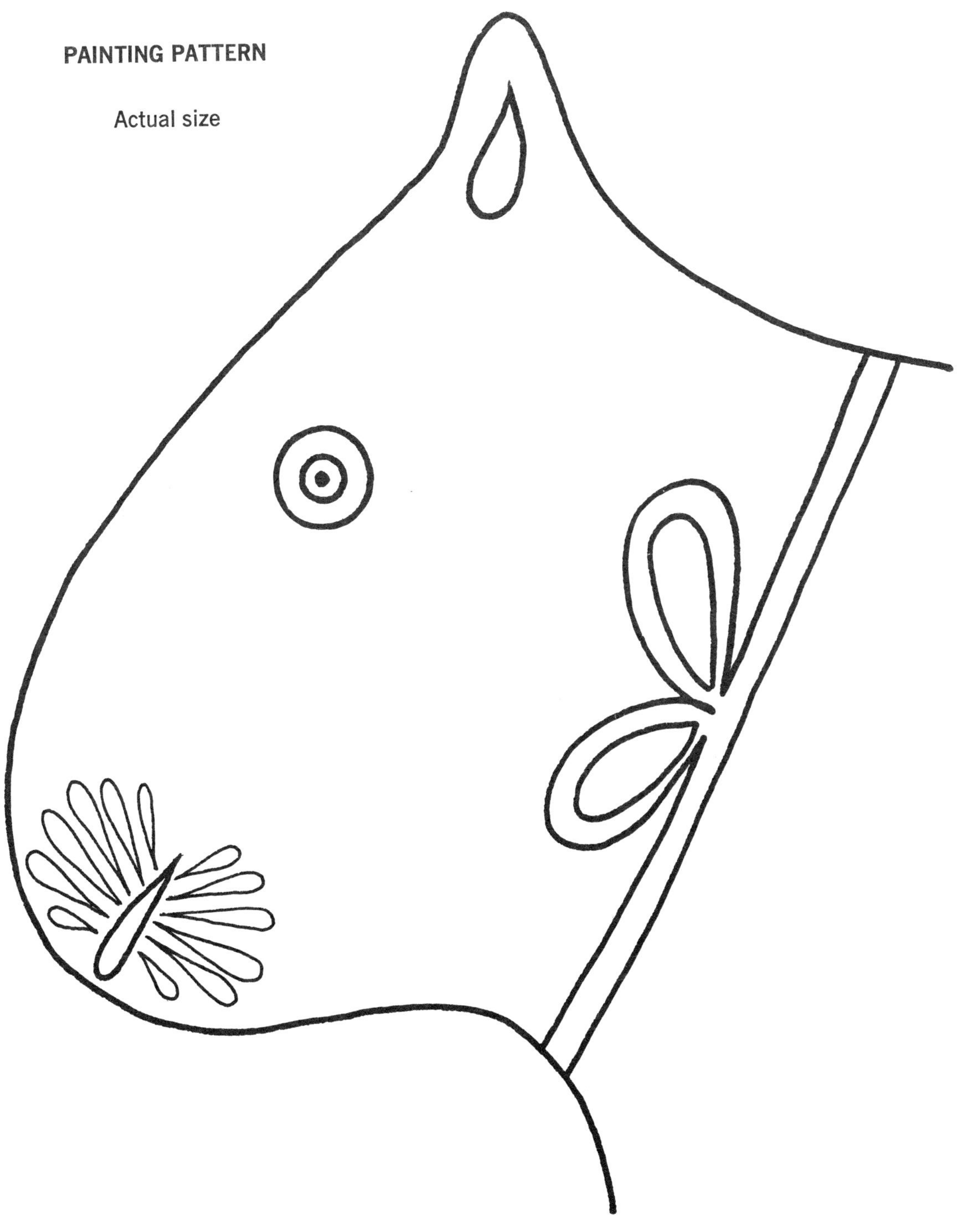

COLOR GUIDE (See color print 5)
Ribbon: light blue
Ear and mouth: pink
Whiskers: brown
Eye: green with yellow circle inside

Spots: cut a sponge in a 1″ circle and dab brown
    spots at random
Trim: blue line at top of seat back and the
    front edge of the seat

Toy Chest

A cheerful and sturdy toy box will hopefully make little ones more willing to pick up their toys and put them away at the end of the day. Our version is simple to build and fun to paint with nursery designs.

MATERIALS:

¾″ plywood (good on both sides)—3′× 5′

1″×12″ white pine shelving for trim—3′ long

5 dozen finishing nails—2″ long

3 dozen finishing nails—1½″ long (for trim)

⅜″-diameter hemp rope for handles—24″ long (optional)

STEP ONE: CUTTING

Measure and cut the following pieces from plywood:

Front and back: Cut two pieces—30″× 12″

Sides: Cut two pieces—11¼″×12″

Bottom: Cut one piece—11¼″×28½″

Lid: Cut one piece—13″×30¼″

Measure and cut the following pieces from shelving:

Trim: Cut six pieces—1½″×3 feet

STEP TWO: ASSEMBLY

Place the front piece flat in front of you and on each 12″ length, start three 2″ finishing nails placing them about ⅜″ from the corners and one in the center. Set a side piece on end and apply glue to the edge. Now place the front piece on top of the side piece (flush with the edge) and nail through the front piece into the side piece (Diagram A). Nail the remaining side piece to the other end of the front piece in the same manner. Then nail the back to the side pieces, forming a four-sided box.

If necessary, sand and trim the bottom piece so that it fits into the assembled box. Put glue on all four edges of the bottom piece and place into position, flush with the bottom edges of the front, back, and sides. Using 2″ nails, drive six nails through the front piece and back piece, and three nails

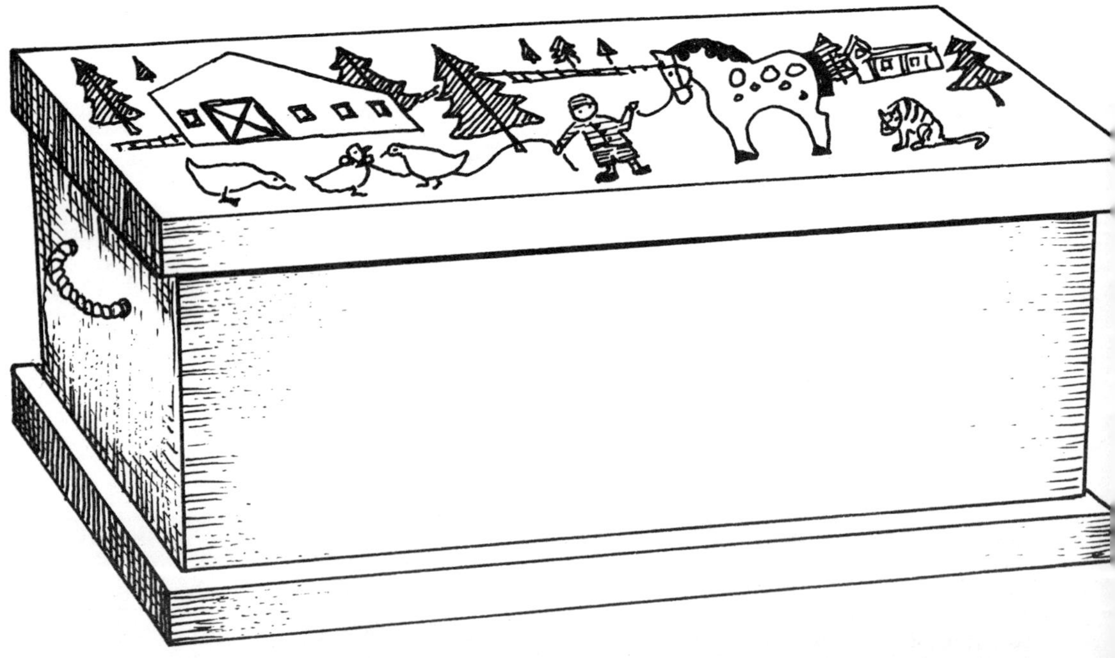

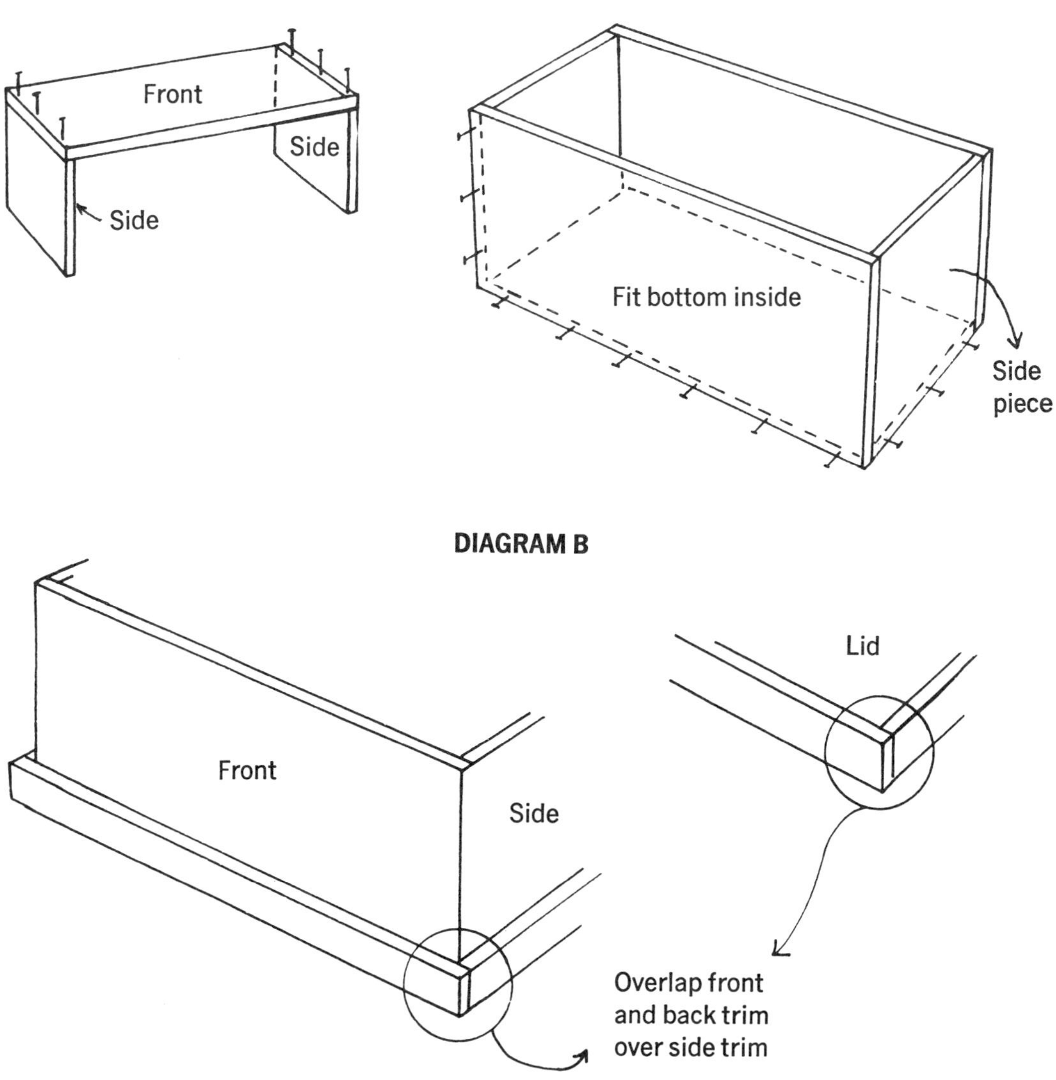

through the end pieces into the bottom piece.

From the $1\frac{1}{2}''$ widths of shelving, measure two pieces the same length (front to back) as the two sides of your box. Cut, then glue and nail these strips to the base of the sides with three $1\frac{1}{4}''$ nails on each side.

Now measure two strips the length of the front and back pieces including the trim. With glue and $1\frac{1}{4}''$ nails, nail the strips into place.

The next step is to nail the trim to the lid. Measure and cut two $1\frac{1}{2}''$ strips to match the $13''$ sides of the lid. Placing them flush with the top edge and corners of the lid, glue and nail them in place. Measure the front and back sides of the box, including the trim, and cut the two pieces to fit. Nail into place. See Diagram B at this point. Countersink nails and fill holes and joints with spackling paste. Sand the entire piece thoroughly.

Now place the lid upside down. Place

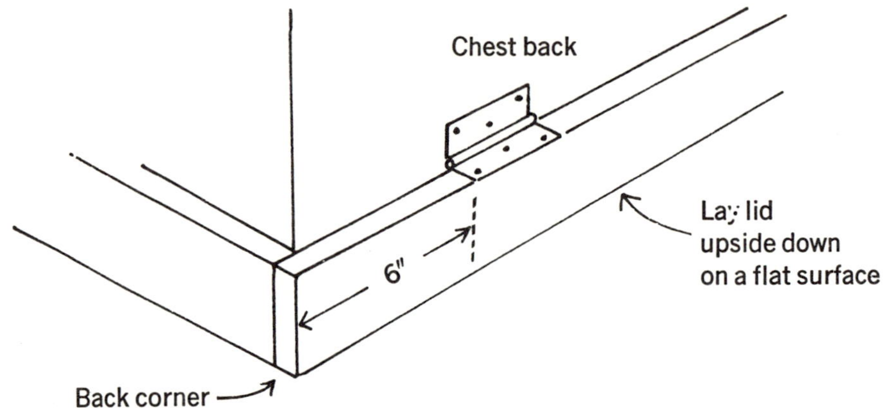

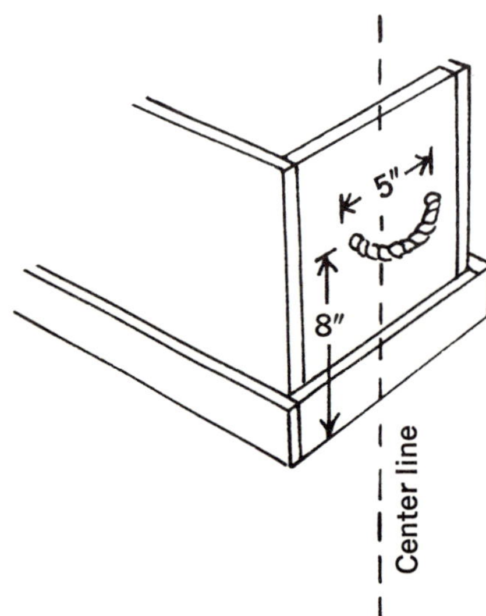

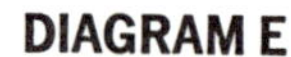

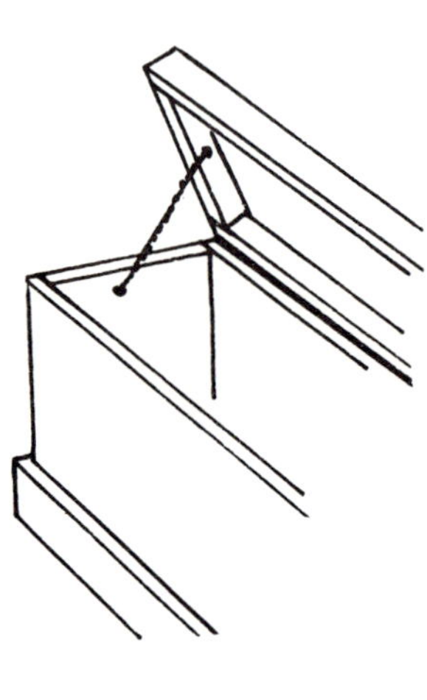

the box upside down into the lid, centering it between the sides of the lid to provide the same clearance at each end. Place the back of the box flush against the back of the lid. Measure 6″ in from each corner and attach the hinges to the trim on the lid and the back surface of the chest as shown in Diagram C.

Rope handles on the sides of the toy chest are optional. To make handles, drill two ½″-diameter holes on each side of the chest, 8″ up from the bottom of the chest, 5″ apart, 2½″ each side of center line (Diagram D). After the chest is completely painted and decorated, knot a 12″ length of rope (both ends) on the inside of the chest with enough slack on the outside for handles.

A chain can be installed on the inside of the chest and lid by using two ¼″ screw eyes and a 9″ length of lightweight chain. Locate the screw eyes on the inside of the chest and lid in a position that will prevent the lid from being forced open too far and yet will allow the lid to stay opened if desired (Diagram E).

LEFT SIDE — A
1 Square = 1 Inch

Join
pattern B
at this
line

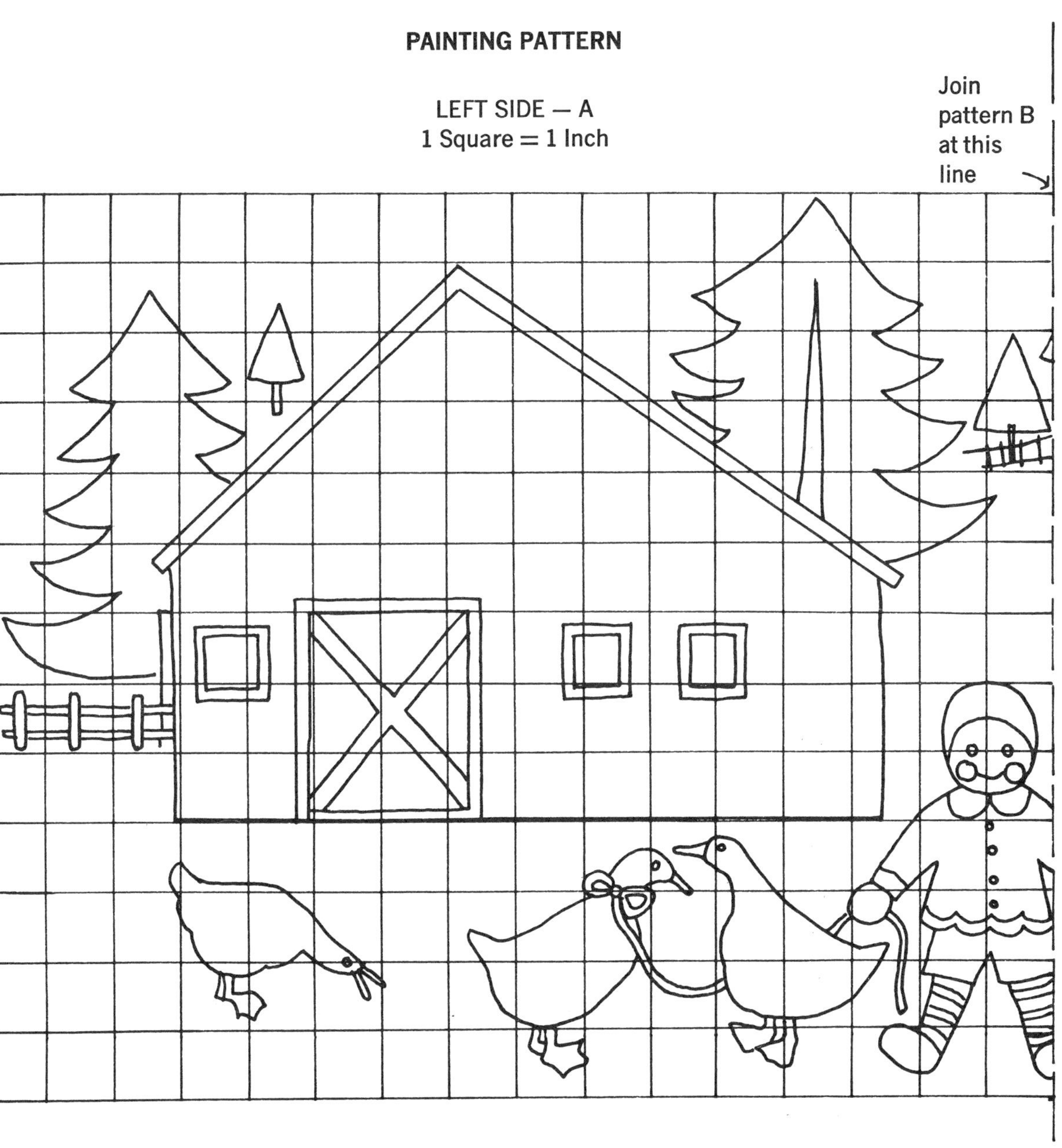

COLOR GUIDE (See color print 6)

Child: Face—light pink with blue eyes, red cheeks and mouth; Hair—brown; Jacket—light blue with pink collar, sleeve trim and scallops, black buttons; Pants—yellow; Stockings—pink with red trim; Shoes—black

Barn: red with black door and white trim, windows white and roof black

Ducks: white with orange beaks and feet, black eyes

Ribbon on duck: yellow

Fence: white (if the base color is light, paint fence black)

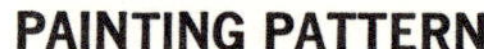

Join
pattern A
at this
line

RIGHT SIDE — B
1 Square = 1 Inch

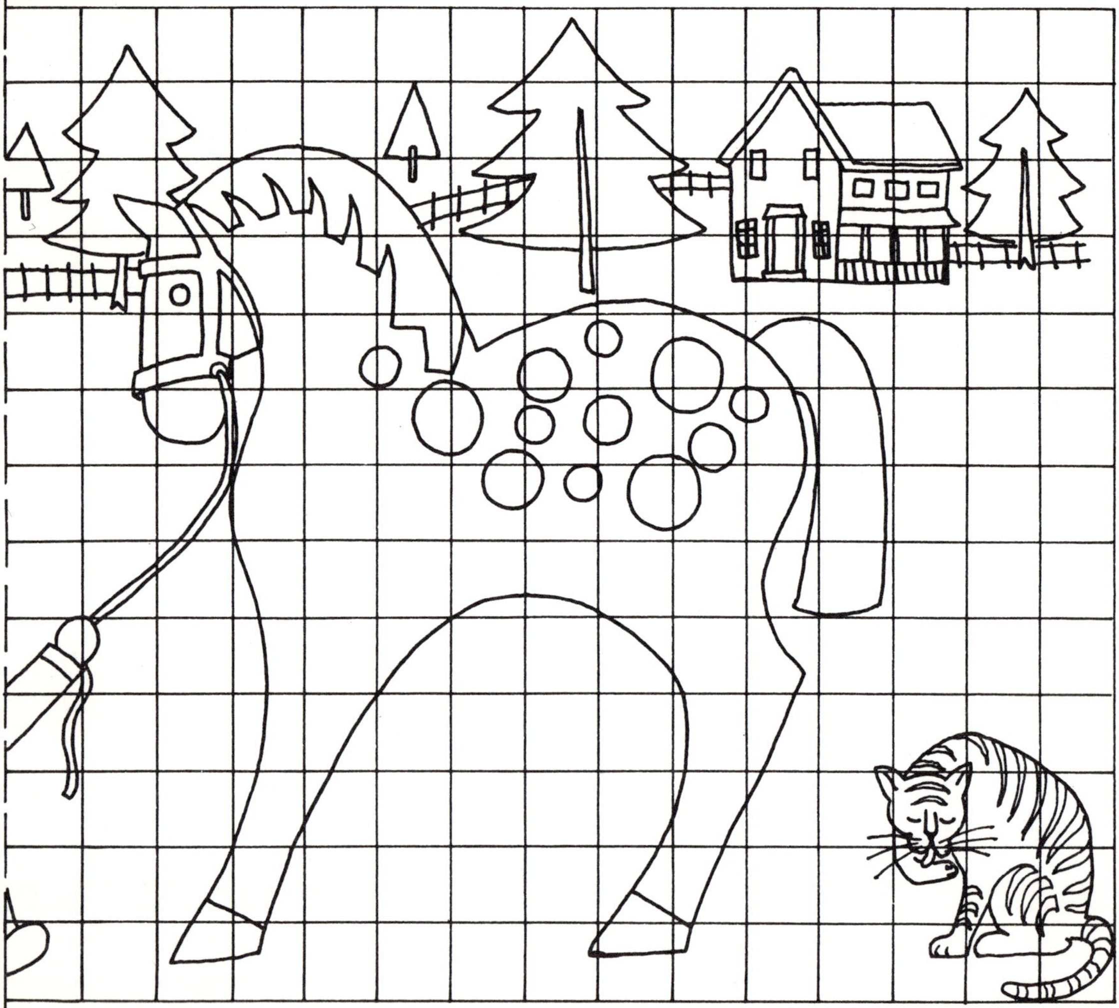

House: light blue with black roof, white windows, door, and trim
Cat: gold with brown stripes and pink tongue, black eyes, ears, whiskers, and claws
Horse: light gray with black mane, tail, and hooves, white spots, red harness, and blue eyes

Pouting Bench

This little pouting bench speaks for itself, and children, whether happy or pouting, love to sit and examine the cheerful designs more closely. The bench is a small version of the Early American high-back pine settle; the one pictured in the color section is painted a rich mustard base color and antiqued, which blends beautifully with wood paneled walls and Early American decor.

MATERIALS:

$1'' \times 12''$ white pine shelving—22 feet
$\frac{3}{4}''$ plywood (good on both sides)—8 square feet
Four dozen finishing nails—2$''$ or 2$\frac{1}{2}''$ long

STEP ONE: CUTTING

Measure and cut the 40$''$ length pieces first:

Back: Cut one piece from plywood—40$'' \times$ 22$\frac{1}{2}''$

Seat: Cut one piece from shelving—40$'' \times$ 11$\frac{1}{4}''$
Front: Cut one piece from shelving—40$'' \times$ 10$\frac{3}{4}''$
Back brace: Cut one piece from shelving —40$'' \times$ 2$\frac{1}{2}''$

Now cut:

Sides: Cut two pieces from shelving—35$'' \times$ 12$''$
Tilt-back braces: Cut two pieces—11$'' \times$

First, the design for cutting on the two side pieces must be measured out with a compass and rule (Diagram A). Draw a 5$\frac{1}{2}''$-diameter circle in the upper left-hand corner of the 35$''$ board. Next, measure 14$\frac{1}{4}''$ up from the bottom right-hand corner, then measure 2$\frac{3}{4}''$ to the left of the right edge and use this as your center point to draw another 5$\frac{1}{2}''$ circle. Now measure 18$''$ up from the lower left-hand corner, then measure 5$\frac{1}{4}''$ to the right of the left edge and use this as your center point to

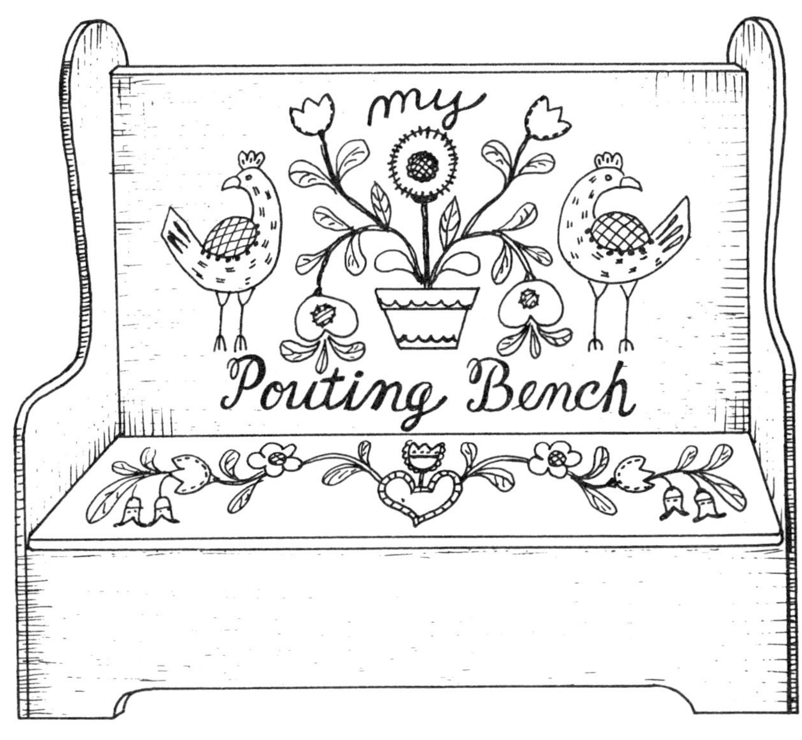

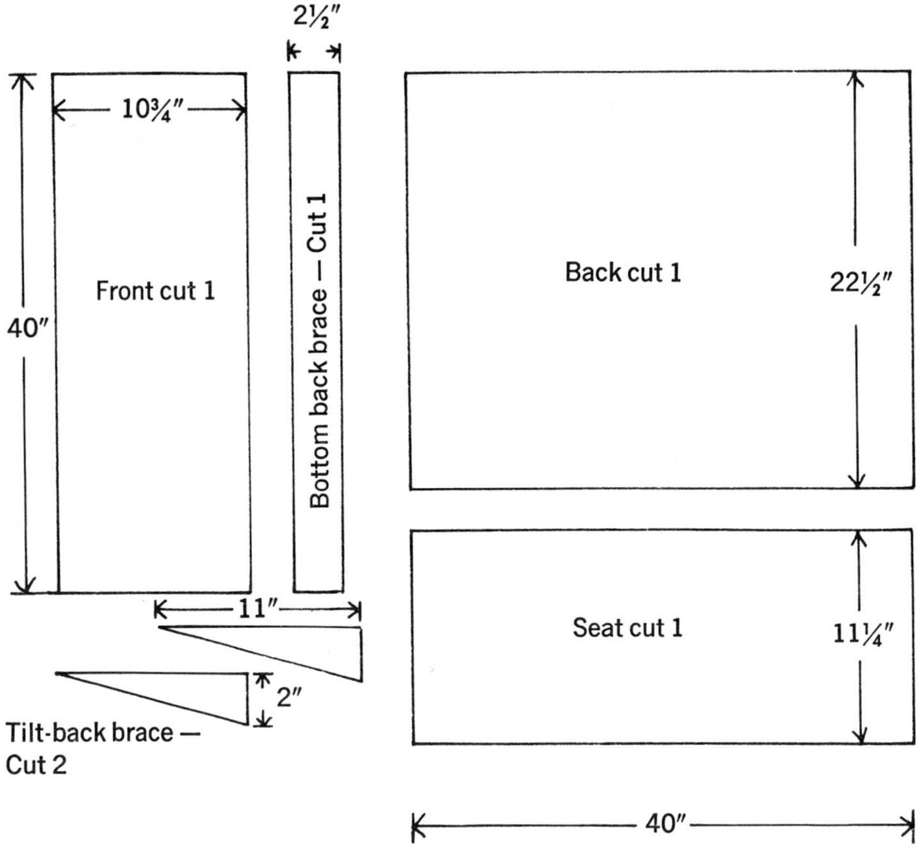

draw a 3½" circle. Finally, connect the three circles as shown in Diagram A of the side piece.

Now construct the cutout design and the **tilt-back angle** at the bottom of the side pieces by measuring from the lower left-hand corner up ½". Draw a straight line from this ½" mark to the lower right-hand corner as shown in Diagram B. This gives the bench a slight tilt back after you cut this wedge off of the bottom edge.

For the cutout design, measure from the lower right-hand corner in 3¾", mark, and then measure up 1½" from the mark. From the lower left corner, measure over 1¾" and then up 1½". Join these two points. Round the square corners with a compass (Diagram A). Cut the design of the side piece with a jig saw or saber saw.

Take the front piece and measure in from both lower corners of the 40" length, 3¾". Then measure up 1¾" and connect the two points with a straight line as shown in Diagram A. Round the corners with a compass and cut with a jig saw.

To make the two tilt-back braces, draw a diagonal line from opposite corners of the 11"×2" pieces and cut the two wedge-shape pieces as shown in the illustration of the Cutting Patterns.

STEP TWO: ASSEMBLY

Glue and nail the 22½" edges of the back piece to the side piece, flush with the back edge of the side piece. See Diagram C for placement. Use five or six finishing nails. Next, glue and nail the front piece on

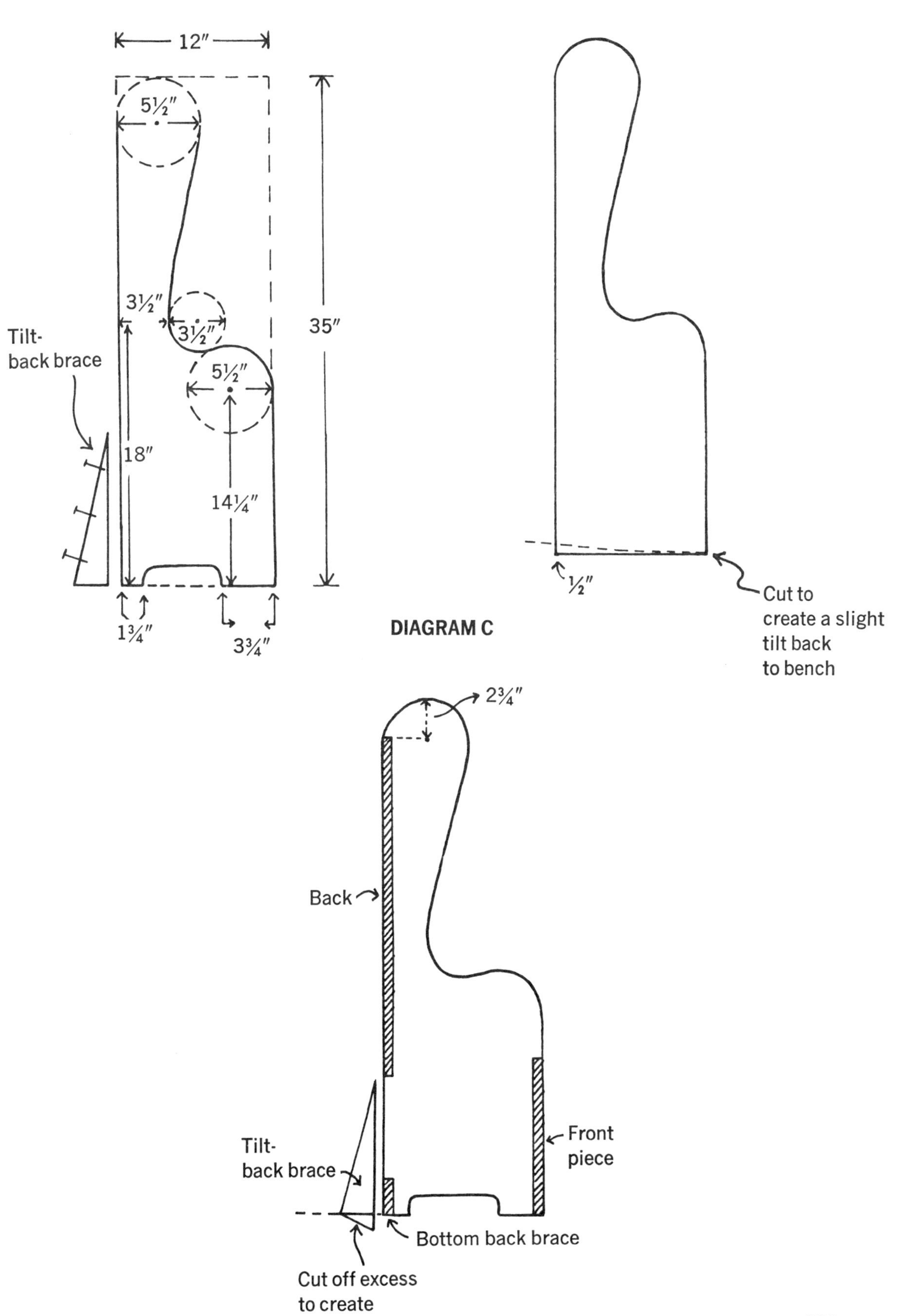

DIAGRAM A
DIAGRAM B
12"
5½"
3½"
3½"
35"
5½"
Tilt-back brace
18"
14¼"
1¾"
3¾"
½"
Cut to create a slight tilt back to bench
DIAGRAM C
2¾"
Back
Tilt-back brace
Front piece
Cut off excess to create a flat base
Bottom back brace

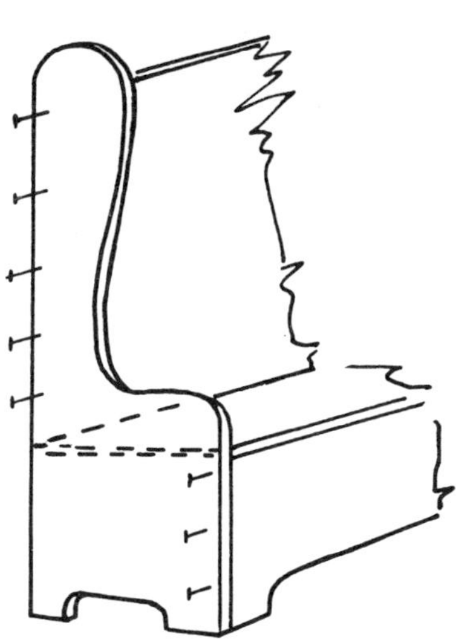

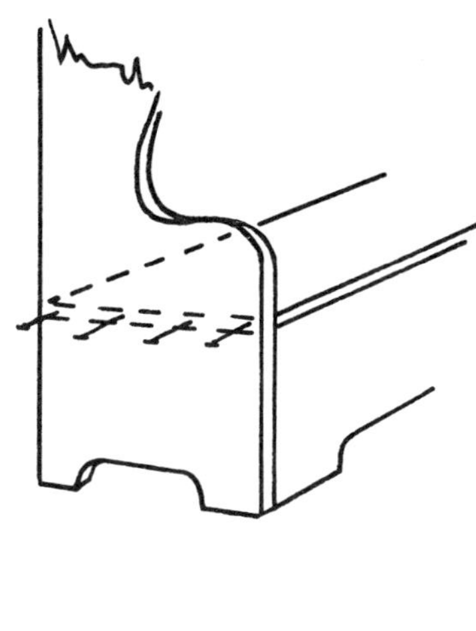

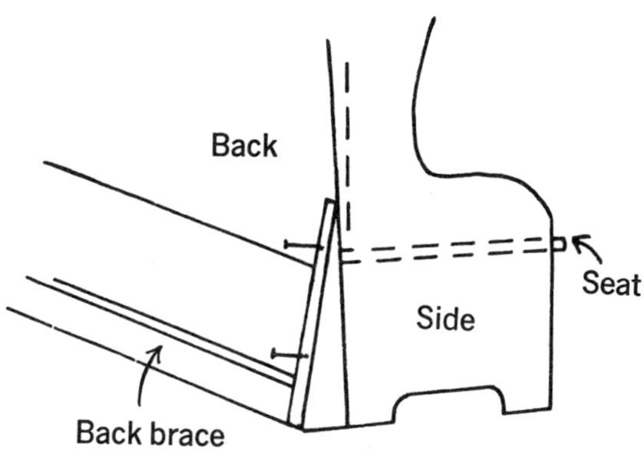

the front edge of the side pieces, flush with the bottom and front edge. Turn assembly over and glue and nail through the other side piece into the back and front piece in the same manner (Diagram D).

Next, butt the seat up against the back, laying it along a line drawn perpendicular from the front edge and the top of the front piece. Nail about three nails through each side piece and seven nails through the back piece. Round the front edge and corners of the seat with sandpaper (Diagram E).

Now add the tilt-back braces. Hold in position and mark with a rule so that the bottom edge is a continuous line when joined to the bottom of the side piece. Cut excess off of the bottom edge of the brace to create a flat base as shown in Diagram C. Nail two or three nails through the brace into the edge of the side piece. With a nail set, set the nails deep, making sure that they go into the side piece. After the tilt-back braces are nailed into place, glue and nail the bottom back brace into position as shown in Diagram F.

PAINTING PATTERNS

SEAT — ½ Pattern
1 Square = 1 Inch

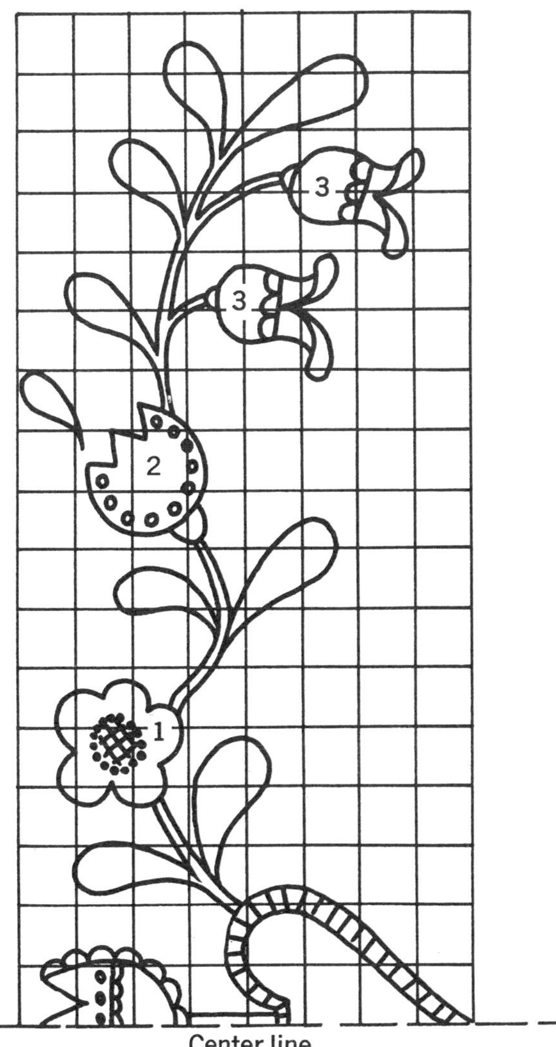

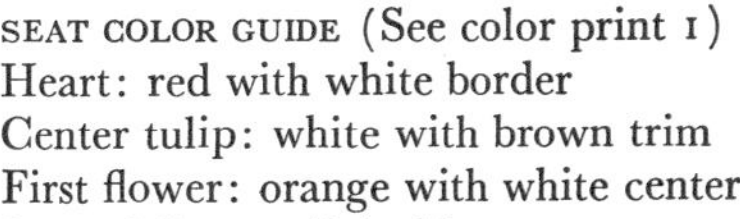

Center line

SEAT COLOR GUIDE (See color print 1)
Heart: red with white border
Center tulip: white with brown trim
First flower: orange with white center
Second flower: light blue
Third flower: white with brown detail
Stems, outlines, and details: brown
Lettering: blue

SEAT BACK
1 Square = 1 Inch

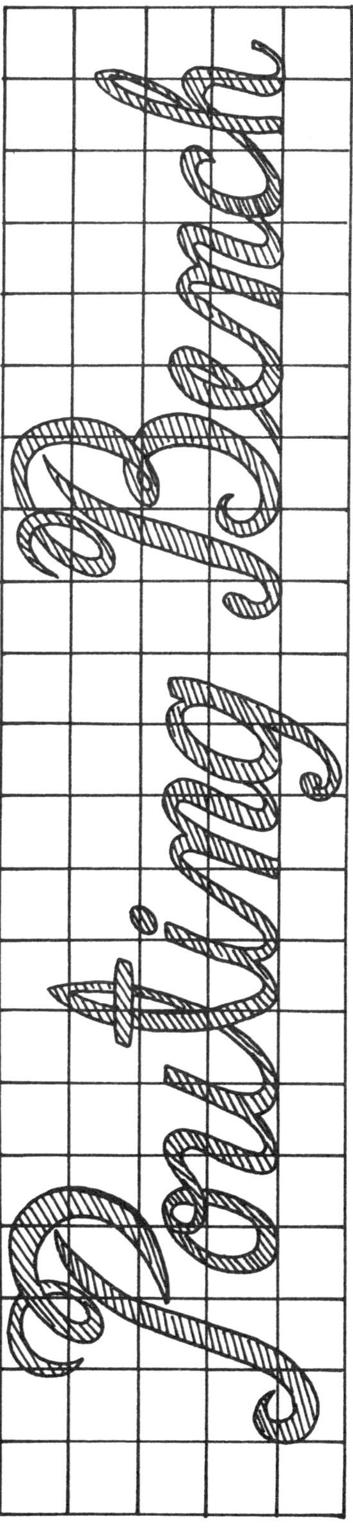

BENCH BACK — ½ Pattern
1 Square = 1 Inch

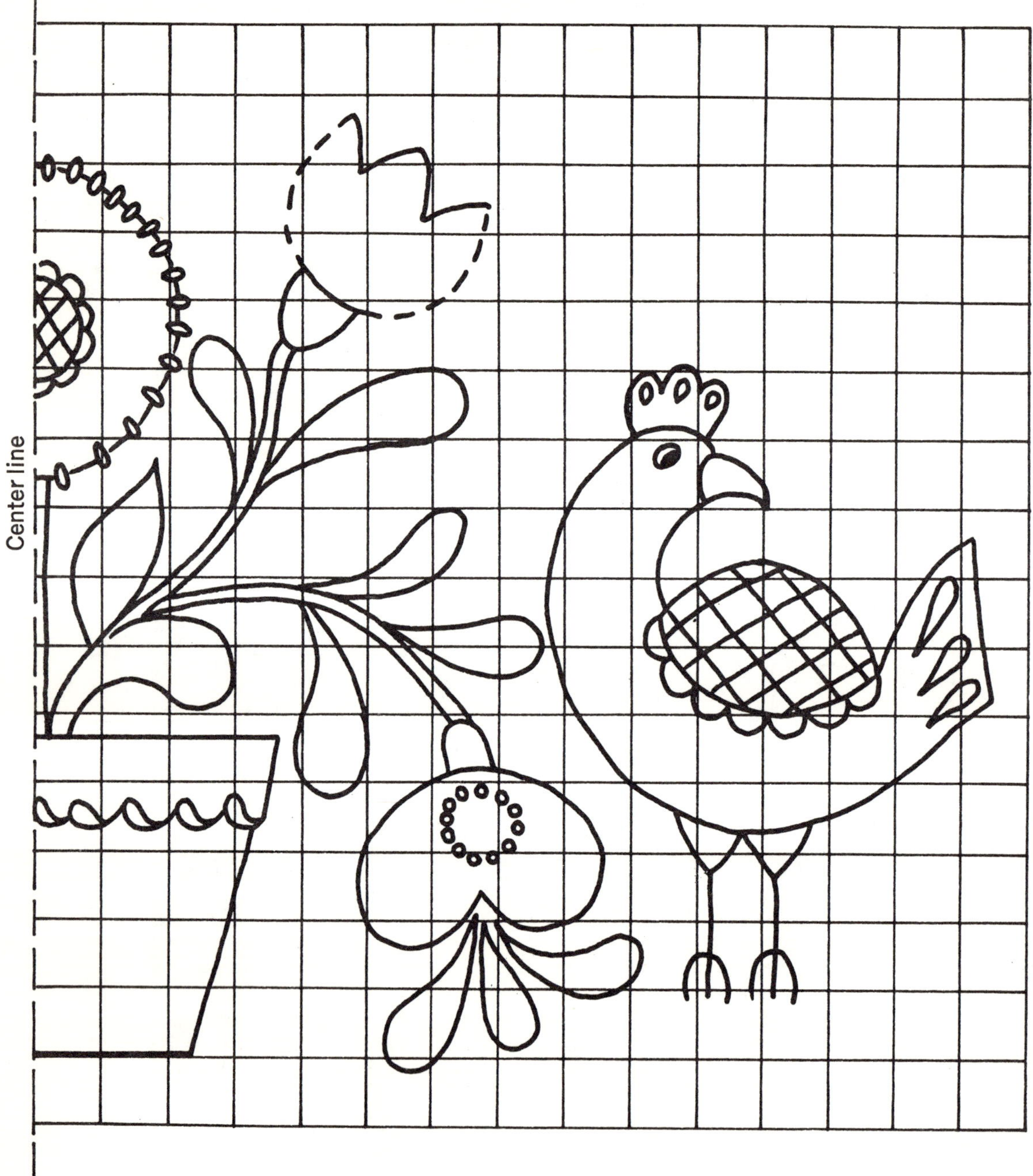

BENCH BACK COLOR GUIDE (See color print 1)
Birds: orange with red wings and comb
Flower pot: orange with red trim
Tulips: light blue
Three flowers: white with blue centers
Stems, outlines, and details: brown

Tote Table

The tote table was designed to be used with two, three, or four tote chairs. Paint the set a favorite color, use the painting design on the chair backs and a rickrack border on the table and chair seats. Personalize the chairs by painting the child's name on the seats.

MATERIALS:

¾″ plywood (good on both sides)—24″×
   24″
1″ white pine shelving—2½″×20″
1¼″ full round (dowel)—66″ long
16 finishing nails—1¼″ long

STEP ONE: CUTTING

Table top: From plywood, cut one 24″-
   diameter circle
Leg pads: From shelving, cut four pieces—
   2½″×5″
Legs: From full round, cut four pieces—
   each 16½″ long

Cut the table top with a jig saw or saber saw. Next, bevel the four top edges of the leg pads about ¼″ for appearance (Diagram A). Using sandpaper, slightly round and smooth one end of each table leg, which will be left exposed.

STEP TWO: ASSEMBLY

Place table top upside down and draw a center line across the diameter of the circle. Placing a carpenter's square on this line with the corner of the square at the center of the circle, establish the other center line so that the circle is divided into four equal parts (Diagram B).

Mark the center lines on the 5″ length of the leg pads. Match the center lines of the pads to the center lines of the table top. Place the four pads 1½″ in from the edge of the table top (Diagram C). Glue and nail each pad in place using four nails, one in each corner.

Before drilling the leg holes in the table top, select a scrap piece of wood and make an angle guide, as shown in Diagram D. This will assist in drilling all four holes at the same angle. Following Diagram A, measure 1⅞″ in from the outside edge of the pad toward the center of the table to establish the center of the leg holes. Now, using a 1¼″-diameter hole cutter, drill a hole in each leg pad no more than 1″ deep.

Apply glue to leg ends and tap them into the holes of the pads. Turn the table up on a level floor and make sure that the legs are even and that the table does not wobble. A slight wobble can be corrected by lightly moving and adjusting the legs before the glue has dried.

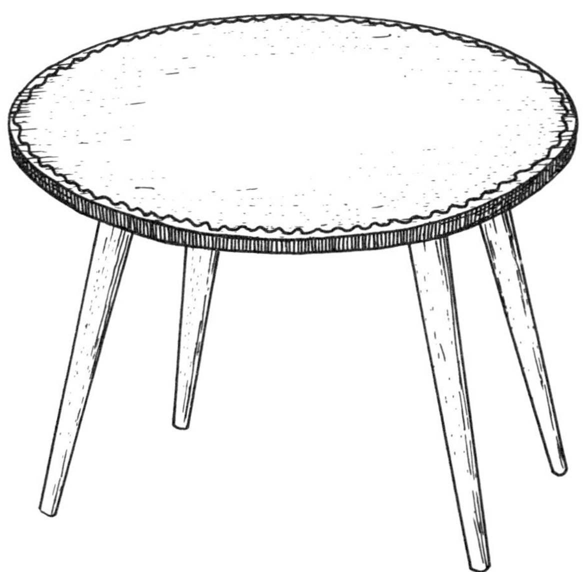

DIAGRAM A

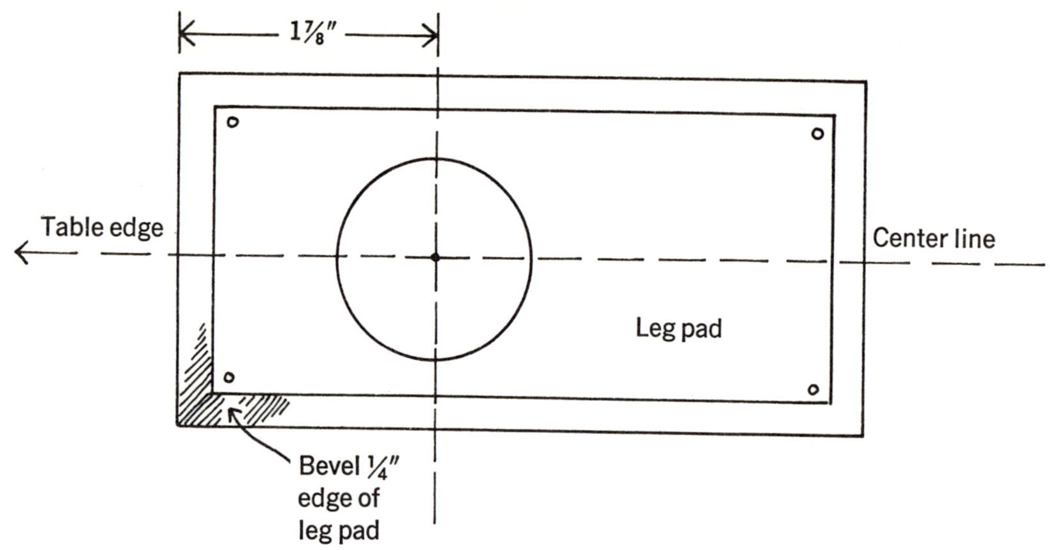

DIAGRAM B

PAINTING PATTERN

TABLE EDGE

COLOR GUIDE (See color print 5)
A simple ribbon line around the table top should be painted in bright green to match the border on the seat of the tote chair

DIAGRAM C

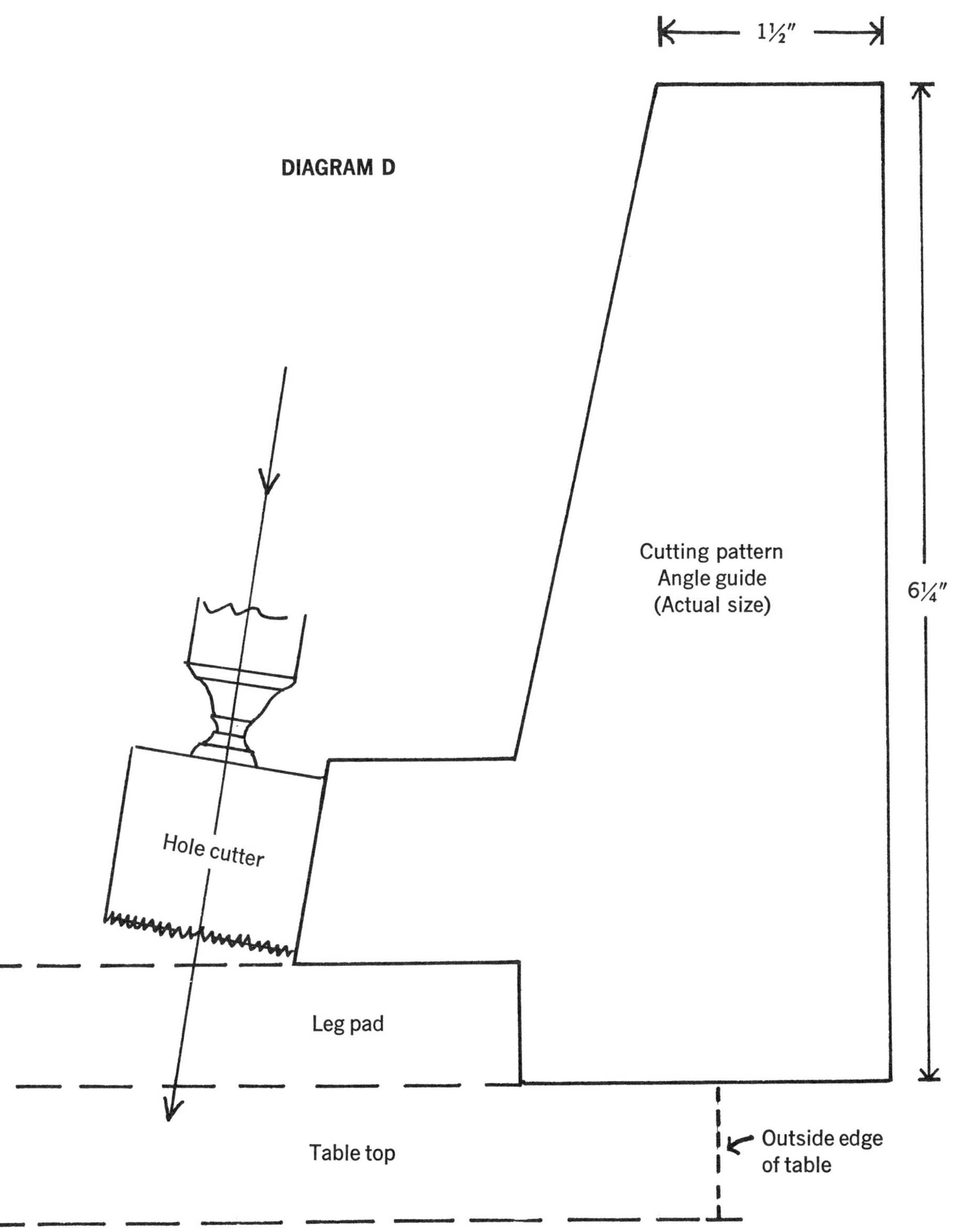

If a vertical stationary drill is available, block the table top up 5½" on the center line of hole being drilled

Tote Chair

Our little tote chair has been a sensation with the young crowd. They use the chair from the time they can toddle until their knees start to touch their chins and even then, the chair is a handy little step stool for hard-to-reach places. For that very reason, short ladies use our tote chairs too.

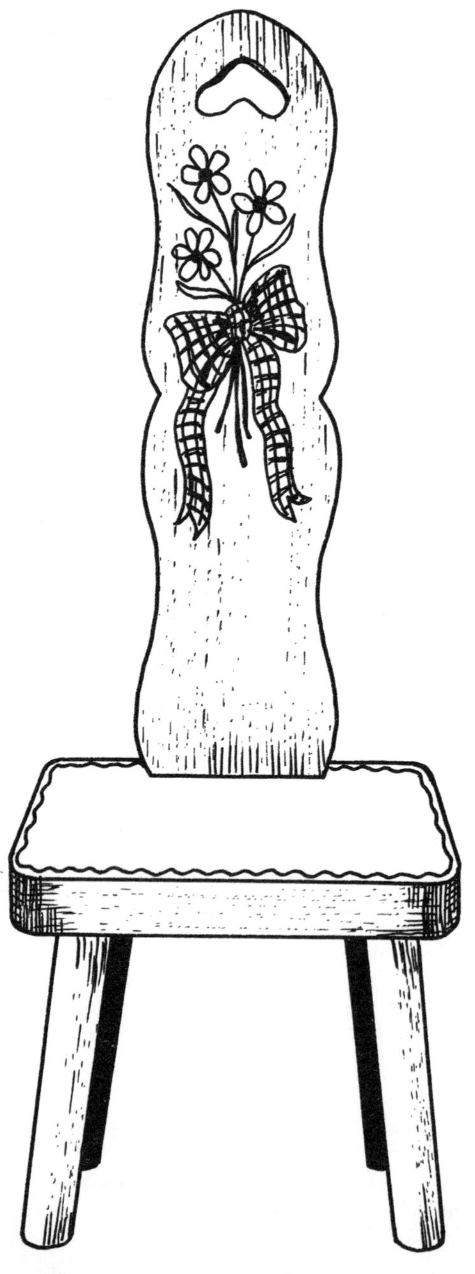

1″×10″ white pine shelving—32¾″ long
½″ plywood (good on one side)—9″×11¾″
1⅜″ full round (dowel)—32″ long
Seven 1″ finishing nails
Three flat-head screws—1½″ long

STEP ONE: CUTTING

Measure and cut the following pieces:

Seat: Cut one piece from plywood—9″×11¼″; also, cut one piece from shelving—9″×11¼″

Back: Cut one piece from shelving—5½″×21½″

Back brace: Cut one piece from shelving—1¼″×4¼″

Legs: From dowel, cut four pieces—each, 8″ long

Enlarge the pattern for the chair back and transfer to the 5½″×21½″ piece of wood. Cut the design with a saber saw or jig saw. To cut the handhold, use a 1¼″-diameter hole cutter to first cut the two outside holes and finally the middle hole. Then with the saber saw or jig saw, cut the remaining wood to complete the design (Diagram A).

Round off one end of each leg piece using a wood rasp and then sand until smooth (Diagram C).

Glue the plywood seat piece (good side up) onto the pine seat piece, matching all edges perfectly. Turn the seat over and drive five 1″ finishing nails through the pine into the plywood. Locate a nail in each corner about 1¼″ in from the edge and one nail in the middle of the seat.

While the glue is drying, draw the cutting pattern in Diagram B on the underneath side of the seat. First draw the two center lines dividing the seat into quarters. Trace one quarter of the pattern for the back, flip the pattern over, and trace another quarter, being sure to indicate the cutout slot. Then repeat the process to trace off the front half of the chair, *omitting* the cutout slot on the front. After the

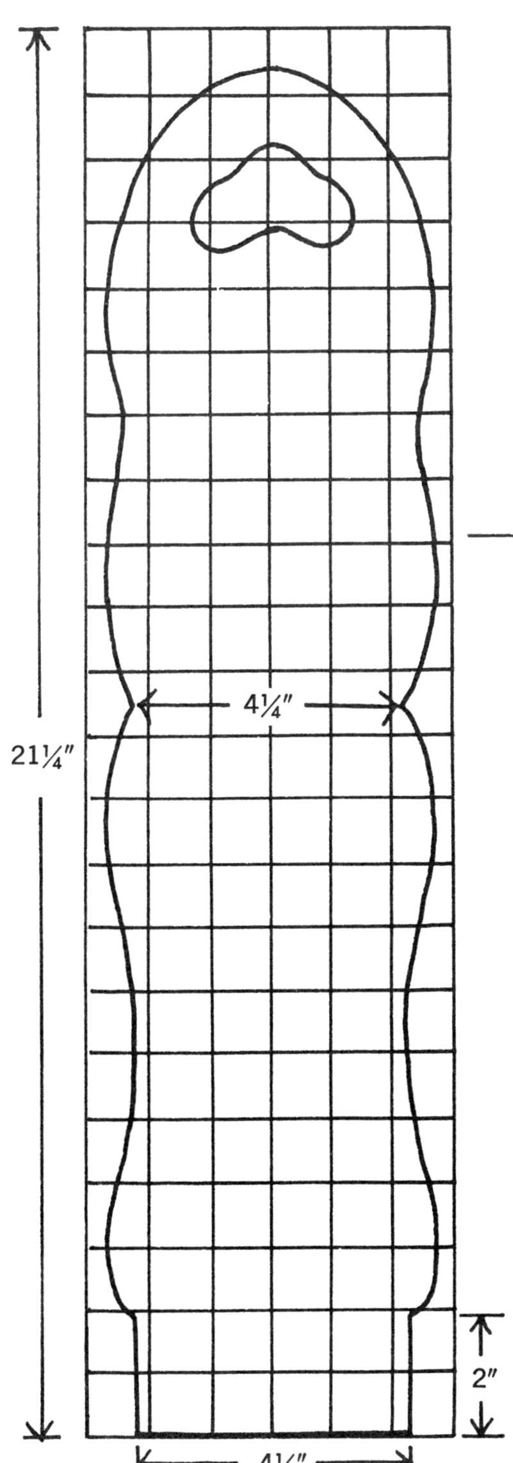

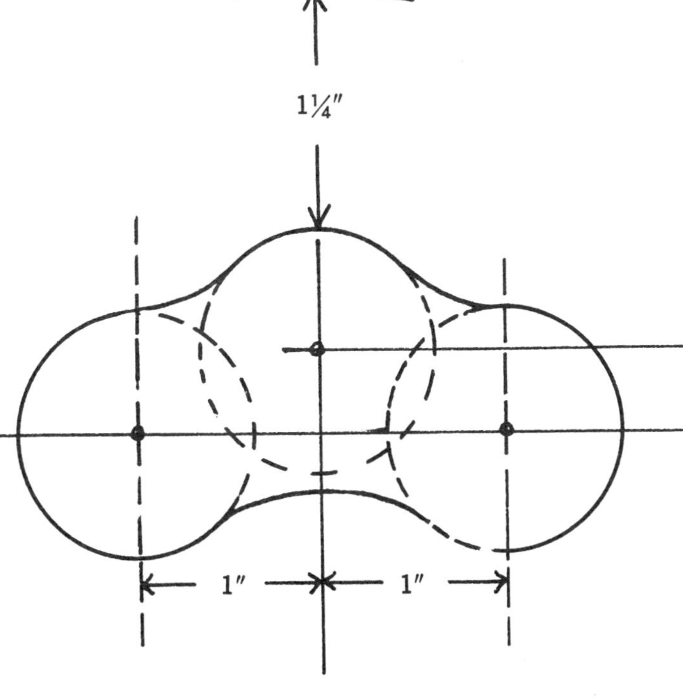

complete pattern has been transferred, round the four corners and cut out the slot with a jig saw or saber saw. When cutting the slot, be sure that the cut is at an exact right angle with the seat top so that when the chair back is installed, it will not lean at an angle.

The holes for the legs must be drilled at an angle of 10 degrees from the vertical in order for the chair to be properly balanced. A guide can be made out of scrap wood which will help you to maintain the proper angle while cutting the holes (Diagram D). The holes should go no more than ¾" deep. Use a 1⅜" hole cutter, and with a seat corner closest to you, drill the hole by angling in from the seat corner. (The hole cutter should be in line with the corner of the seat.)

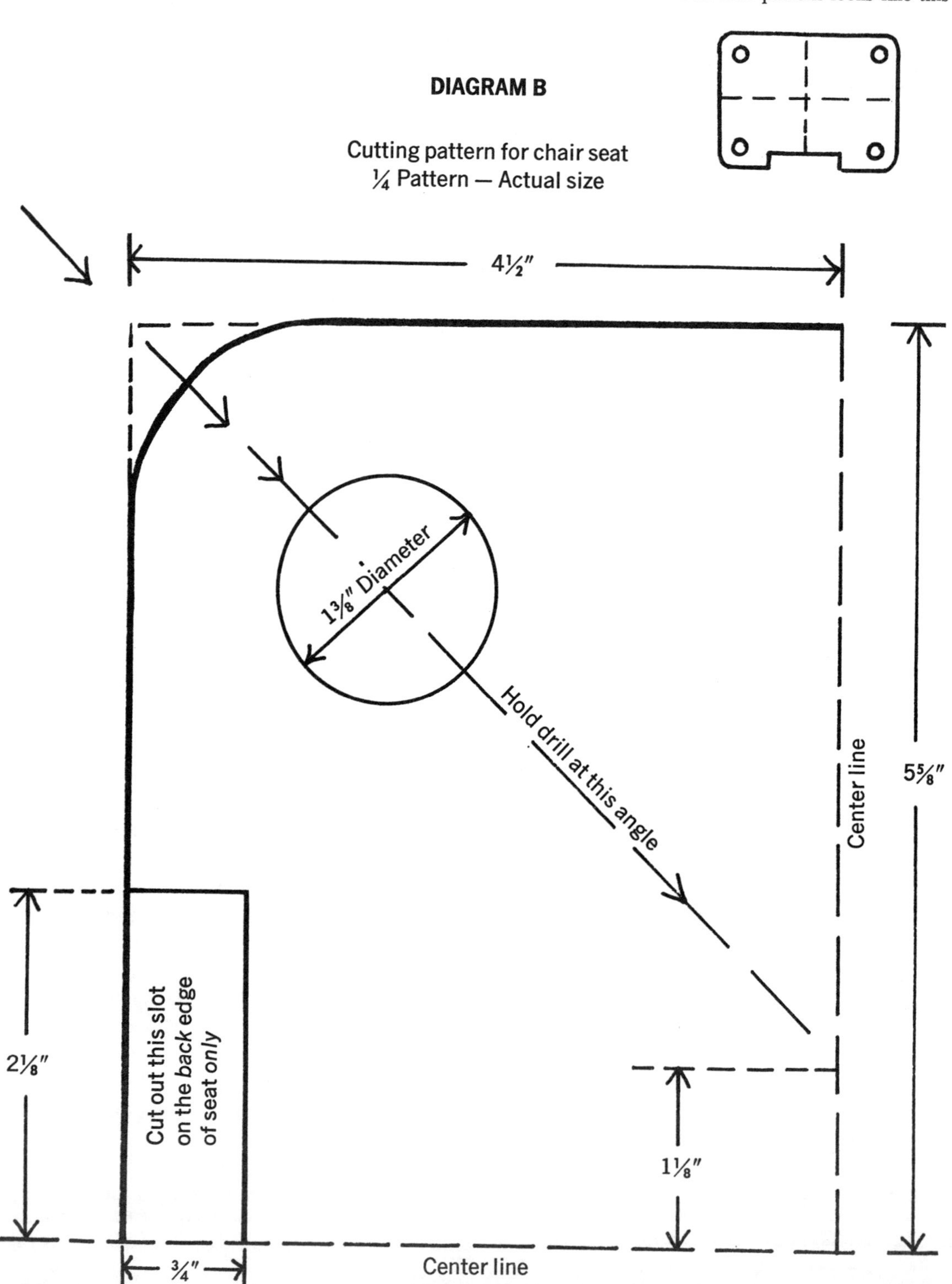

Full seat pattern looks like this

DIAGRAM B

Cutting pattern for chair seat
¼ Pattern — Actual size

4½"

1⅜" Diameter

Hold drill at this angle

Center line

5⅝"

Cut out this slot
on the back edge
of seat only

2⅛"

1⅛"

¾"

Center line

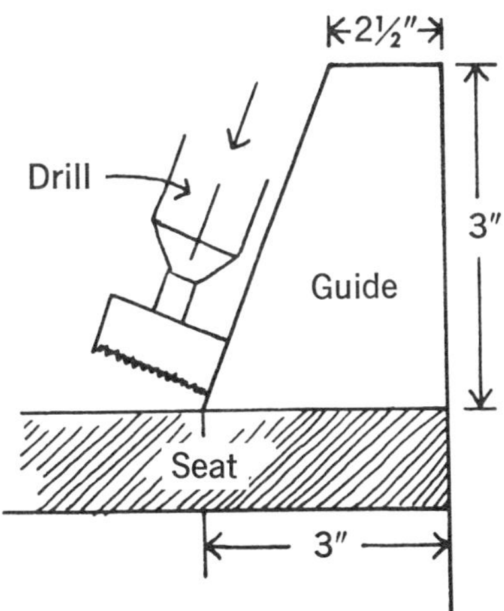

DIAGRAM C

Drill hole for chair leg at a 10° angle, going no more than ¾" deep

DIAGRAM D

Make a guide as shown from scrap lumber

DIAGRAM E

Position of back brace

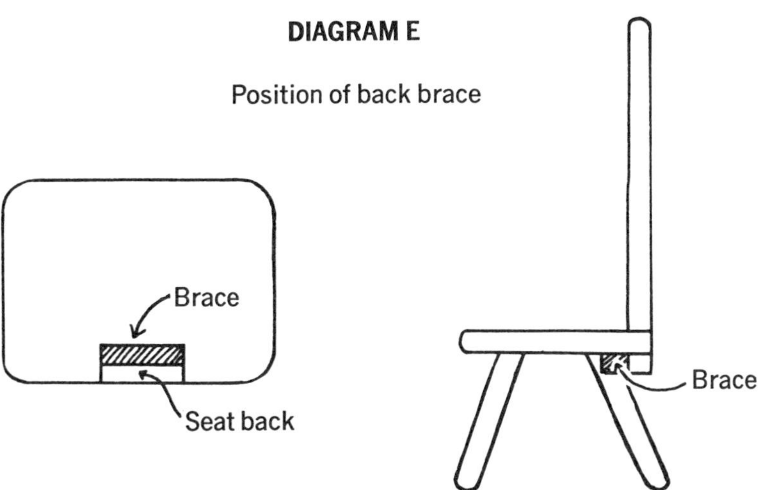

STEP TWO: ASSEMBLY

With sandpaper, smooth all sharp edges and corners. Place the seat upside down on a flat surface and with glue and two 1″ nails, nail the brace into place with its edge flush with the cutout slot in the seat. (See Diagram E for location.) Next, place the chair back into the cutout slot with the bottom edge of the back flush with the bottom edge of the brace. Using glue and three screws, locate two screws into the seat and one screw into the brace, as indicated in Diagram E.

Finally, place the chair upside down on your workbench with the back over the edge of the bench so that the seat is on a firm surface. Apply glue to the leg ends and drive them into place in the holes. If the fit is too tight, sand the leg tips lightly for easier assembly.

PAINTING PATTERN

1 Square = 1 Inch

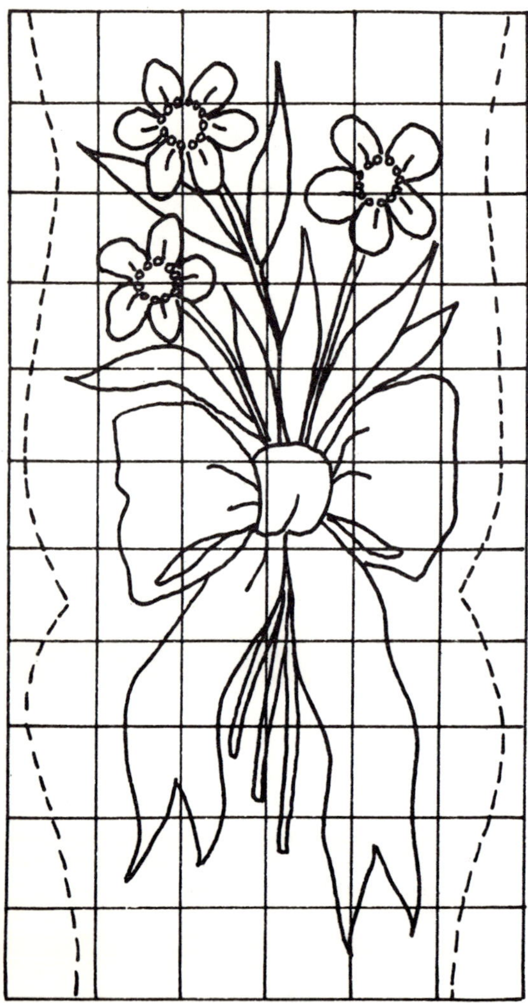

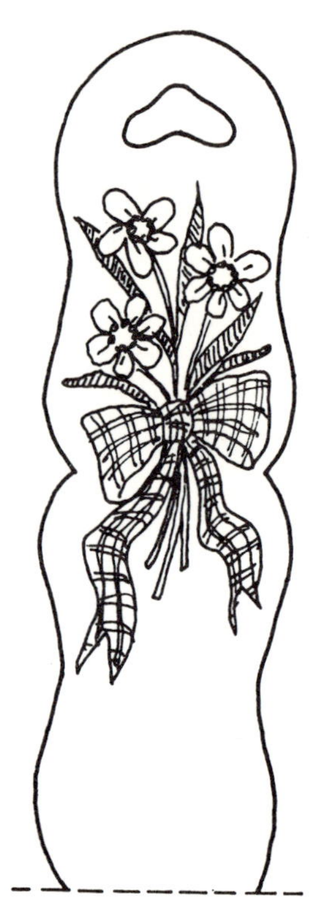

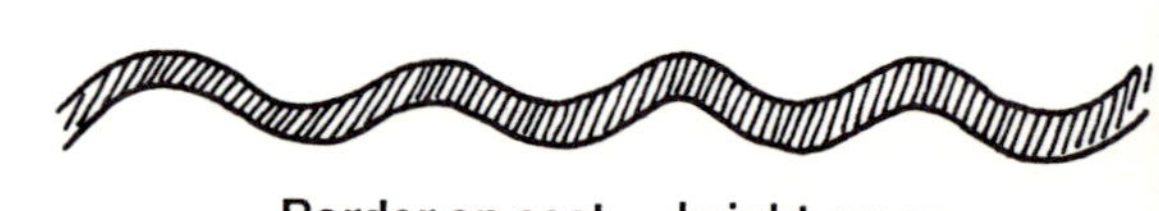

Border on seat — bright green

color guide (See color print 5)
Flowers: gold, blue, red, with white centers
   circled by green dots
Leaves, stems: dark green
Ribbon, bow: bright green* checks, outlined in
   black
(* use permanent Green, light)

Turtle Stool

It should be a pleasure to build this perky little turtle which serves as an unusual step-up stool for tots. You will find that it is quite stable and not prone to tipping over.

MATERIALS:

1″×10″ white pine shelving—6′ long
20 finishing nails—1½″ long

STEP ONE: CUTTING

Measure and cut the following pieces:

Head: Cut one piece—12″×6″
Top: Cut one piece—13″×9½″
Legs: Cut two pieces—16″×5½″
Neck Brace: Cut one piece—5″×6″
Stringer: Cut one piece—6″×1⅝″

Begin with the top of the stool by drawing Pattern A on the wood and cutting it with a jig saw or saber saw. Next, cut the two leg pieces (Pattern B), being careful that the grain of the wood is running in the direction shown on the pattern. The next piece cut will be the head (Pattern C). Again, check the grain of wood for proper placement of the pattern. Cut the neck brace from Pattern D as shown. To cut the stringer, measure a piece 6″×1⅝″ and cut. You now have a total of six pieces to sand and assemble.

STEP TWO: ASSEMBLY

Center the neck brace on the head piece, as shown in Diagram A, and drive two nails through the brace into the top edge of the head piece. Measure and mark a center line on the inside of the two leg pieces. To attach legs, locate the leg piece center line 1″ forward from the back edge of the neck brace (Diagram B). Now locate the stringer, as shown in Diagram C, and nail into place through the leg pieces using two nails on each side. Drive another nail through the stringer into the back end of the head piece. Be sure that the top of the neck brace is absolutely flush with the top edges of the leg pieces in order to provide a level surface for the stool top.

On the underside of the top piece, locate and draw a center line in both directions. With the top upside down, put the assembled base of the stool in place, being careful to match all center lines. Drive five nails through the neck brace into the top. Turn the stool over and drive three nails through the top and into each leg piece. Countersink the nails and fill with spackling paste.

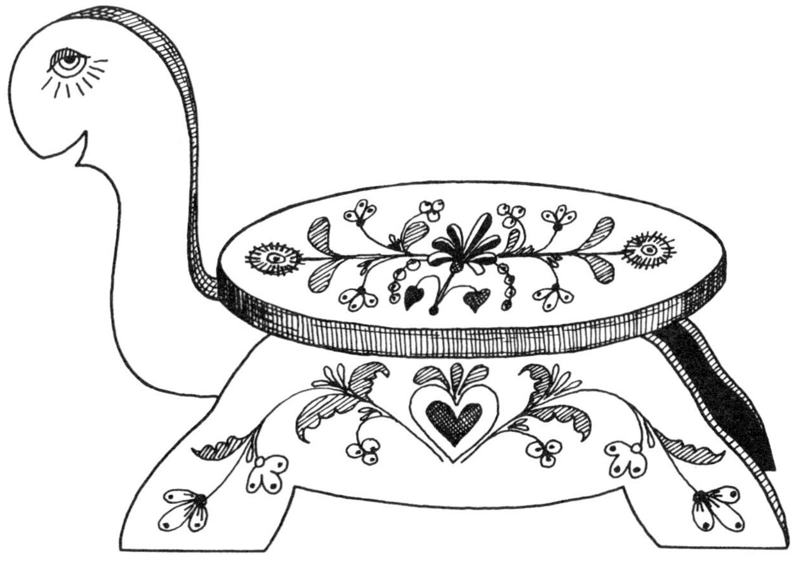

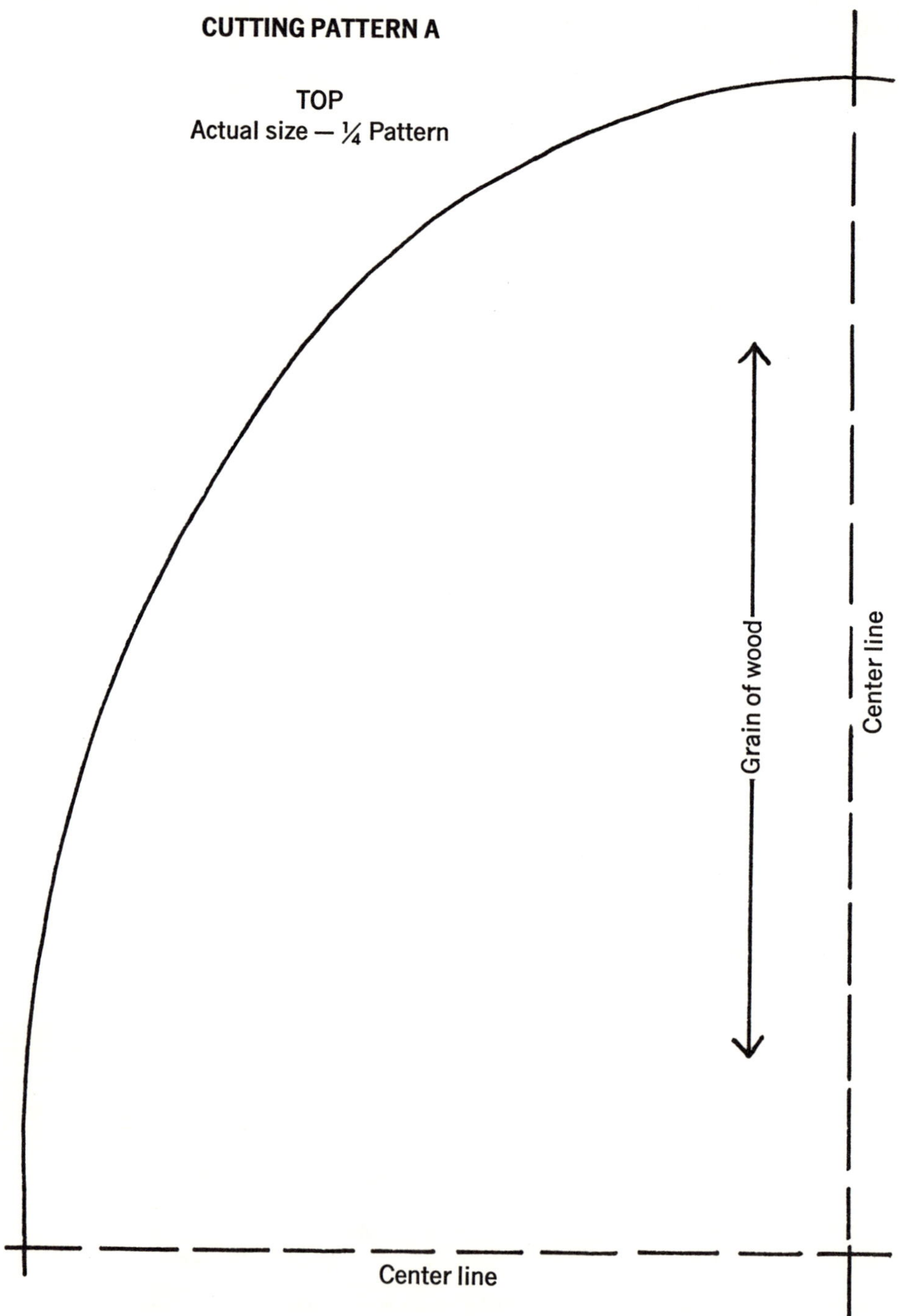

CUTTING PATTERN A

TOP
Actual size — ¼ Pattern

Grain of wood

Center line

Center line

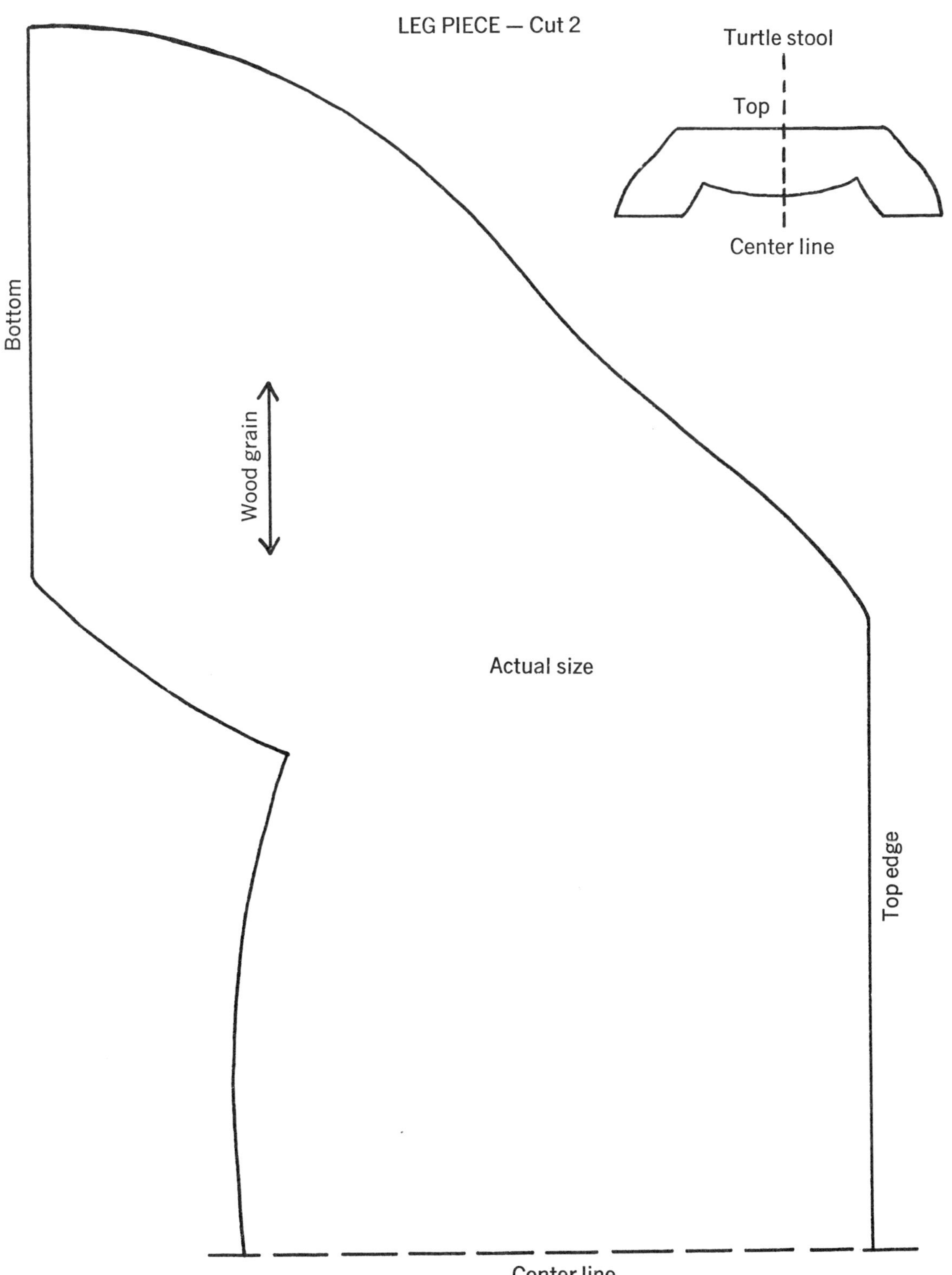
LEG PIECE — Cut 2
Turtle stool
Top
Center line
Bottom
Wood grain
Actual size
Top edge
Center line
(reverse for other half of pattern)

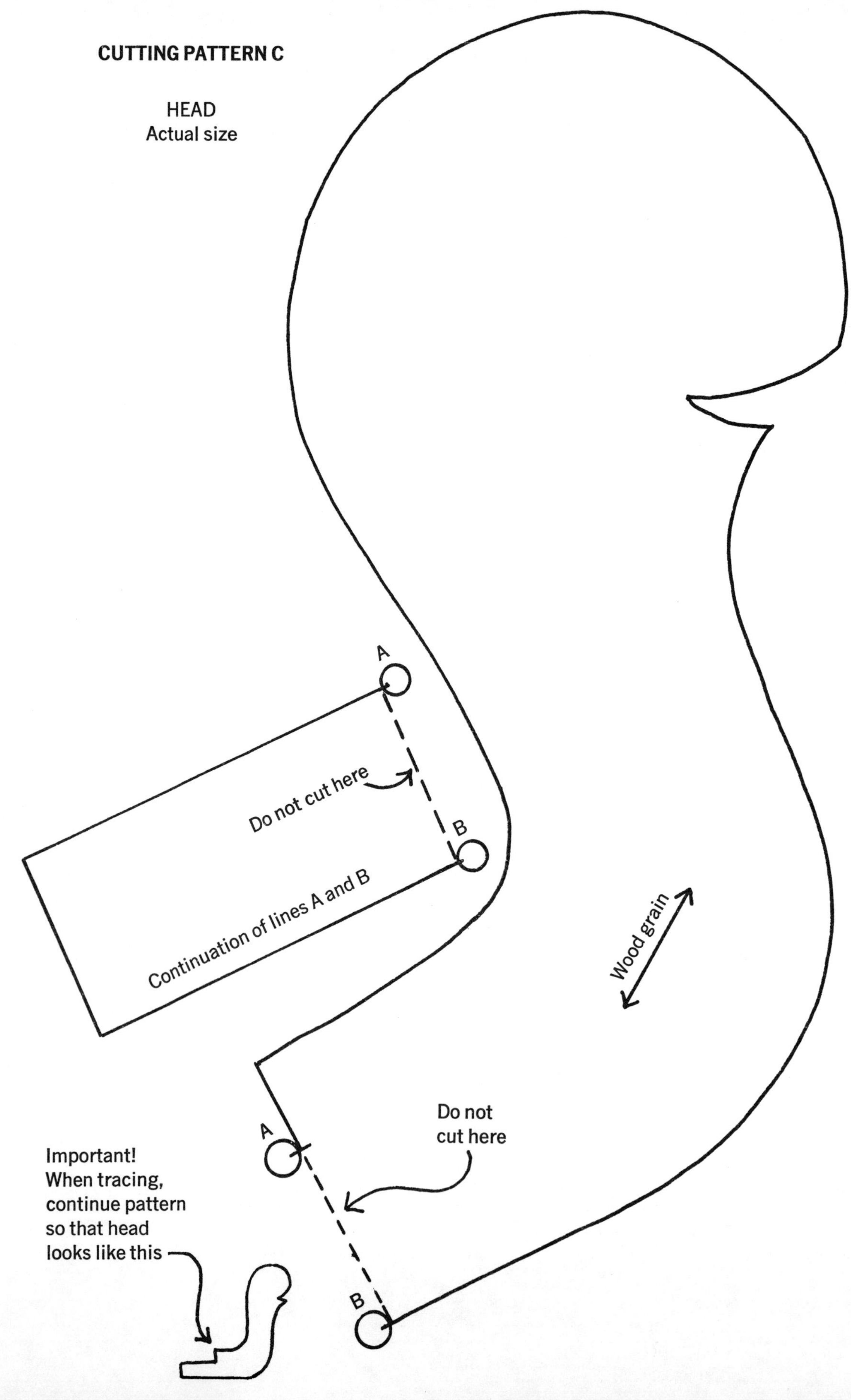

CUTTING PATTERN C
HEAD
Actual size
A
B
Do not cut here
Continuation of lines A and B
Wood grain
A
Do not
cut here
B
Important!
When tracing,
continue pattern
so that head
looks like this

NECK BRACE — Cut 1
Actual size

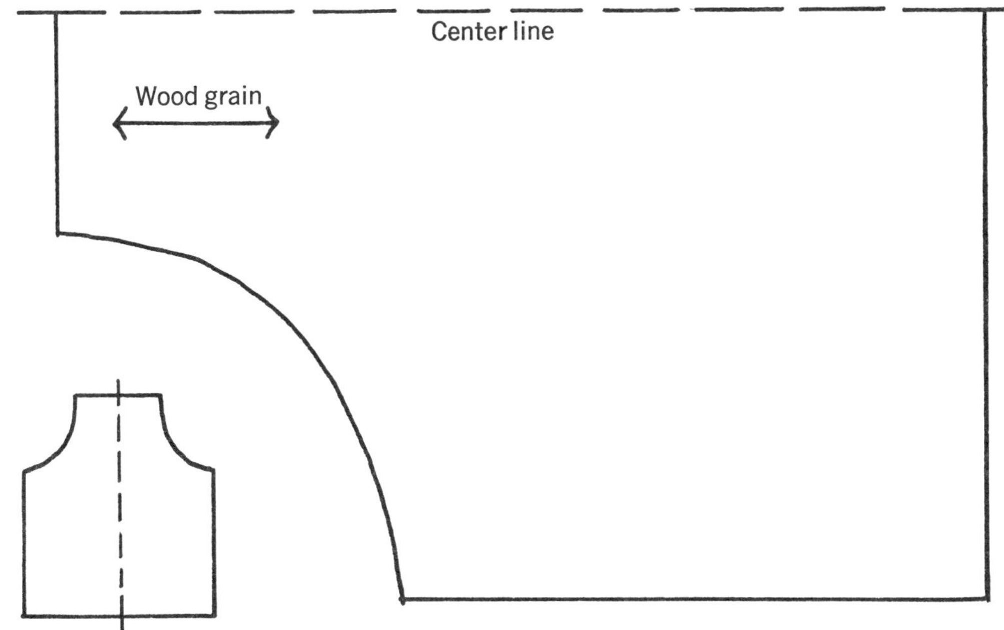

DIAGRAM A

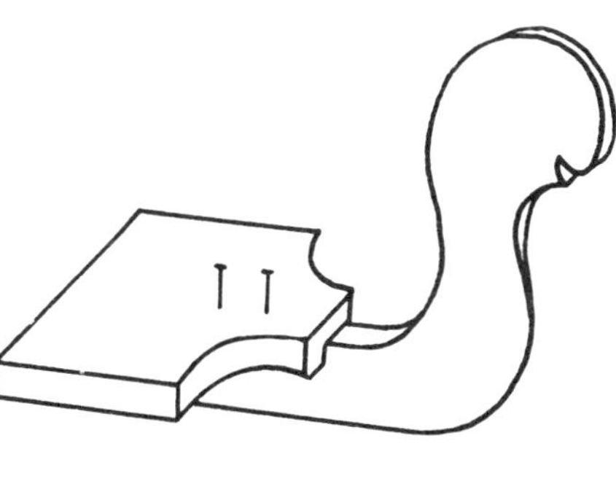

DIAGRAM B

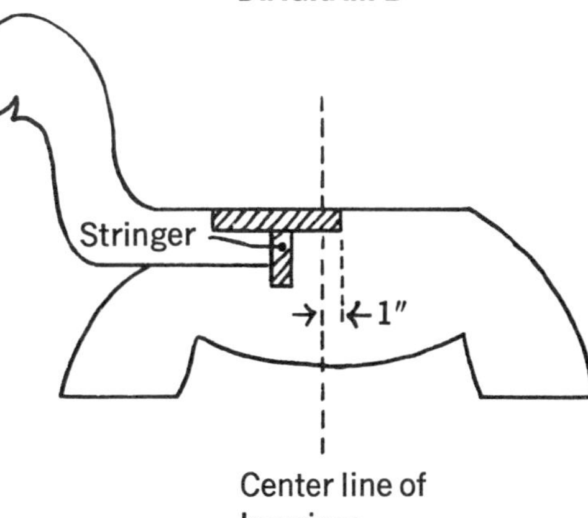

Locate center line of the leg piece 1″ forward
from back edge of neck brace

DIAGRAM C

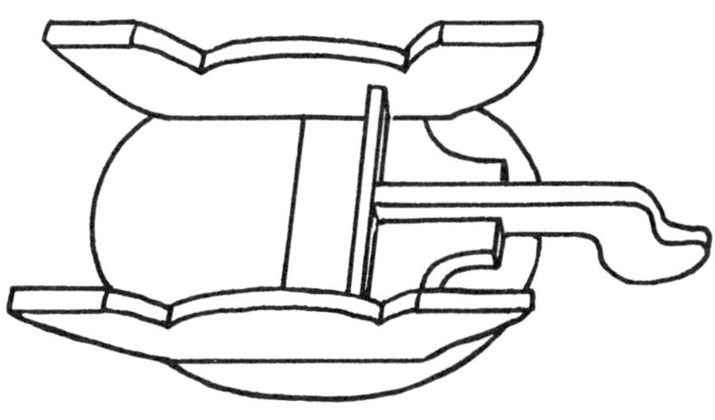

Bottom —
view of stringer
on neck brace
(proper position)

TOP
1 Square = 1 Inch

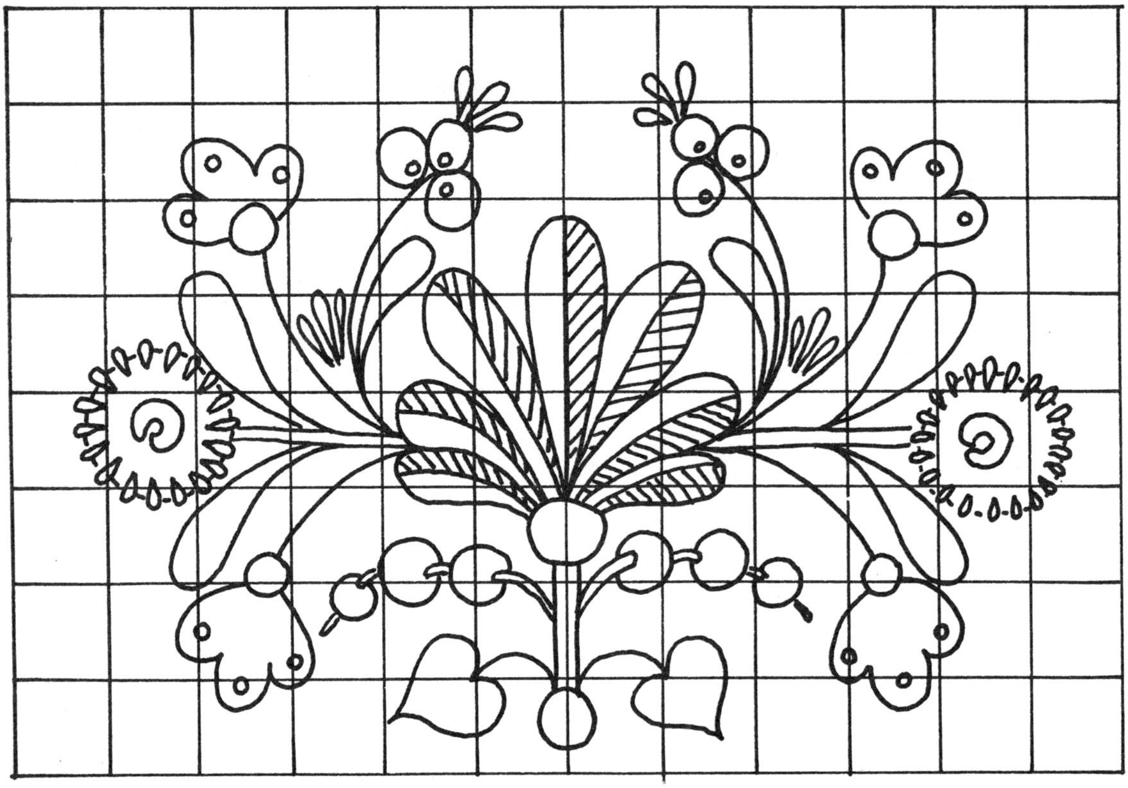

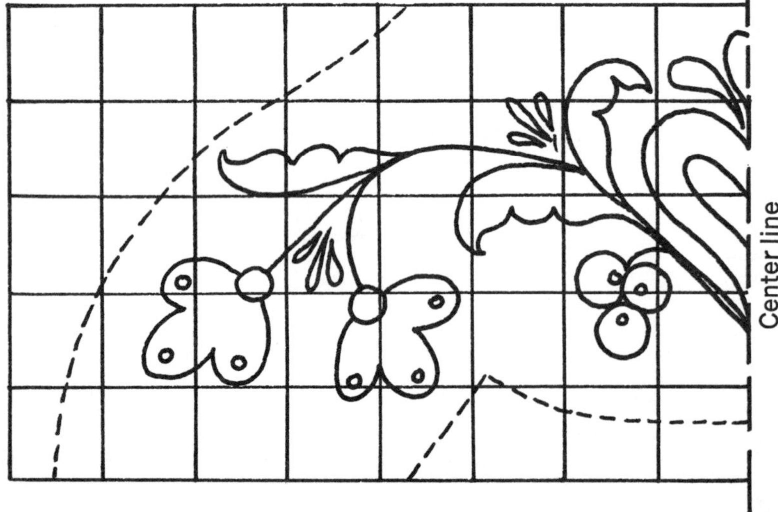

LEG — ½ Pattern
1 Square = 1 Inch

Center line

EYE — Actual size

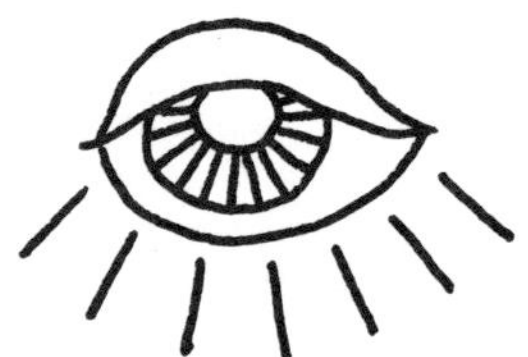

COLOR GUIDE (See color print 5)
Leg design: Heart—red; Cherries—red; Buds—yellow circle with 3 blue petals; Leaves—green
Top design: Center flower—gold; Round flowers—gold; Cherries—red; Buds—red; Leaves—green
Turtle eye; Iris—blue; Pupil—black; White of eye and lid—white

A Loverly Stool

Our loverly stool has been a big hit with the children, but we find that the mamas love it too. Not too big and not too little, it has graceful lines and a heart cutout that we borrowed from the Pennsylvania Dutch who love to put hearts on just about anything. It makes a stool suitable for any room in the house.

MATERIALS:

1″×12″ white pine shelving—5′ long
  (plywood may be substituted)
1½ dozen finishing nails—2″ or 2½″ long
⅜″-diameter dowel—3″ long

STEP ONE: CUTTING

Top: Cut one piece—10″×18″
Ends: Cut two pieces from Pattern A
Stringer: Cut one piece—14¾″×3⅜″
  from Pattern B

Before cutting the individual pieces, you may find it easier to locate and cut the heart design in the two end pieces first. Do this by first drilling two overlapping holes with a 2″ hole cutter. These will form the top of the heart (Pattern A). Complete cutting the lower part of the heart with a jig saw. To make the stool easier to assemble, drill two pilot holes (slightly smaller than your finishing nails) on the center line of the end pieces; the first hole should be ½″ down from the top edge, and the second hole should be 1″ below the first.

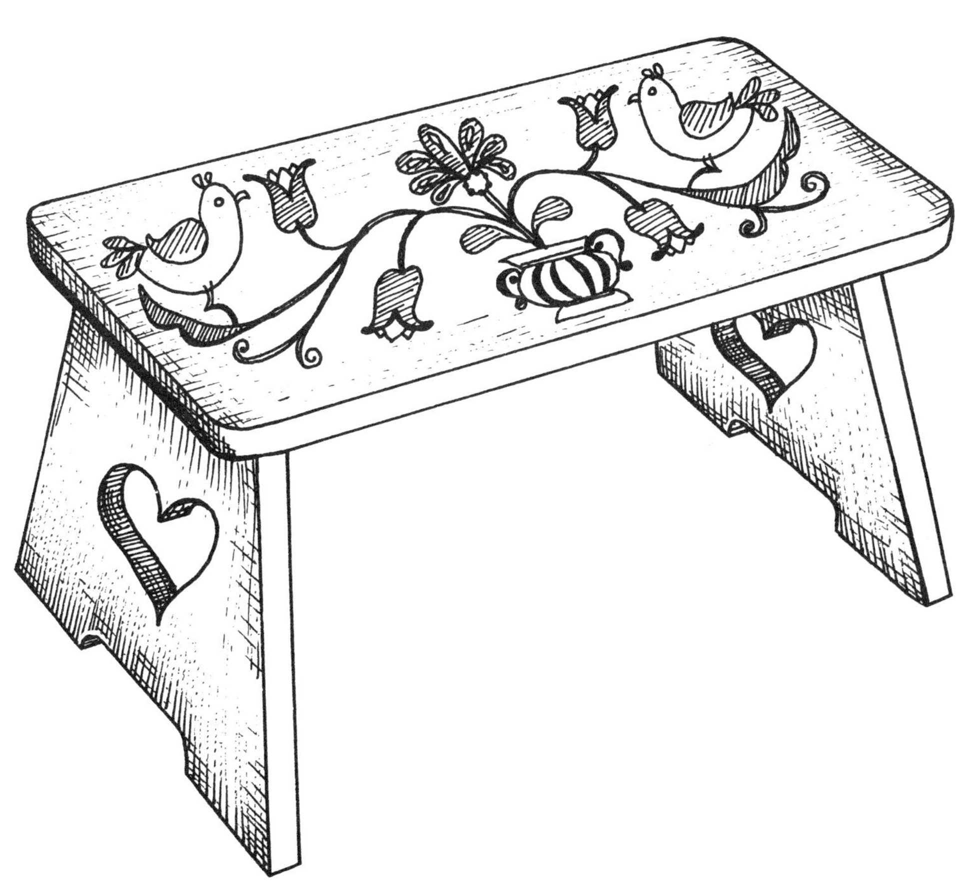

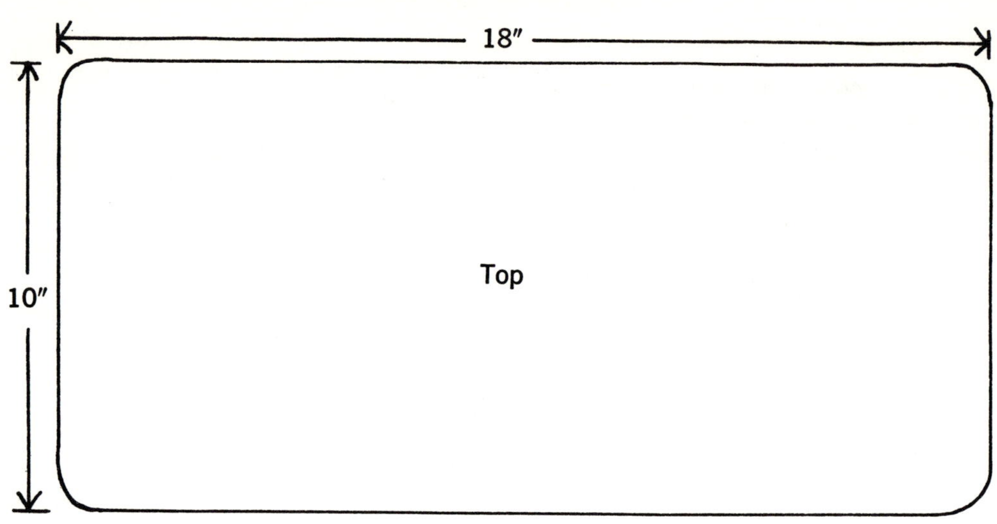

18"
10"
Top

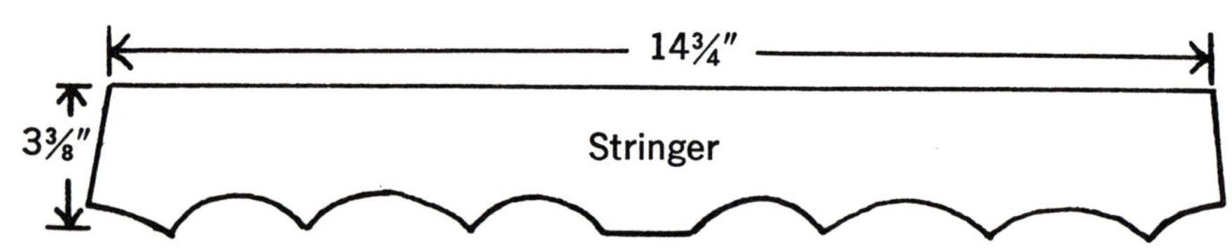

14¾"
3⅜"
Stringer

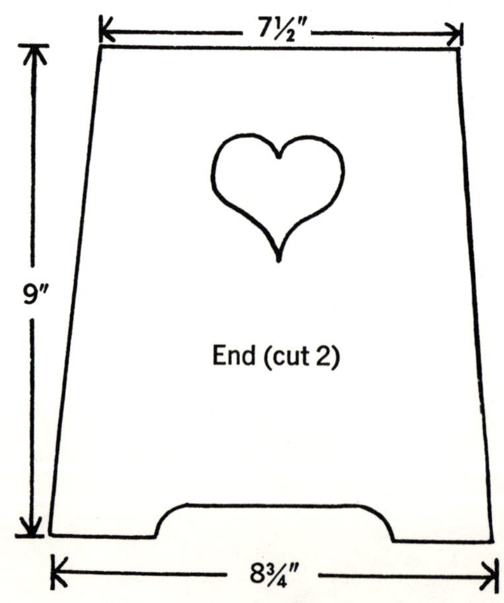

7½"
9"
End (cut 2)
8¾"

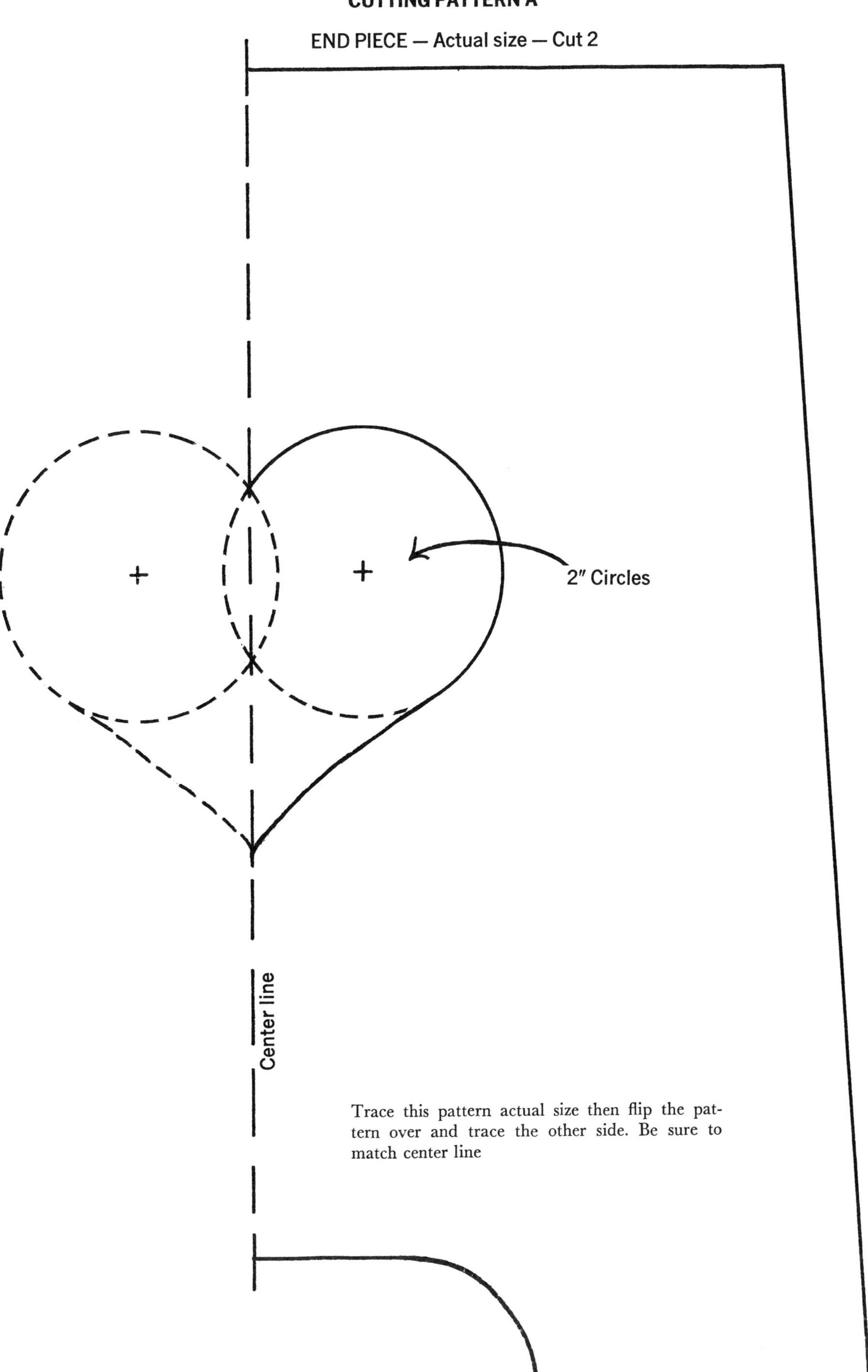

CUTTING PATTERN A
END PIECE — Actual size — Cut 2
2" Circles
Center line
Trace this pattern actual size then flip the pattern over and trace the other side. Be sure to match center line

CUTTING PATTERN B

STRINGER — Actual size

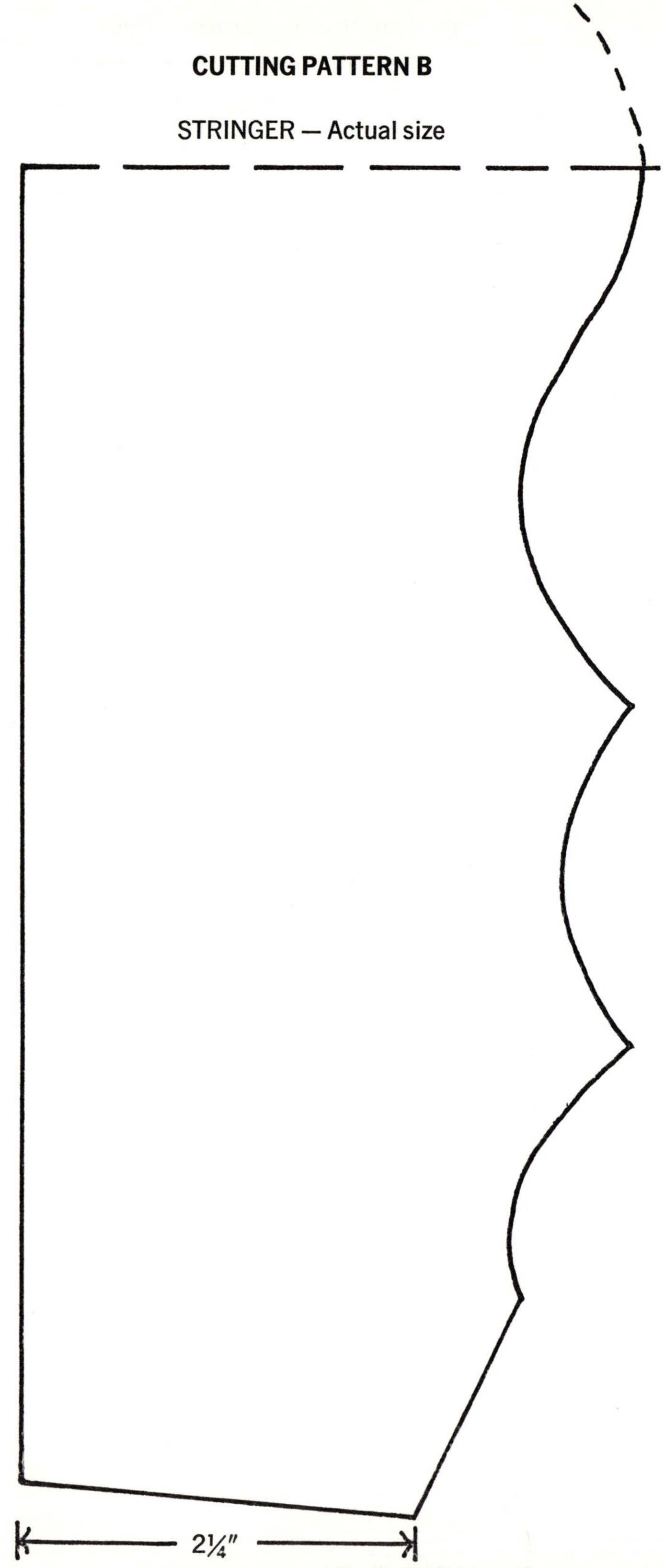

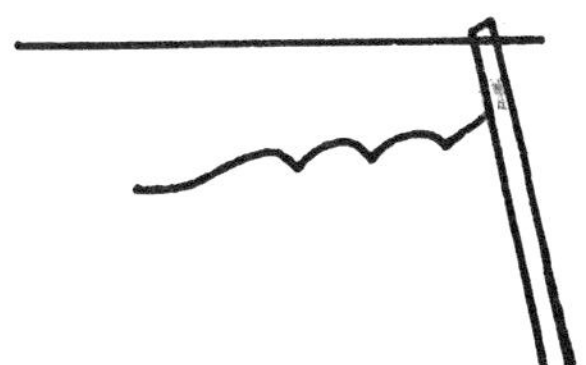

Bevel the top edge of end piece to match top edge of stringer

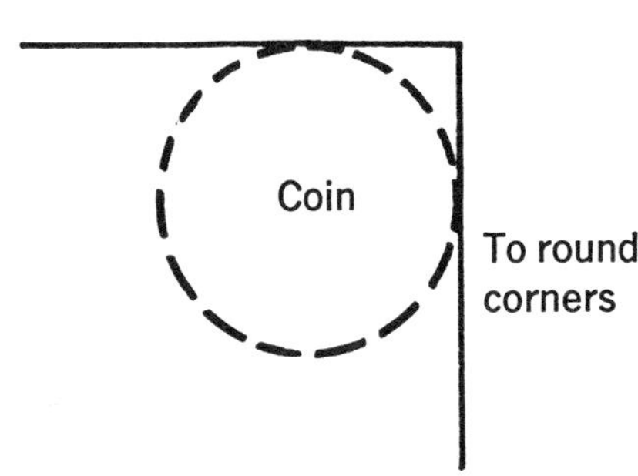

DIAGRAM A

Now, cut out the four pieces following the patterns you have traced onto the wood. Round off the four corners of the stool top with a compass or a coin (quarter or half dollar) and cut the corners with a jig saw or saber saw, as in Diagram A.

STEP TWO: ASSEMBLY

The first step is to nail the two end pieces onto the ends of the stringer. To begin, apply glue to an end of the stringer and position it on the center line of one end piece, matching the top edges. Join by nailing through the pilot holes you drilled when cutting the piece. Do the same at the other end and allow the glue to dry. Because of the angle of the stringer, the end pieces slightly protrude above the top of the stringer. These should now be sawed off flush so as to provide a flat surface for the top.

With the top piece upside down, position the assembled stool base onto the top so that it is centered. Apply glue to the top of the stringer and carefully turn the complete stool upright. Nail three nails through the top into the stringer and two nails through the top into each end piece.

To give the stool a pegged look, drill a ⅜″ hole on each end piece about 1¼″ above the heart. Make the hole about 1½″ deep. Cut two pieces from the ⅜″ dowel, each about 1½″ long. With sandpaper, round off and smooth one end of each piece of dowel. Glue and drive the dowels into the drilled holes leaving the rounded ends protruding about one fourth of an inch.

PAINTING PATTERN

½ Pattern
1 Square = 1 Inch

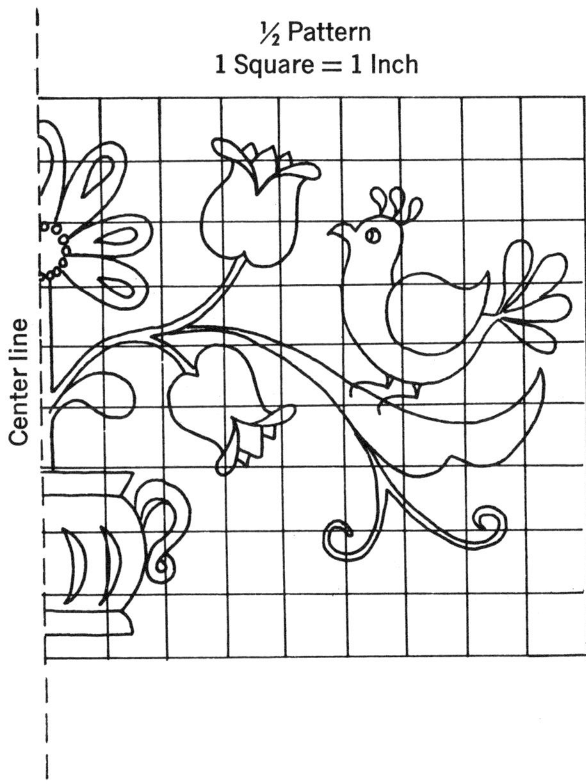

COLOR GUIDE (See color print 6)
Vase: gold with brown details
Center flower: red petals, gold base, blue center in petals
Tulips: blue with red center, light blue spikes
Birds: red body, blue wings, blue tail feathers and comb
Leaves: green

Chapter Seven

"Something for My Room" Patterns

Sweater Rack

Besides being an attractive accessory to a room, we hope that this sweater rack will encourage tidiness among the small fry. It is very handy for hanging sweaters, caps, and lightweight jackets. Mother could use one in the kitchen for coffee mugs or hand towels and pot holders.

MATERIALS:

One piece 1" white pine shelving—8"×16"
One piece of ½"-diameter dowel—12" long

STEP ONE: CUTTING

Cut the piece of shelving to measure 7½"×16". Locate and draw a center line 8" from one end. Trace the pattern on half of the board and then flip the pattern over to complete the other side. Cut the design with a jig saw or saber saw.

For the heart, measure up 6" from the bottom edge and draw a parallel line (parallel to the bottom edge). From each side of the center line, measure $\frac{9}{16}$" and with a small nail make a center point for the drill. With a 1¼" drill or hole cutter, drill two holes as shown and finish cutting the heart shape with a jig saw or saber saw.

Now draw another parallel line 2½" up from the bottom edge and mark the four center lines for the pegs. The first peg is located 2" from either side and the other three pegs are spaced 4" apart. Make a center hole for each peg. Finally, drill four ½"-diameter holes, ½" deep and at a

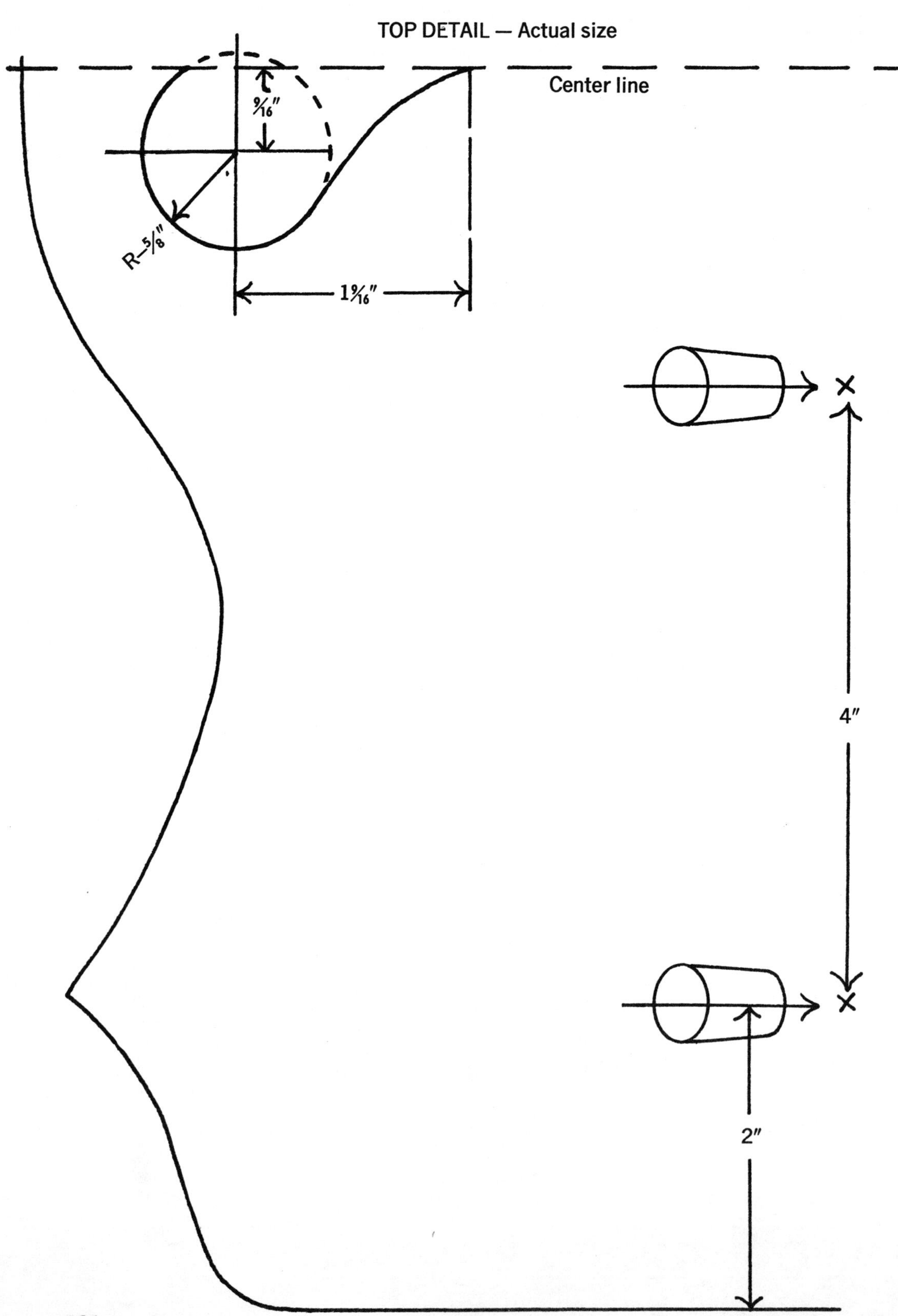
TOP DETAIL — Actual size
Center line
9/16"
R–5/8"
1 9/16"
4"
2"

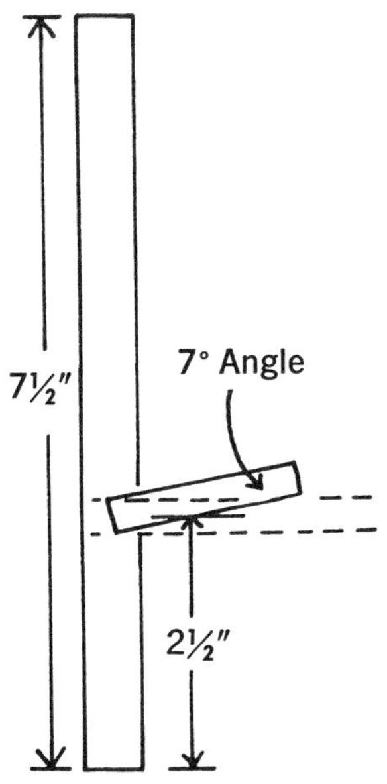

Drill holes at an angle so that pegs will tilt up slightly

slight angle so that the pegs, when inserted, will tilt up (Diagram A).

Cut the dowel into four pegs, each 3″ long. The outer end of each peg should be rounded off slightly with heavy sandpaper or a file.

STEP TWO: ASSEMBLY

Using white glue, insert the pegs into the four holes, tapping lightly until each peg is left extending 2½″. If you have difficulty fitting the pegs into the holes, a light sanding will help.

PAINTING PATTERN

1 Square = 1 Inch

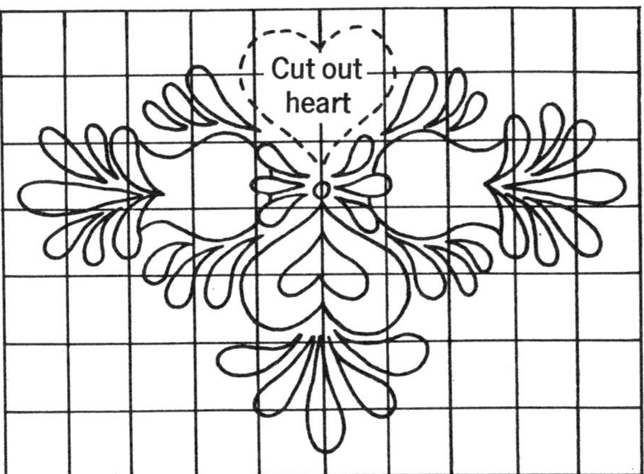

COLOR GUIDE (See color print 3)
Heart and tulips: orange
Small heart inside large heart: blue
Tulip tips: blue
Strokes at end of tulips and below heart: brown
All other strokes: green

Book Ends

This set of book ends is simple to make and can be made from odds and ends of material. Consider them for gift giving for they add color and interest to any room; the painted design we offer is for a nursery, but the book ends are also charming with fruit or vegetable designs in a kitchen or with a floral design for students away at school.

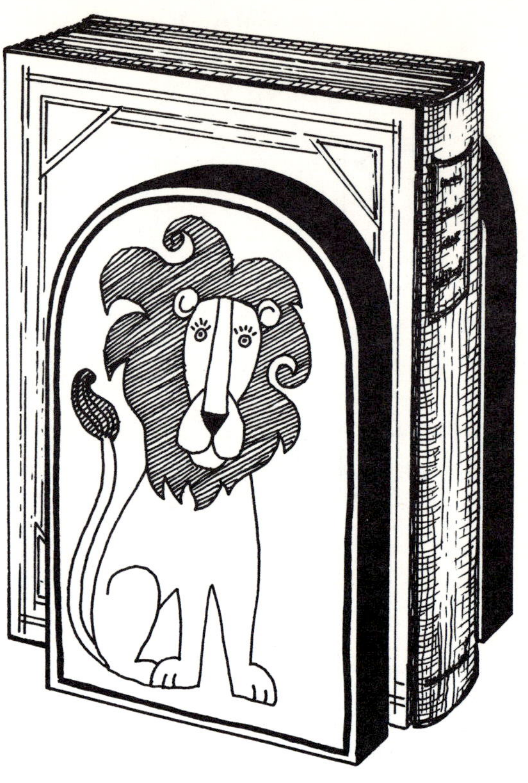

MATERIALS:

Two pieces of 1″×6″ shelving—7¾″ long
One piece of Masonite board—⅛″×3⅛″ ×7″ long
Four flat-head screws—½″ long

STEP ONE: CUTTING

Using the pattern, measure and cut the two book ends from the shelving. On the straight bottom edge of each book end, measure over from one side 1³⁄₁₆″ and, with a carpenter's square, draw a line. Measure the same distance from the other side and draw a line. Still using the square, draw two lines ⅛″ up on the front side of the book end and connect these lines as shown in the sketch. This slot can now be cut out with a saber saw or jig saw.

The Masonite feet can be traced from the pattern and cut with a saber saw or jig saw. Drill two ³⁄₃₂″-diameter holes through the Masonite feet (see location in Cutting Pattern). On the bottom side of the Masonite, use a knife or screw driver to slightly bevel the holes so that the screws can be screwed in flush with the Masonite surface. Finally, with a file or fine rasp, shave the small end of the foot, 1″ back from the edge in order to provide a tapered surface to slide under the books.

STEP TWO: ASSEMBLY

Before screwing the two parts together, thoroughly sand and remove all rough edges from the Masonite feet. Place the large end of the Masonite foot into the slot at the base of the book end with the smooth side of the Masonite facing up and the large end flush with the front edge of the book end. With the Masonite in place, use a drill or nail to make a starting hole into the wood. Attach the two pieces with a flat-head screw. Repeat with the other book end assembly.

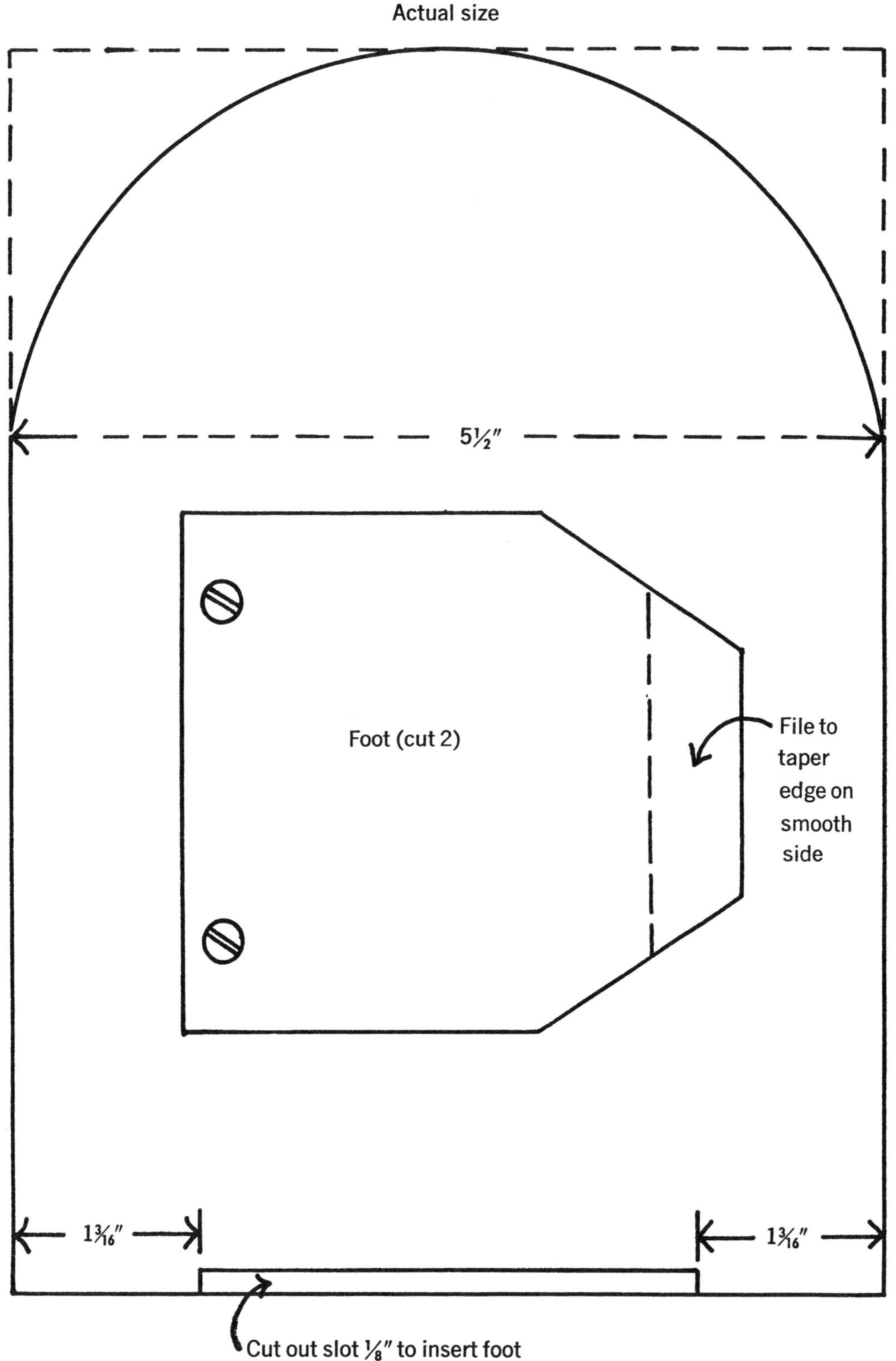

Actual size
5½″
Foot (cut 2)
File to taper edge on smooth side
1³⁄₁₆″
1³⁄₁₆″
Cut out slot ⅛″ to insert foot

PAINTING PATTERN

Actual size

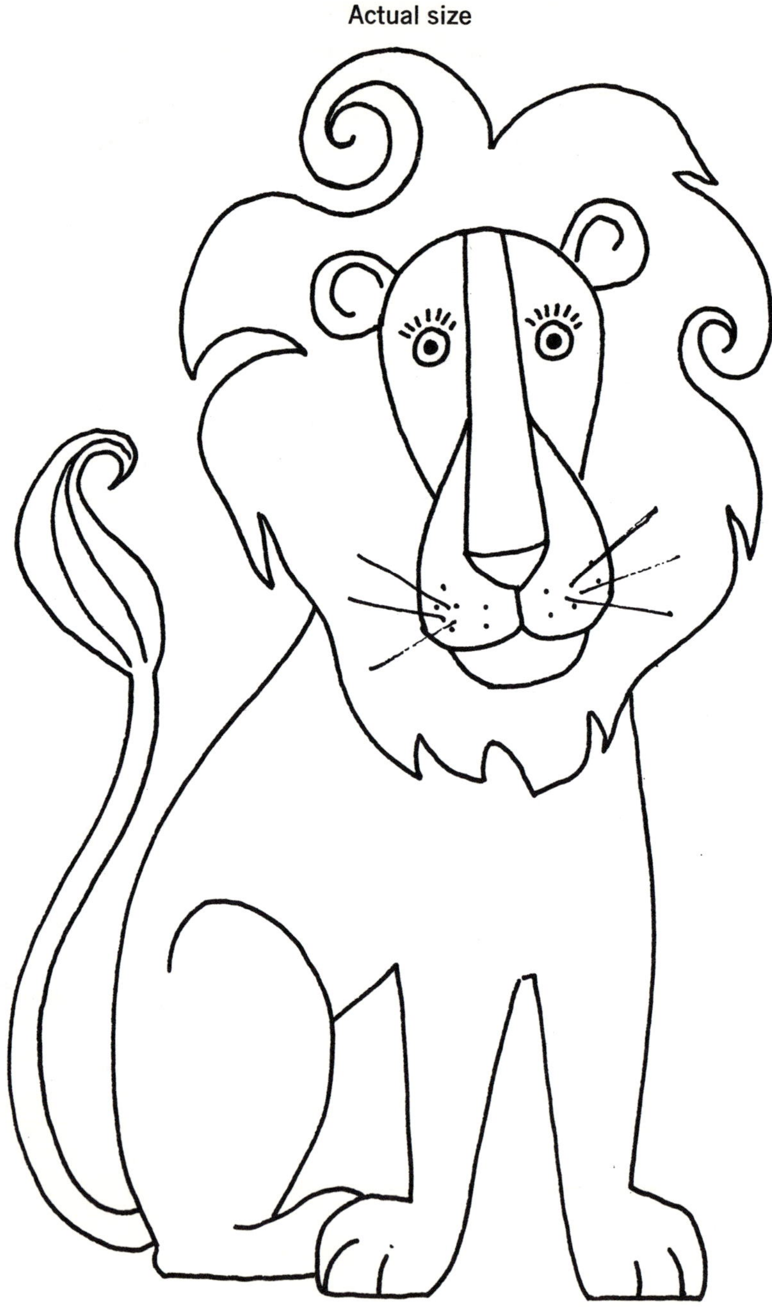

COLOR GUIDE (See color print 5)
Body and face: gold
Length of nose: white
Tip of nose: pink
Mane and tip of tail: orange
Eyes: green